Growing Wings

&

Children

GROWING WINGS & CHILDREN

Moving Beyond our Identity into a Shared Humanity

ALISON FEATHER ADAMS

For Kate

Editor: Joanne Weaver

Cover Art: Alison Feather Adams

The following people have supported me on so many levels while writing this: Barbara, Anita, and Joanne have met me with integrity, honesty, and inspiration. Mikhael has remained committed to learning, laughing, and growing with me as my partner, at work and at home. Our children, Harrison, Kate and Alex, have kept me on track by spreading their wings authentically in response to me growing mine. I have been very blessed by professional and personal relationships with wonderful and gracious people who give incredible depth and meaning to my life.

Order this book online at www.trafford.com
or email orders@trafford.com

Most Trafford titles are also available at major online book retailers.

Printed in Victoria, BC, Canada.

ISBN: 978-1-4269-2178-0 (soft)
ISBN: 978-1-4269-2177-3 (hard)

Library of Congress Control Number: 2009913594

Our mission is to efficiently provide the world's finest, most comprehensive book publishing service, enabling every author to experience success. To find out how to publish your book, your way, and have it available worldwide, visit us online at www.trafford.com

Trafford rev. 1/11/2010

 www.trafford.com

North America & international
toll-free: 1 888 232 4444 (USA & Canada)
phone: 250 383 6864 ♦ fax: 812 355 4082

Also by Alison Feather Adams

Healing through the Eyes of a Woman

Contents

Preface

Growing wings for some of you will make more sense to think of in terms of spreading the wings you have already realized you have! However, for many of us, when faced with discontent and confusion, the last thing we are aware of is spiritual metaphors for what are very real problems we face in our lives. Perceptions are both intriguing and deceiving for they are not easily isolated or identified as being our personal filter of what exists, especially when the human factor of emotion adds such conviction to the reality they project for us. For women it is not as simple as one might think to recognize where we awaken to find ourselves. There is no definite beginning or end to our search for identity, and in seeking reassurance for our place in the whole scheme of things, we often unknowingly isolate ourselves from finding relatedness to higher ideals once we are in relationship and have children. Our identities may seem defined to those in our lives, but in our minds it all melds together and the pull to fill the spaces where we believe our family, friends and colleagues rely on our being there is difficult when a thread of our own inner workings breaks free of our conditioned fabric. Calling in the repair team is simple if we know what the problem is, but how many of us actually know where or how to find objectivity about our self when it is through relationship that we experience who we are?

Navigating through our challenges in life is frightening if we awaken to find ourselves without safe ground under foot, and we are stuck in our process of thinking that plays tricks on us without our knowing it. Thinking is not our enemy, nor are our emotions, but when in the midst of personal change, the grey hues that inhabit our internal world can overwhelm our common sense to constructively direct our thoughts towards unveiling clarity about ourselves. We are not unlike children claiming to be bored, and no matter what suggestions are given, there is nothing that's going to shift us into exploring a solution to our dilemma until we are *ready and willing* to seek resolution beyond how we currently see and experience our reality. We remain bored because we choose it, but in our minds, we don't think we are the cause for remaining in such a state. In summoning the courage to reach for the little threads that lead us towards this clarity, we transform the need for comfortable answers that satisfy keeping our current identity with self justified, and into reaching for greater meaning and experience that fulfills our hearts desires.

When you're not feeling fulfilled or happy, imagine that you are in the fog trying to find your way out. You can see faint outlines of familiar things but there is nothing concrete to guide you. Just taking the single impressions like strands of a thread that catch your attention, and allowing them to reveal themselves is the beginning of finding your way through to clarity. In tuning into the impressions each strand makes on you, without trying to define or identify them, you can become accepting of the feelings that stir within you. Enter this process without categorizing your perceptions as good or bad, right or wrong, but just feelings that represent *an identity* you have yet to recognize being attached to, or as the case may be, severed from acknowledging that it exists in you. It's not unlike the experience of walking through the outer strands of a cobweb and feeling it across your face but not being able to see it. It is not until we explore where it may lead that we see the intricate workings of the spider's web and the parts of nature that have become entangled in it. When we are feeling stuck in life, the aspects of self are like these parts of nature that get caught in the web of our inner workings.

In recognizing our relatedness to the people around us, we embark on bringing awareness to who we are in relation to them and then have the ability change in relation to our self. These threads of relatedness create resistance for us, and in avoiding venturing near and disturbing them, we allow our thoughts to run us, rather than harness our ability to direct our thoughts constructively. As we allow ourselves to follow these threads they weave themselves into common experiences we begin to recognize, and they begin to inform us in ways that move us swiftly to a greater capacity within us to grow. The path towards awakening to who we are beyond our known identities starts in the fog, and that seems to be just the way it is, whether we like it or not. Those threads that initially appear very personal in nature to us begin to unravel and weave their impressions into our life. As some of these themes and common fabric started to become visible to me, I became less attached to how I personally related to these ideas, and actually began exploring and making enquiries with other women about how they experienced them in their life and relationships.

I am not sure if experience has proven to be a good or bad thing as I have opened the doors to many of my own limited perceptions that I honestly couldn't believe existed unconsciously within me. In a good way, liberating these unconscious perceptions unmasks the drama of daily events that are very humorous once we break free of the idea that we must maintain our integrity reliant on others perceptions of us. In an unexpected way, once embarking on this process, we awaken to the possibilities we have yet to become aware of. Once realizing where we have abandoned our hearts' dreams without knowing it, we wonder what else we currently don't realize about ourselves. Are we all so different? I think not! We establish some bad habits in relating to others along the way and the one that beckons the fog to close in around us is when we determine who we need to be based on what others think or accept about us. We leave our heart's truth dangling out in the storm, and reach for a life line we believe will guide us, when we change to be what we think another will recognize and respond to in us that will keep the relationship in tact. The minute we change in order to be what is accepted and recognized by another, we have abandoned ship on embarking on our own journey to discover True Self. We have allowed another's perceptions of us to define who we are. In doing this we limit our capacity to experience greater fulfillment in sharing with them from a bigger pool of awareness. Finding a lifeline that transforms our current experience with them becomes an invisible option. Our relationships remain limited, and inside us, the various parts of self that seek expression are left dormant to begin to stir and become restless and dissatisfied. In growing our wings, we may recognize these parts in us, and a greater context emerges that shows our relatedness to so much more beyond current self's acknowledgment or identity. In a sense, we reclaim our power by taking ownership of unrecognized self acting through us, and meet it with humility. We reclaim our innocence, and with it, the world becomes a place of wonderment and magical beauty for us, as do our interactions with the people in our life. Spider webs become beautiful works of art and ingenuity when we are not victims caught in them.

As women, our emotions blend and stir through our thinking process, creating influence and molding our perceptions without us taking too much notice of their influence. Many women have told me how much they think about things as if it is not a good thing. I had a man in one of my workshops that openly said, "Are you trying to tell me that people actually think about this stuff!" My response, "Yes, and can you honestly tell me, you don't?" A common truth was revealed: Men and women think a lot, but we do it differently, and many don't acknowledge that the noise going on between their ears exists for a reason. For the record, the man who confronted me about this, and then acknowledged that he did think about these things, turned out to have incredible intuitive as well as healing abilities. I am so glad we both met on this one, because remaining the unrecognized skeptic was closing him off from the part of himself that would link him with his gifted true nature. Our thoughts can become the enemy instead of an ally that can help us recognize unconscious energies active within us that seek to be liberated into positive virtues.

Working with my patients in the clinic, there were basic threads that kept catching my attention while I was writing this book. I started to become aware of how many women don't really respect men or experience with men relationships with depth and emotional presence, because of statements like " are you trying to tell me…" putting a halt to their own expression. How many of us, as a result of encountering the masculine energy of *telling us* what to do, unknowingly side with *suffering* rather than *empowerment* to change how we perceive our ability to meet the challenge of relating to others in meaningful ways. More specifically, through exercising choice, we can enable self to grow relative to the greater dimensions of who we are, rather than holding out for the change we think is needed for our partners, but never expect to happen. Our partners become the sounding boards for the voice of self that we can't hear coming from us!

When I first started exploring these dynamics, I felt a little crestfallen to think that I might be committed to an ideal about men and women's equality in the world that maybe wasn't realistic. What if my own life was a dream that I would awaken from to find I was alone. I have a wonderful man in my life, and many of the men I know are wonderful people. I sat with that one whirling around in my head for a few moments before I decided to leave logic at the door, not entertain unfounded fear, and start noticing the actual quality of the energy expressing itself around me. Aside from outward appearances, it occurred to me there is a lot of unrecognized masculine energy being expressed by women and men, and much of it is creating roadblocks at a time when receptivity to new ideas and creative thinking is calling us forward. In exploring my own ideas about this, I came up against my own masculine energy that was very allowing of others, but wasn't very allowing of me to voice how I see women's ability to harness constructively and authentically their own masculine energy. The masculine energy I'm referring to is not about our competence as much as how we are *choosing to express* our competence with the people in our lives, be it at work, in the community, or at home. How do we move past our identities as women and men and the unconscious impressions that are part of us, if we deny these energies exist within us in a limited state? This aspect of vanity is not easily recognized when society endorses focusing on the outward appearance of our face in the mirror each morning.

A voice inside me warned that women aren't going to like this. I may be seen as a traitor to my gender for suggesting that maybe men aren't the villains after all. In waiting for change in them, are we betraying our own ability to grow beyond what keeps our comfort zone of accepted relationship in tact for us? Accepting that they may not change, and being able to nurture growth in our children and ourselves without waiting for them to understand or listen to us, is a difficult journey to embark on that others know how to support. Where does this leave the conditioning we have about how we support the love we have for our partners? Are we willing to ignore our ability as women to further develop the depth and fulfillment possible in relationships because we don't want to admit we may have to change how we experience ourselves? I am not dismissing the reality that there are men who's actions do not reflect honor or respect for their mates, despite their outward claims to be supportive and attentive partners. However, holding our breath, suppressing our anger and discontent, and waiting for men to get us through osmosis, and give us permission to spread our wings with them, isn't serving building faith in where relationship can fuel growth for us. It is possibly serving to isolate us from experiencing greater intimacy and shared respect that can be mutually appreciated.

Our culture encourages walking in unison with our partners, or walking away and taking what you can with you as if somehow they will be taught a lesson by paying for what they did to us. This vanity is imbedded deeply when we think it is within our power to teach another a lesson that is theirs to learn, as much as it's ours. We may transform this notion of duality and entertain the possibility that we can honor our own journey and honor their journey, with faith that they will strengthen one another, not dismantle union. If we walk away rather than independently acknowledging what is important to us, we miss the development and experience of interdependence. If as women we see men expressing a masculine energy that we don't like, or relate to, then maybe it is time to recognize it is our own unrecognized masculine expression being mirrored back to us. We cannot see past this expression in them because we have yet to unveil a masculine energy within ourselves that has the capacity to be compassionate with ourselves. In not accepting the challenge to unveil these unconscious energies within us, we miss relating at the deeper level we yearn to experience with others. Our desire to change our partners into what we believe they are capable of but not expressing with us is a reflection of what we have unknowingly severed ourselves acknowledging as active, and disowned, within ourselves. The unwritten social contract of the *collective masculine* is up for renewal and it's through our own hearts that we will birth awareness of our ability to choose with discernment what we as a shared humanity wish to nurture at this time.

The emphasis on nurturing self, recognizing our needs, fostering the development of the feminine energy is on the forefront right now, but without a *masculine energy within us* that is allowing of this emergence, and ability to focus our resourcefulness, we are in a headlock with ourselves. Addressing this duality and expressions of confrontation we see in daily life requires expanding self into new levels where the masculine and feminine qualities are acknowledged and transcended to serve a shared humanity. We may support self in its ability to be guided by higher truths and ideals. We may choose our experience of reality, and unveiling more of what already exists relieves us of our personal need to justify our identity relative to it. We can change if we are willing, and begin living in acknowledgement that we are learning and growing with one another in our capacity to live consciously aligned with abundance and compassion.

Most of us operate under the assumption that is we can't see something, it doesn't exist. Many things exist and have always existed even though we have not yet come to recognize, let alone realize or identify them. To think that the current world is demonstrating and expressing full reality will breed hopelessness unless we reach out with our hearts and minds to see beyond self's current lens of identity. We seem to be experiencing and supporting a reality that assumes we are running out of time, resources, and sustainability to support our selves and our planet. Maybe it is merely time to entertain more expansive ideas, and perceptions beyond self's current identity and build new references for our progress beyond self's idea of importance, so we realize we are running out of *our idea* of time, *our idea* of resources, and *our idea* of sustainability. What exists and supports humanity as stewards of this planet will remain unrealized as long as self is not recognized as limited in its experience and comprehension of life. We seek self's potential and maybe we are missing developing a relationship that integrates self with soul's potential where we are a shared humanity.

Growing Wings & Children is about allowing new dimensions of who we are to become integrated with our current identities of self. To expand who we are in our roles and our assumed identities as females is to mature in our ability to harness greater awareness of the resources available in energetic terms to us. To grow wings is to expand our faith in what is unseen and unrecognized as realistic for most to invest in, but brings meaning to our relationships and reason for being. This book is not about developing strategies for dealing with life's challenges, or what to do about the people we relate or don't relate to in our lives. It's about *getting real* and gaining faith in life's inherent harmony so we can recognize our own resistances, and move through them to change what keeps us from experiencing harmony within us, with one another, and with this planet that supports us all.

Chapter 1

Our Outer World Mirrors
Our Inner World

Trust the masculine to allow the feminine within you to receive,
nurture and birth conscious creation,
that breathes and beats with the heart of humanity.
Open your eyes to see the invisible,
open your ears to hear the inaudible,
open your heart to feel this presence,
and through knowing this truth you will begin to experience,
the purpose of your own being.

When we look back through the history of humanity, the development of consciousness has provided a consistent cord that blends and intertwines the findings of science with the perceptions of the humanities to bring us to further understand who we are. That cord serves to inform us as individuals of our capacity to incorporate higher ideals with what we currently don't recognize as ourselves. The sciences have offered the observations, identifications, enquiries through experiments, and theoretical explanations of natural phenomena. The humanities on the other hand have explored understanding the relationship of things in a different way, through *feeling* and a blending of ideas and concepts that exist within our basic nature as human beings. Be it the artist, the poet, the musician, the astrologer, or the philosopher, the humanities have often sought understanding of these identities through feeling one's way *through* discomfort, expressing oneself in what appears to be abstract terms, rather than seeking to explain phenomena in concrete form. In our search to understand who we are, we have cultivated skills that affect our outer world, and in experiencing the response, we are given the opportunity to recognize our actions as a reflection of our inner world seeking knowledge and identity. We have faced constant challenges, if not by our global circumstance, then by our personal experience, to expand awareness in ourselves, our roles, and the meaning of this existence to us as human beings.

It seems that it is in times of great suffering when we unveil our personal unrecognized resources and unrealized abilities to transform our circumstances into opportunities to grow greater faith in who we choose to be relative to them. In recognizing our unconscious attachment to societies accepted identities, we face extending our own identities to meet them compassionately. For example, the *archetype of the victim* can see a world that is against them and that puts up obstacles impossible to overcome. The victim, once recognized and accepted in this state, has the opportunity to be further realized by the individual. That same victim begins to see that there is choice and an ability to exercise courage to transform oppression into liberation for itself. It may not seem to directly liberate anybody else, but for themselves, the victim may allow greater dimensions of what exists into their awareness and experience. We may now relate to this transformed archetype as the *magician*, but the two are not essentially different in that they take what exists and work with it. Having faith, they may transform their perception of who they are relative to it. It's how we work with what life shows us that determines the depth of experience we become capable of experiencing. As individuals, we decide how we wish to work with what life gives us. Take a handful of clay and give it to a magician and he might create a work of art or a useful bowl to catch rain. Give the same clump of clay to a victim and they don't see what can be made with it, they see only that it is formless, lifeless, and useless as it is, as all they see is clay as an isolated object, separate from their own capacity to hold it. There is nothing relative to the clay; no connection to anything else that the clay enables within their capacity to imagine. The magician allows the clay to become part of him and allows it to take shape and become an expression through them. Recognizing what part of us is being exercised at any given moment takes practice. Once conscious, magic enters the picture all on its own through our imagination and faith in its existence within us.

As we have come to identify what our outer world reflects about its growth, its imbalances, its challenges to find harmony and peace, we have *come to recognize our internal workings* as human beings facing the same challenges but through our personal experience. In recognizing the play of duality in our external world, we find the origins of this same duality existing within us, if we dare to look. Awareness of our inner workings has brought us to take the step of claiming responsibility for the *experience* we have of the world. In a sense, we learn to be masters of our own world, because we have faith to summon growth within ourselves to meet what we encounter externally with courage, and let it in to inform us of its potential.

Just as our diversity in cultures and beliefs are challenged to coexist peacefully beyond perceived duality, we as individuals face the same challenge *within* us. There are qualities in us that influence how we approach and work with life, and more importantly strengthen our relatedness to life. We have moved from a society where men were identified as the masculine, and women the feminine, and through developing our awareness of these qualities, we have realized that both exist within us as individuals to constructively exercise. Our challenge becomes to move through exercising these as separate qualities, exercised in separate situations, into a more cooperative process that blends with the divinely inherent qualities of both. As we consciously develop awareness and acceptance of these expressions and qualities in ourselves, we can more easily relate to what is currently active and unrecognized as an identity we have yet to develop more fully within us. As we recognize our part *in allowing experience* to educate and mold us into greater capacity as people, we are moving from codependent relationships into the realm of interdependent relationships that serve sustaining a shared humanity.

In general terms, if you are a person who relates to factual information, technical data and documented proof, and you tend to categorizes things into right and wrong, good and bad, and have no problem remaining detached in the midst of indecision, than you respond from the *masculine energy* within yourself. If, on the other hand, you tend to observe things around you to gain understanding, and although you have a critical eye, you are more than likely to direct your analysis towards yourself and your own inner workings, then you are responding from the *feminine energy* within yourself. Quite simply, the masculine energy operates much like the *gears* on a machine, and there is a specific division between thoughts, feelings, and actions, much like the way science isolates phenomena in order to understand its dynamics. The masculine has the capacity for competence and compassion, but there is often distinct division between each of the modes of operation, and should the gears get jammed or the focus on one gear be interrupted, there can be great confusion and frustration.

The feminine energy on the other hand is more of a *blending* of idea's and emotions, and although there is the same capacity for compassion and competence as the masculine, it is expressed differently. There is a need for harmony and cooperation with this energy, that when not present, a sense of being overwhelmed keeps one from engaging with responsiveness. The feminine energy has subtly influenced how we as individuals receive and gestate information that science has identified in another context, but not understood. The masculine is focused, whereas the feminine is present. The masculine approaches things, the feminine receives them, and the two in balance are necessary in order for us to open ourselves to greater perceptions and understandings of who we are, and how we individually and collectively influence our outer world.

As the sciences have led us beyond the facts and data into abstract observations and explorations about the nature of the universe and the workings of not only the parts but also the whole, we see the line between the sciences and the humanities becoming an increasingly grey area. The blurring of the line between the sciences and the humanities is very much like the blended feminine and masculine energies. The further science ventures, the more like poetry it appears! The further we delve into our own depths of consciousness with awareness, the more soul's intelligence makes logical sense. We now have a consciousness that supports integrating these two energies with a *more intelligent energy* that transforms our need to keep things segregated in order to keep balance for us into allowing life through us.

In our discomfort and our suffering as a community, we are now entertaining and consciously exploring the integration of *Greater Other Dimensions* of our existence into our equation of survival. Spirit has always been part of the human experience, but more than ever its presence and influence is becoming more evident in ways that we are able to appreciate and accept as valid by both science and the humanities. Science has validated much of the physical and nonphysical phenomena present here, while the humanities have fostered faith in where the creative mind and heart is leading us. These two fields of enquiry, although approaching each other from opposite ends of the same spectrum, are leading us to the same realizations about how the world works, and how we as individuals are integral to its evolution. Each is becoming more accepting and allowing of the value and necessity of the other as the concept of synchronicity is becoming a visible reality. Some in the Western Medical community are seeing the significance of Energy Medicine in ways that make sense to them. There is increasing evidence that demonstrates how we think and feel affects our health and wellbeing. In our discomfort, we summon the courage to be led beyond what we believe is threatening, to find out what exists and is inherent in both approaches and within us as individuals.

The opposition within us, between the masculine and feminine energies, is reaching out for something beyond our current identities, to gain understanding through a more objective lens then self. The same phenomena that is appearing under the lens of microscopes and the expressed ideals of the humanities is opening our awareness to Greater Other Dimensions beyond what we currently recognize with our naked eyes. Our mind, in its agility and vastness, is the conduit that will take us to trust this truth if we develop faith in our skills to harness its potential. We have an agreed-upon name for this intelligence. We call it *energy*, and no group or sect, or school of thought, can object to this name as it is science-based and easily related to by all cultures and belief systems. As it reveals itself, *because we have sought to understand it*, we are gaining greater understanding and appreciation of its sacred role in all life. It is appearing and responding to our enquiries, be they under the microscope or through our prayers, to be what others since the beginning of time have known to be *GOD*.

Before we awaken to recognize self
we will experience a loss of meaning and purpose to who we are.

❧ ❧ ❧

There are times in all of our lives when we look around us and see nothing we can relate to or identify as relating to us. We are lost and we can't find our way home. We don't know what the next step is and we become consumed with a search for meaning. We plead for some sign that we are going to find peace somewhere within us, or that we are at least headed in the right direction! Our experience of life so far seems to have done nothing to prepare us for this challenge. In the midst of this realization, we stand naked of *an identity* that we can accept for ourselves. The more we seek, the more opposition and discomfort we seem to encounter, not only with others, but also within ourselves. Without our realizing it, we focus on all that we are not. The negative aspects of ourselves overwhelm us and seem to fragment us further. We cling desperately to the past when all seemed to be well while knowing the real solution to our problem lies elsewhere. This is not the way that we want to experience life. We have lost our place, our sense of belonging, and have lost faith in our personal power to change it.

The only thing that seems real, is a gut wrenching void inside us that life as we've known it has some how slipped out of our grasp and we don't function well here. We wonder if we have somehow missed the primordial loop of acceptance that assures us we are going to be all right, and that we are doing what we are supposed to be doing. Moreover, as busy as we find ourselves, our *doing* seems endless and empty. We become tired of seeking the magic pill that everyone else seems to have forgotten to share with us. We seem to have somehow slipped from our moorings into a deep abyss where there is nothing but darkness, a darkness that we cannot relate to or find our way out of. Worst of all, we fear that if we honestly speak of this discontent, it will sever us from the relationships we currently value. In this moment of realization, we are no longer the person we were and cannot figure out who we are now. All we can focus on is what our external world mirrors to us about the hopelessness of our personal physical reality. We are all too aware of what we are not, and will never be. This is the experience of *isolated-self*, and it becomes our experience of reality when we find ourselves here.

Recognizing self enables us to shed our identity
and stand naked in our truth:
to stand ready to be clothed by grace.

≈ ≈ ≈

The discomfort of self, when we unknowingly attach to it exclusively, can become entrenched in an illusion that it represents who we are in our entirety. Our life will continue to mirror back to us this limitation, as long as we remain consciously separate from knowing it for what it is, relative to our spirit. Becoming aware of the role that archetypes play in our experience, and how self relates to these archetypes, or collective energetic patterns, can help us to build a foundation in which spirit can be realized through the acceptance of our humanness. One of the most common archetypes is *the victim*, and although we may not recognize how our thoughts and perceptions revolve around believing we are *victims*, we continually draw experience to us that will further endorse this belief. As long as we keep functioning with this unrecognized belief that sees who we are in a certain way, we miss the opportunity to accept who we choose to be relative to that identity. In becoming aware of what we currently have bought into as our reality, and consciously deciding to grow past it in awareness, we take a huge step into the unknown. Without the desire to seek and know the various aspects of who we are beyond our current experience of these archetypes, we remain isolated, and the door to a greater awareness of self, or a more expanded understanding of who we are beyond the victim, or the martyr, or the orphan, remains unconscious. Often *limited-self* unconsciously identifies with these archetypes in relation to the roles we play in life and misses realizing the choice we all have to be who we choose to be within these roles. *Who we choose to be* defines the roles *in relation* to us, whereas the archetype that is currently recognized and endorsed limits us from perceiving *what is possible for self* to express within that role. When self is attempting to expand beyond its current identity, it meets resistance, and often the illusion of who we are affiliates itself with an archetype, such as *the victim*, rather than the expansiveness that our true being is offering us. We unknowingly believe we are *the victim* as a mother, or as a wife, or as an employee. The archetype permeates itself into these various parts of self so we come to experience its many nuances, until we recognize it as being with us, and choose more constructive expression and understanding of it. Where we experienced the *angry victim*, or *frustrated victim* before, we realize we are an individual *who feels* angry, or frustrated, or *having the experience* of victimization. The victim is not who we are in our entirety.

Our children, in their innocence, verbalize more openly what they feel as they feel it, but often we don't recognize its significance in relation to us. Archetypes are pools of reference, but a child hasn't yet learned to identify or rationalize such things even though they experience them. It is often when a limited expression of one archetype is strongly demonstrated within a child's environment that we begin to see the *symptoms of their struggle* with accepting it first surface. As a parent this is the gift of our children's innocence, and to receive it we must open ourselves to receive them as they initially express themselves, recognizing what it mirrors of us. We may grow in our understanding not only of them, but of ourselves if we meet them constructively when it surfaces. As they begin to develop a sense of self, they attempt to reconcile this archetypal pattern. Of course, it is often within the home that they challenge the imposed projection, and those within the home are the ones demonstrating the limited expression, so it is easy to see how they could become conflicted before they even get out of the gate. When they meet external resistance, and it is not respected as a part of their growth and encouraged to find constructive expression, it can be turned inward to a belief that something is wrong with them.

When I ask the young children in my office to tell me the most important thing they'd like help with, they don't tell me about how their stomach hurts, or they can't sleep or are in pain. They tell me they're having a hard time with friends, and they don't like school because of it, and they admit this as if they are the only person in the world with this problem because they are different and others don't like them. In their admission, there is sense of relief. They honestly don't know how to expand themselves in the situation. We attach to emotion without acknowledging its influence, and depending upon how we see ourselves in relation to everything outside of us, our body responds with fluidly or becomes constricted. The archetypes are energetic patterns that influence us and depending upon how we learn to identify ourselves from the models in our life, they can influence how we perceive life, and who we believe we are. Archetypes influence how we as individuals respond to challenge, and those that we don't like as they exist within us, we don't allow to grow in expression, because we don't know a substitute for it. Interestingly, the child's stomachache most often occurs at school, not at home. When circumstance changes, and there is an opportunity for resolution but we cannot perceive it, the part of self that we have stashed inside rears its head to get our attention, by creating discomfort. Discomfort is what we experience because we are being beckoned to step out of our conditioned comfort zone, expose this part of self, in a situation where *another may allow it to transform* into something that expresses our magnificence. In the home, in this case, the exposed vulnerability gets shut down because to move through resolving it requires that the parents recognize their limited understanding of what the child is attempting to express beyond their own experience. As parents, are we allowing of our children to think independently and voice their thoughts even though they don't jive with our perceptions?

Let's relate this to the example of the clay with the victim and the magician. If, as parents, we are unknowingly committed to seeing the clay as a victim would see it, then when our children express a desire to make something with the clay, we tell them it is impossible. It's not because we don't want them to be successful, but because we want to protect them from disappointment or harm. When they go to school, they are encouraged to get dirty and make something with a clump of clay. I'd get a stomach ache too, if inside me there was a fear to allow such an experience for myself, because "it is impossible" and I believe that I am sure to fail or be humiliated in allowing myself the experience. Our personal perceptions see our outer world as either for or against us, and our choices and physical health reflect these beliefs. To give treatment for the stomachache without resolving the conflict that exists on this energetic level is to miss the *gift of the symptom* to guide us towards greater awareness of who we have the ability to choose to be, independent of another's idea of what is possible for us. No parent in the world would knowingly hurt their child, or limit their ability to be successful, but often in our unrecognized patterns of relating to life, we pass down our fears instead of encouraging those we love to look challenge in the face and give it their best shot. There will always be another chance to try another way if at first they don't succeed.

This experience is the same for adults, but as adults, we aren't as flexible at accepting sudden change for the good, as we no longer acknowledge our own innocence as a valid experience. We are conditioned not to build up our hopes, or expose our true self, in order to avoid the experience of disappointment, failure, rejection, or isolation. We'd rather stick with the familiar and struggle in the hope that things will change for the better. We unknowingly justify staying where we are emotionally and spiritually, wallowing in our discomfort, or fighting our inner dragon, but not revealing our perceptions openly. We rely upon the sympathy of others, or convictions of others, and avoid taking responsibility for our situation because to reveal our sensitivity is too threatening. It is a heavy existence, in both mind and body, and the density of these feelings makes relating to spirit very difficult. We personally hold the power to change this for ourselves, and as much as others may be able to see how our pain has become self-inflicted, we remain blind to our part in choosing to stay this way. It is very natural to be caught in this web of powerlessness, when unrecognized anger, grief, and fear are running our lives.

In openly revealing our discomfort when it rears its head, we allow another into our experience to remind us of who we can potentially be. For every person we do allow in, we also invite in another depth of realization about who we are, and have the opportunity to be relative to him or her. Revealing self turns the fear of humiliation, rejection, and defeat into the experience of being clothed in grace so we may stand as we are openly and with humility.

> *The illusion of isolation knows no alliance, as self*
> *has chosen to stand against the world.*
> *The illusion of inclusion knows no enemy, as self*
> *has chosen to identify with our world.*
> *Truth transcends all illusion, when self seeks to stand*
> *as a likeness of God, within our world.*

ꝏ   ꝏ   ꝏ

Recognizing an archetype or collective identity in another is easier than recognizing an archetype in ourselves. So often what sets us off in others is simply a mirroring of our own negative characteristics back to us. When we are upset by the actions or words of another, we don't realize that they are simply responding to the energy we put out in hopes of being recognized. In recognizing the limited perception as we hold it within ourselves, we are given the opportunity to expand it into a greater understanding, and expression available to us. We carry our story in our energetic field, and although it is invisible to most, everyone responds to it automatically before we say or do anything. It is this story, expressed by our energetic body that determines how others respond to us. We can change this field for the better by being more open and at ease with who we are. In allowing in life, we expand our knowledge and experience of it. The more positive and enriching our field becomes the more positive and enriching our experience of others will be. We move about in the world confident in how we feel and think about ourselves. We feel safe enough to be receptive to others influences without doubting who we are relative to them. We can have the most horrible emotional scars and experiences, but if we decide to become a richer person for having had them, then they fill that field with strength, not demoralization. This invisible field grows bigger and bigger the more we trust ourselves to experience life and others, because we endorse our faith in humanity. We believe in ourselves when we extend our consciousness outward to blend self with the boundlessness of spirit. We never *feel alone* when spirit enters our awareness and becomes our experience even when we appear to be physically alone.

One perception of *limited-self* is its experience as *the victim*. As long as this alliance with the victim persists, *limited-self* will always see the effects of another's actions as negative and personally against them. Limited-self remains separate from letting in *any* experience that can broaden their understanding of this part of themselves. This cycle becomes self's experience over and over again. Our perceptions repeatedly confirmed through this cycle create a self-fulfilling prophecy that we don't realize we have the power to change. In unintentionally attaching our identity to that of the victim, we *become* the victim, and we perceive everything around us through the eyes and ears of the victim. There is a subtle difference between being a victim and being victimized. When we identify ourselves as a victim, we feel powerless. When we identify ourselves as victimized, there is an opening created by us to receive spirit, which enables us to change our experience of the situation. As subtle as that distinction may seem, it is profound in terms of what we set up for ourselves to experience and perceive as our personal reality. As an *individual,* we may find ourselves in a situation where we *feel like a victim,* and because we do not believe the victim is who we are, we open ourselves to possibilities that allow us to transform the experience of the victim. If an aspect of self attaches to being the victim because that is all we can identify with, we continue to experience being the victim. What we hear and see from others is through the eyes and ears of the victim, not who we are as individuals with choice and resources at our disposal.

We have all heard stories of people who have done courageous and inspiring things in the face of horrific challenges. These examples demonstrate that it is *how* we move through challenge that is the key, not whether or not challenge exists. Life challenges come in many forms. We lose a loved one, we are diagnosed with a terminal illness, or we lose our job. How we respond to these challenges determines how we will emerge from the ashes. There is no question life is full of surprises, many of which are not gift-wrapped and tied with a pretty bow, and neatly labeled for us to recognize as a gift for us. We have to shake off the tendency to become complacent and accepting of a negative fate, and seek to liberate the resourcefulness that is within our grasp to exercise.

Loneliness is the experience of not growing,
to fill the space allowed for us to expand in the absence of a lost loved one.
We are invited to know them more intimately beyond their physical form,
as we embrace their presence,
and grow in awareness of being with them.

∼ ∼ ∼

The fear of death has a huge influence on how we handle challenge. We become so protective of our physical life that we place unnecessary limits on what we are capable of experiencing. We place these same limits on what we allow our children and loved ones to experience because we are afraid of losing them. If we identify ourselves as mother or father or spouse, then to loose one of these relationships means losing our sense of place in life. When people physically leave the earth plane, and die to their physical form, there can be a space created that we perceive as absence. It feels like a void in all the places they were present in our lives, and we miss them. If we unknowingly have relied on another for our identity, then the space that remains feels like a loss, as if part of us is missing and is impossible to retrieve. When they first go, we are aware of emptiness where they once existed for us, and resided in our daily life, and there is tremendous emotion present for us in letting them go. Once we accept our loss, and allow ourselves to enter the process of letting them go, through acceptance of our own fears in living without them, we begin to move through a process of our own, and there becomes awareness in what appeared to be emptiness before. The *embodiment* of their spirit left, and in that place once occupied by form, is a space for us to grow into. That same emotional energy that surfaces as grief, once accepted and moved through opens us to the fluidity of the greater dimensions of emotional energy that becomes spiritual energy. This now fluid emotional energy enables us to feel and know the subtlety of spirit, and we consciously can begin feeling their presence in a new way. The part of them that holds meaning in our hearts is still there, even though their physical presence has dissolved, as we have become more spiritually conscious. It may be through this natural cycle of life that we draw closer to embracing awareness of spirit, and become less attached to our identity and more aware of our soul.

Birth and death mark significant passages of actualization, and when we begin to perceive life in new ways, we expand our experience of it. When people leave us, whether they leave to go away to school or they leave us for another relationship, they are giving us the opportunity to strengthen our faith in life, to move past the limited experience of our adopted identity. To find faith in spirit is to reach out with our minds into the unknown, to enter consciously the experience of knowing spirit, and be open to receive a greater experience of life. For many of us, a loved one's death forces us to reach out in search for the return of experience with them. In our reaching out, we allow ourselves to enter the realm of spirit, where they are alive at this higher frequency, and can become known to us in a new way by our feeling their presence. There is life perceived at this subtle level of awareness, but not in the way we have come to expect it or trust that it exists in the physical form. Life is not limited to our world of material proof as we have come to understand it. There are many dimensions to experience. Do you doubt that you think just because you can't see your thoughts? As humans, we have sensory awareness built into our physical experience that once accepted, explored, and developed, can enhance our understanding of what is real and what is an assumed identity of ourselves in physical form.

With every experience that endorses the *limited-self's* experience, comes the opportunity to endorse our spiritual awareness. We remain spiritually immature when we refuse to reach a greater understanding of ourselves or the meaning of relationship with others. Others are continually blamed and dismissed for their wrongful actions, when it is *isolated-self*, caught in its emotional response that is protecting itself from pain and holding onto limited perceptions. We continue to *feel* hurt, and we even say things like, "I am hurt."; " I am misunderstood."; "It's not fair to me."; instead of acknowledging our feelings as part of our experience, not as a way to define who we are. Changing our internal dialogue from "I am hurt" to "*I am feeling hurt*" shifts us into accepting that self is experiencing hurt, not becoming it! In not recognizing our emotions as an energy that we experience as a person, as self, our isolated-self is kept from exercising its ability to grow beyond this limited perception into a greater experience of itself, because emotionally it is stuck in the hurt. Self has identified itself with the hurt and nothing else beyond it that can reveal a greater reality. Isolated-self remains intact, exactly as it is in its hurtful, unconscious emotional state, completely cut off from a greater experience of reality. We suffer here, and it becomes a self-fulfilling prophecy to remain in the experience of the victim, separate from spirit that has the ability to expand our understanding and alleviate our experience of being alone.

Choosing to be Heaven on Earth
is accepting that there is more than what we know in this moment.
We must find our wings and merge self
with a greater consciousness.

ᴥ   ᴥ   ᴥ

How in the world could one experience a positive expression of the victim? Who would consciously choose to suffer? Most of us will deny that the victim is part of us, and yet we all have this energy present in our psyche. It is how we choose to see ourselves in relation to the victim and whether or not we recognize it when the victim archetype is engaged. It is not a question of whether or not it exists, it is a question of in what context and state it exists within us. Are we experiencing the victim as an accepted and recognized energy, one that poses no threat to our survival, and enables us to develop other aspects of ourselves that otherwise would never be explored? Or is it a contained and disdained energy that we believe is disempowering and impossible to transform? We alone have the power to choose to experience it as friend or foe, light or shadow, because we as an individual stand relative to it, not as it. Until we can merge *our self* with *the victim*, transcending the suffering seems like an impossible task. But without this discomfort, we would not develop awareness of other dormant attributes in ourselves. Often we separate *who we really are* from self, as if containing and isolating self, will somehow keep it from infecting the other parts of us we feel are vulnerable. Who we are in our entirety goes beyond our self's experience, and includes the *Greater Other Dimensions* of our being. So begins the *process* of inner alchemy that opens us to accepting a greater reality that spirit has the ability to bring to our experience of self. Our physical bodies are subject to the laws of mortality, but spirit is eternal, and nothing can dampen its ability to enlighten and foster our faith in any situation, no matter how horrific the circumstances may be.

We all experience the victim energy because it is collectively present in our realm of experience as humans, so as a collective archetype it can fuel growth for us personally, because self *feels* its presence and self is motivated to develop strengths as a result of being challenged. How we experience the victim is a direct reflection of how we perceive who we are. And also how we can change our perceptions of self to better *meet* challenge, look it in the face, and give it our best shot at *who we are*. The more we consciously acknowledge that the victim exists within us, the broader our awareness of the victim archetype becomes. Our ability to change suffering into *a conscious choice to grow* emerges. We *enable* the magician, not by disabling the victim, but by accepting the victim exists, and we have the courage to work with it! In recognizing its appearance in us, we may choose to know its there, but keep enabled to work with life beyond its threatened influence. When we recognize more of ourselves, we see the diversity and the vastness of the archetypal energy, beyond the positive and negative impressions possible within an identified realm. We may have the *feeling* of injustice, and the *experience* of being dismissed, but the actual archetype is not personal in nature, and unless we allow it to take over and dictate who we are relative to it. Think of an archetype as an umbrella to define a specific flavor of experience that we collectively relate to, and endorse or *transform* through our own experience of it. An archetype is not in itself emotionally defined, but because we experience an archetype through self's emotional responses, such as through grief, fear, love, and anger, the definition of it becomes personal for each individual. Archetypes can enable self to recognize itself, which can be helpful in understanding what we have unconsciously become in our limited beliefs and assumptions about who we are.

Self has its own unique collection of perceptions that define us as individuals, and our beliefs and understanding of a particular archetype are often emotionally founded. The two, archetypes and self, although I am defining them as separate, are very intricately intertwined from the time we become aware that we are individuals, and this is often why we become stuck. We allow our perceived limitations to define us and dictate how our lives will play out. Self and archetypes operate on many levels and appear to us in many forms. There are many aspects of self, and each aspect can, without knowing it, attach itself to the identity of a specific archetype. If one aspect of self has been imprinted by a painful experience from the past that our circumstances forced us to endure alone, we are left isolated in our pain. When we witness this part of ourselves in others, or it seeks expression in us, we associate it with negative attributes and shut it down. We avoid people who reflect it, and we avoid situations that antagonize it in us, and in doing this we miss growth to experience anything different about it. The victim sits with the *clay of life* stashed in the back of the cupboard drying out and collecting dust, pretending it doesn't exist, while the magician has long moved on to other experiences that allow in more to work with. The magician's clay bowl continues to fill with rain, and provides sustenance when there is thirst, but it is "in play" with the universe to realize greater potential, not stashed away in hopes of it disappearing.

Often the constructive expression of the same archetype is one that our life leads us to develop, and we are stuck because we have an unconscious disdain for this experience of ourselves without recognizing its origins or knowing that the ability to change it rests in our own hands. It would be great if the positive and negative attributes were easily recognized as belonging to the same archetype. Unfortunately, we don't make the connection when emotions enter the picture. The magician isn't going to hang around for a long time trying to convince the victim to try to make something of the clay. Remember the child who complains about being bored. "Go figure it out for yourself", is more than likely the message the victim hears after the magician offers encouragement and is dismissed for their input. The victim hears how they have been abandoned, and brings into play another archetype, like *the orphan*, and explores the influence of that archetype with the same limitation but with a different slant on the perception. The magician knows that the victim is capable when the victim is willing to hold their own power, because the magician owns their own victim and chooses who they are relative to it. The magician also knows that the lesson is not one for them to teach, for we each have something valuable to learn in relation to our personal journey. Perhaps the magician will learn another level of *the victim* and discover yet another expression for it that gets added into the collective pool of consciousness for others to draw upon when they seek knowledge of it. A bowl to catch rain is but one expression!

The aspect of us, as a disdained archetype, becomes our own isolated-self, compartmentalized into a fixed perception that we continue to believe has no resolution. The emotional component leaves us with the impression that we can't detach from our experience. We become *the victim*, or *the rebel*, or *the orphan*, when in fact self is lost in the illusion of these energies being only what it knows from its experience so far. We fail to see that it was our experience of that archetype or adopted role model, in that moment, which we are allowing to define us, not *who we are* beyond it. We unconsciously believe that we have no choice but to experience ourselves this way. Without understanding that we have the ability to choose for ourselves, we remain dependant on another's perceptions of us to inform us as to who we are. In turn, we perceive others with the same qualities from this fixed perception, and miss experiencing anything else from them. We often remain dependant on another's perceptions of us without realizing that we have accepted these perceptions as our own, and as such, *we may change them at will for ourselves.*

Situations change and we may be in a different position, not reliant on another, when we experience that energy challenging us again. As with the example of the child with the stomachache, when we consciously begin working with life, our discomfort can be used as a *positive indicator* that it is time to let our resistances down to *allow in the clay of life* to inform us of it's possibilities for us to express another way. In holding onto our fixed perceptions as stagnant truths, we don't allow in anything that can show us greater truths. That one portion of the archetype that we previously experienced becomes our reference for that archetype, and we often decide at the moment when the impression was made, that we are never going to be like that because it is bad. That archetype shows up often though, and not always in that one particular expression. But in whatever form it appears, we respond unknowingly to our own limited-perception and assign negative qualities to it. We form judgments about these expressions, and more importantly, the people expressing them, when we fail to recognize them and accept them in ourselves. This can make the archetype a very misunderstood and seemingly restrictive energy, when in fact it consists of many expressions that are inclusive of many positive as well as negative attributes that can enrich our awareness of who we are beyond them.

Children are innocent to these underlying dynamics, as are many of the adults in the role of fostering children's growth. The assumptions we all make put self on autopilot, and when we find ourselves lost in the fog, we shut ourselves off from letting in life to know it more expansively, and keep focused on trying to see what we're set on finding. We remain blind to our part in allowing this to happen. If as role models we do not embrace our own individuality, it is difficult for us to foster growth for our children within respectful limits. Children need to explore roles for themselves that foster their development into unique individuals. As adults we also hold the knowledge of innocence and in recognizing our ability to align with it, we too may further explore roles and foster development of our unique expressions as individuals. We all develop tastes and preferences through experience, but if we nurture growth without clarity about what criteria is being met, or more importantly *who's criteria* is being met, not only children, but we as well, can believe we are inadequate because we don't meet an unrecognized standard. Measuring up to another's expectations of us can create anxiety because we are challenged to figure out what they want. We try to *please* them as long as we are dependent on them. How do we successfully meet another's standards while building faith in learning to think for ourselves if we are denied acknowledgement for our part in the process? If we are to move more effortlessly from a codependent society into one that is interdependent, the skills that allow us to know what is in our hearts must be nurtured so we gain faith in our competence to be independent. What we discover on our own journey must be considered valid criteria for finding our place in the world. We must accept and honor what we discover as true for ourselves and then allow in the *clay of life* to integrate with self so we become a greater expression in our outer world. If as adults, we judge reality by what we think, and never venture to expand our thinking because we are questioned by those with less experience, we miss growing wings that show us a greater experience of reality.

It is through reclaiming consciousness of who we are,
that self gains the knowledge to become more.
We realize we alone decide for ourselves,
who we choose to be in this moment.

❧ ❧ ❧

Children repeatedly test their boundaries as a way of discovering who they are relative to others. Adults do as well, but not as openly. We begin to make connections between what our outer world demonstrates to us about the perceptions of our internal world. When the boundaries are introduced with love and respect, we learn to constructively respect them in return, and gain security from our ability to work with them in ways that makes sense to us. We earn the privilege to move beyond these boundaries as we gain confidence and awareness of self because we are encouraged to do so by those who support our growth. Our inner world gains security when, as children, our first experience of our outer world is stable and consistent. Self can feel and act out these feelings in an effort to learn more about its identity and relatedness to others. When a newborn cries, its caregivers initially act out a laundry list of possible comforts. Is the baby hungry? Is the baby dry? Does the baby need to be held? Is the baby tired? On another level, a caregiver that allows the baby into her own being intuitively knows when she is needed and how to respond. In this way the baby learns to trust that her needs will be met thus setting up a lifelong deep-seeded sense of security. The foundation of security is anchored by the experience of *dependency* being accepted and allowed without any resistance. There is nothing to impede her actualization of self beyond dependency.

When a three-year-old misbehaves at mealtime, she learns that there are socially-accepted rules of conduct that make communal dining a pleasure for everyone. She learns these lessons in the loving environment of her home, where she is accepted as being an important contributor to the family's experience together. Her *independence* is supported as she begins to express herself and is met with constructive boundaries that are allowing of her development of her unique contribution. There is nothing to impede her learning constructive expression for herself as she becomes aware of her independence.

The teenager who didn't get asked to the Prom and questions whether she will attend or not, is encouraged by secure adults to attend because it is important to her, regardless of whether or not she has a date. (As adults, how many women won't attend an event alone, even though it is of great interest to them?) The teenager as an individual is supported for having the security to honor how she feels and thinks about herself, independently of another's willingness to accept her. In each case, the help comes in a way that is appropriate for the child's level of development. The depth of the help offered depends on how responsive we are able to be to the true needs of the situation. If our goal is to solve the problem, we miss the opportunity to be supportive of their personal journey, which only they are capable of choosing to embark upon once they feel secure.

We give our children boundaries to keep them safe, but through the eyes of children, they appear to be restrictions on their boundlessness unless they are part of choosing how they would like to cooperate in honoring them. Sadly, instead of giving children choices about what they can do within our criteria when they challenge us, we tell them what they can't do! There's that masculine energy with the decision already made about what will and will not be allowed. It's no surprise that this attitude meets resistance. Two-year-olds outwardly demonstrate their protests in response to the word "no" for this reason. As self enters their awareness, and they practice asserting it, the masculine energy of exercising choice also enters the picture for them to experience. The last thing the developing masculine energy wants to hear from anyone else is a "no" that dismisses their own developing thinking process. Where two-year-olds outwardly demonstrate their protests, adults dig in their heels in more subtle ways. It's not the "no" message as much as the delivery of the message that evokes confrontation with our own masculine energy. The dismissive "no" can be demoralizing when heard by the fragile self. The dismissive "no" from the masculine energy has no interest in a dialogue with its audience. It has come to its decision without any attempt at communication. It is devoid of respect. We could engage co-operation in our children if we told them what our criteria is and asked for their suggestions. A resolution could then be reached that would satisfy their desires and our role in ensuring their wellbeing at the same time. In this way, the same masculine energy is exercised compassionately because it includes a nurturing component that honors our feminine receptivity, and we earn their receptivity and trust in return because their masculine energy is honored as valid by us.

We always have choice as individuals, but learning discernment comes through experience, and we can't expect to develop this constructively without practice in making decisions from early on. For a child, experiencing security in relating to opposition on the home front encourages them to set their sights on experiencing positive outcomes when they find themselves in conflict with others who think differently than they do. They meet new experience without the assumption that intimidation and frustration will be the outcome when meeting resistance with others. They simply *assume the best in others* because they have experience that endorses *knowing the best in themselves.* The boundaries for physical safety are obviously not flexible for young children, but on a self-development level, there is more to be considered that includes acknowledging their inner sense of security to be who they are. Defining boundaries to our children becomes very difficult if we do not know *ourselves* or have the security within us to welcome challenge. We must be flexible in how boundaries are defined and implemented. If we take a moment to consider what the purpose of the boundary is; whether it's to ensure their physical safety or our personal comfort, we would more easily recognize our children's abilities rather than impress our own fears upon them. In the moment of determining what we are protecting, their safety or our insecurity, we instantly recognize how to relate to the best qualities in them, and elicit a cooperative response that honors their goodness and reinforces the goodness in ourselves. In fearing for their safety, we may inadvertently be sending the message that we do not have faith in their ability to think for themselves and understand the concept of safety relative to their experience of their outer world.

That emphatic "no" expressed to a sensitive child is perceived by them as a restriction on who they are rather than a concern for their wellbeing. Those initially-defined boundaries implemented with care become the experience of an *ever-expanding trust* in themselves, in us, and ours in them. Our children experience faith in human nature as a reality, and develop faith for honestly relating their needs to others in constructive ways that are mutually respectful. We summon growth in our own abilities to relate constructively to our children when we encourage them to challenge imposed limits hand in hand with expanding their level of awareness in honoring the world in which they live. Our children begin mirroring a positive reality that our own inner world has consciously chosen to experience with them.

> *A young child's drawings reflect how they see*
> *themselves relative to their outer world.*

≈ ≈ ≈

Let's say you are seven years old and you are asked to draw a circle on a piece of paper. When you are finished you are to stand up at the front of the class and share your drawing with your classmates. Deciding to draw a big circle covering the surface of a piece of paper or a small dot in the corner reflects your personal perceptions, and what is pleasing to oneself. If this is seen by someone across the room, it takes into account something more than one self, as there is another purpose involved, beyond the mere rendering of the picture. Purpose to a young child is about expressing oneself, and it is not taking into account anything but the moment in which it is being expressed by them. It is all about self in the beginning, because the child is exploring what he can do and who he is relative to his outer world. The focus on developing the masculine energy is strong early on, but the feminine is very much present also. In a child who is not encouraged to recognize his ability to choose what he thinks about things, the masculine energy can be left undeveloped. When the child is met with another's criticism, his feminine energy is left exposed and is experienced as vulnerability. The sensitive ability of his feminine to birth greater consciousness is not *allowed* but rather *defended* by his masculine. Criticism, when not constructively or respectfully given, is missed as a gift to be received, and instead becomes the experience of being judged.

When we are young, we approach new situations from a place of boundlessness before experience is present that demonstrates limitations. When entering another more expanded situation like a daycare or a classroom that involves functioning with others, the purpose goes beyond just considering oneself. But the masculine energy is not secure in its abilities yet, so it's very impressionable. In the classroom, if the child goes ahead and makes the dot in the corner, and then experience a lack of enthusiasm in his classmates because they don't understand what he is trying to say, he has learned something about the importance of taking into account something outside of himself. If those fostering growth in the child encourage him to try another way next time that enables him to share his ideas with others more effectively, he may increase his awareness and not be reduced to feeling inadequate. Self is in charge of making decisions. While others may point out the things he might wish to consider in the process, ultimately no one can make him do things a certain way, without forcibly taking hold of him. *How he feels about the experience* is what makes him open to change. The good feelings of acceptance encourage the exploration of other possibilities. Bad feelings simply force us to doubt our choices, retreat in the opposite direction and completely shut the door to further cooperative exploration.

It takes very big, secure people to make room for others to make mistakes and be given the time and space to recognize and work through them constructively, without feeling less for having made the mistake in the first place. Big people have learned through their own experience that there is no such thing as mistakes, just opportunities to broaden awareness. We don't know what we don't know, and admitting our ignorance is difficult if others form opinions about us that make us feel inadequate and small. Chances are that for the child who has drawn himself as a small dot on the page, the experience of being exposed in front of a classroom is already perceived as threatening, before anything happens. As the circle grows, so does our energetic field, so does our capacity for greater awareness and interaction with others outside of us, because we allow more into our awareness. Children are learning how to think for themselves, and allow in those around them without getting overwhelmed or lost in the process.

Our own disappointments in life as adults are not so different from those experienced by a child. We just have more layers of emotional impressions that cloud our ability to recognize what is important to us on a deeper level. We can choose to continue expanding our own thinking, and be that clear voice for the children that depend on us for their growth. As with *the victim*, so many people in our children's environment actually believe they are inadequate, so it doesn't take much to endorse this belief in them through our own masculine expression with them. In being *big* with others, modeling a *compassionate masculine energy* when dealing with others, we create space for exploration. They in turn become bigger people by making choices that enhance their awareness of the situation and their awareness of others beyond self. Mistakes met by the masculine energy asserting its position through criticism are belittling and bring doubt and fear into one's experience instead of sparking a desire to explore the challenge from another angle. In avoiding challenging situations, or avoiding constructive feedback with our children, we can inadvertently give them the message that we believe they are vulnerable. Sometimes we need to challenge them so they learn to stand up and voice what is important to them. Investing in their sensitivity as a magnificent virtue to support is a lot easier if we are secure with our own sensitivity. Having faith in our children is the best support we can be for them for we endorse their innocence and ability to learn constructively. If we have given up the faith in our own process of growing, then how are we to be a credible advocate in their eyes?

It is interesting to watch the process of self-realization unfold as it's mirrored in our children's eating habits. They like certain foods and dislike others. They keep their food in separate categories on the plate. They often don't want to try new food or mix up the food on their plate. They eat one thing at a time, and as they become more aware of self and more comfortable with exercising their ability to make what they believe are good choices, their food tastes expand and their courage and flexibility in going through their discomfort of trying new things expands right along with this greater awareness. They become more receptive to entertaining new ideas and they gain confidence. When there are only so many choices and one is left to figure out what to do within those limits, this process takes us naturally to a greater awareness of self's likes and dislikes.

In today's society we have an abundance of food choices, many of which are seductive treats that are available on a daily basis. When our children turn up their noses at the food on their plates, we rifle through the fridge offering many, many alternative solutions, in an attempt to accommodate their tastes. Just think of the insanity of this approach for one moment, as the child is limited in experience and exposure to really recognize what they need physically to be healthy. This is an emotional response on our part to *keep them happy*. We want a short term solution to their discomfort. In our frantic attempts to pacify, we teach them to avoid discomfort and back down in the face of challenge. Whether the issue is food or starting school or dressing appropriately for the weather, how we respond in the situation models awareness for them. As adults, if we don't recognize our own emotional responses, we miss recognizing the difference between actual physical needs versus the emotional expressions of our children. How we respond to our children is an excellent mirror reflecting back to us where we need to grow in our own awareness of self.

The new mother who hears her newborn scream at the top of its lungs when it needs something must be ready to calm the child. If she doesn't trust herself, she is reliant on a check-list to figure out what the baby wants. If she has been allowing and accepting of her personal journey, she is open to receive the energetic impressions from the baby and will allow the scream to inform her of the baby's need at that moment, past how it is being outwardly expressed. Mothers discern the subtle difference in the way the baby's cry feels inside themselves, and respond accordingly if their masculine energy is secure enough for their feminine to receive and birth greater consciousness for themselves. What happens if we operate exclusively from learned responses and don't recognize that the needs change for that baby, as does their ability to express it, as they develop? More refined and expanded expressions may be supported in the child if we don't automatically give them food, or a toy, every time they scream a certain way. We may support another in more fundamental ways once learning to identify our selves. Becoming a mother, or actualizing the *mother archetype*, brings the gift of expanded awareness if we trust ourselves to nurture greater consciousness in ourselves that extends our understanding of others. If we have never developed past being dependent on learned responses, it is hard to support independent expression in others. Not unlike the baby's outward physical growth, our own inner world grows in tandem with our children as our capacity to experience a deeper, more fulfilling relatedness to life emerges. In children's innocence, we let them into us, and our own parameters of experience are expanded to realize our own innocence again.

As adults, many of us are emotionally disabled, and because the emotional body is not recognized or honored as being a valid expression of self, we are limited in our own resourcefulness and tolerance of younger, expanding minds that challenge us. We meet challenge by offering solutions that keep *our* own emotions at bay, when sometimes the solution is not hiding in the fridge, but sitting right there in front of us. It is not visibly on the plate, but inside that little person who relies on us for creating and maintaining safe boundaries that will foster their growth. The masculine energy, when expressed by a young child, triggers our own undeveloped and insecure masculine energy that knows safe limits. When we can't feel our emotions we can't help them recognize their own feelings. Their protests get louder and their insecurities surface in the ways that are sure to get our attention, like not eating, not sleeping, and becoming disruptive when we are occupied with something that interests us. How can we help them recognize their inner needs, physically, mentally and emotionally if we can't discern our own feelings and values that need to be supported to remain healthy and vital?

When children are ill, they often become cranky, irritable, and very annoying in their demands for our attention. They don't recognize what is going on, and we tend to think it is ploy to get our attention. We may be correct about that, but it is often *not* because they are emotionally needy, it is often because they don't know how to communicate the discomfort they're physically feeling. When they are frightened they express their fear emotionally in order to evoke a response. A lot of children today are living on what amounts to garbage. An inadequate diet can be responsible for all sorts of negative behaviors. When children are not focused or attentive, or they are outwardly disruptive, we look for what is wrong with them. It is *what is right with them* that we are missing. They are responding to the garbage food we're feeding them, or as I mentioned earlier, they are expressing the symptom of conflict from not being recognized in their innocence, learning to exercise who they are constructively. Without proper nutrition, this type of behavior is often what they demonstrate. By changing their diet from processed, genetically engineered food to healthy and living, organic food, we will see the reflection of this vitality in their clear behavior. We will also know they are properly fueled to meet challenge of growth on all levels with the foundation of physical strength and alertness for support. Their inner world, when challenged, will become conscious of discomfort that they learn to work with, rather than physical disease that drains their energetic as well as physical reserves.

In becoming deaf and blind to our own energetic anatomy, we have developed a particular distaste for outwardly displayed negative emotions in others. We learn to disassociate from them. When our children are not responding the way we would like them to, we ignore that they are mirroring back to us what we have modeled so beautifully for them. We choose to side with the mental energy of the masculine to avoid investigating beyond their disruptiveness; if they are unhappy, we don't honor the fact that they are *feeling unhappy* and then suggest they may choose to focus on something that makes them feel better. Instead, we distract them by taking them shopping, letting them watch television, or anything that will take their mind off of their discomfort. In illness, as in many other forms of discomfort, we aim to find things to keep us from *being with it,* to understand what the illness is expressing that is not right for us. It is difficult to avoid discomfort when it is our immediate experience. Trying to avoid feeling uncomfortable doesn't resolve the problem, it just suppresses it. Physical imbalances in children often go unrecognized until they are acute and outwardly apparent, like a high fever, vomiting, or eruptions on their skin, because when we hear the emotion initially, we ignore the importance of what physical and energetic imbalances it may be expressing for them.

How many people wake up with a fever or headache, take an aspirin, and charge ahead with their plans for the day, eating and drinking what they assume has no impact on their health, and feel as if nothing is wrong? I suppose after finding something that provides relief, they feel that the problem is resolved. Once the bad feeling is felt no longer, there is no desire to change an existing routine or perception of themselves that is hurting them to hold onto. They will repeat the same routine and experience of themselves day after day and believe they are just fine, until the aspirin doesn't work, or a new pain surfaces that isn't alleviated by just one aspirin. It isn't even a consideration to stop and rethink what they may be doing to create the discomfort, be it the food they feed their bodies, or the thoughts they feed their minds about themselves, for that means being unproductive in concrete terms for one day. When symptoms of discomfort first appear, we often dismiss them as irrelevant and useless, and we ignore our ability to choose to stay in bed and deal with it, or realign our thinking and doing with a healthy experience of self.

If darkness is what we perceive in others
then we have yet to unveil our own true light.
Darkness is what we will continue to see,
as long as our own shadow is left unrecognized.

ॐ ॐ ॐ

When there is physical trauma and physically we heal, there is also an emotional component that is harder to heal because it is not visible or readily recognized as being left unresolved. When we are emotionally traumatized, we can literally shut off from feeling any emotions in order to preserve our integrity and remain functional. This *one aspect of self* that experienced being a victim becomes completely associated with that *victim-energy*, as this is the only thing it knows of itself through the experience. Part of us believes *we are the victim* because of the emotional component left dormant to preserve itself. Our personal experience of the victim has been influenced by the situation or relationships that existed for us at that time. We become very good at keeping these invisible emotional wounds protected and out of sight, but they are still energetically in us, and have not been given an outlet to be expressed and recognized as valid by us. In recognizing that, as we grow, our ability to choose consciously what we wish *to be* expands as well. We become aware that there are other possibilities than the one we have unknowingly become attached to, and only we can choose to open our hearts and minds to what may be beyond our personal experience so far. To continue to seek resolution through others honoring our hurts and injustices becomes a tangled maze, and we become lost in remembering just how we got there exactly. It never occurs to us that another is not able to satisfy our need to be acknowledged or able to give us permission to expand ourselves beyond their understanding of who we are.

We wear these emotions we've dissociated from like an outgrown piece of clothing that we can't bring ourselves to throw away. They appear upfront and visible energetically in our energetic anatomy, as if they were stains on our shirt sleeve, but the shirt is so comfortable we don't even recognize we have outgrown it. Just as visible as those stains, but on an energetic level, we send out unconscious signals to others that show them what is buried in us, and then we get upset at them for responding to it. At a higher level of consciousness, beyond the existing identity of self, the victim doesn't want to remain the victim as self is defining it, but we are the only ones who have the ability to change it by consciously making a different choice.

Days go by, weeks go by, and often years go by, and because of our nature as humans we are very adaptable and seek growth, we learn to work around our disabled aspects of self that experienced this *victim* energy. The victim energy is not exclusively attached to one part of self, as over time it has added its filter to many other parts of us in hopes of transforming into a fuller more realized expression. The victim doesn't wake up suddenly one day to realize that the magician has been there all along. There are other players brought to the fore within us to help us realize our abilities long before we are ready to acknowledge the magician's perception of life. Upon consciously embarking on our journey, we go out into the world to try on a few hats, exercise our *warrior* abilities so that we gain confidence in exploring these inner chambers where we believe our dragon resides. After awhile we don't even know how we have compensated, except that whenever that *victim* energy shows up in our lives, we relive the initial emotional hurt, and experience ourselves identically to the initial experience. The awareness of our victim grows the more we embrace our own journey, for we are growing, and it is appearing more at odds to what we are discovering about ourselves beyond the initial experience. This one aspect of self that was experienced in a limited way has remained isolated in its hurt and in its *perceptions of itself* at that time. It's as if it is frozen in time and has never grown or *evolved past that expression* of the victim. This aspect of self sees only injustice and helplessness as a result. In our current journey we may be exercising the *warrior*, but the *martyr* is creeping into our experience as long as these inner wounds are not resolved.

Just like an outgrown shirt, we unconsciously reach into the drawer, pull it out, and put it on because we associate comfort with it and never revisit our choice to continue to wear it. In our minds we see it in exactly the same way as the day we bought it. Like the familiar shirt, the actual current situation or other person involved is reduced to these limited impressions. That is all we can see because *emotionally* that is how we have contained it. It remains our personal truth. We cannot see in another that which we have yet to know in ourselves. If darkness is what we perceive in others, then we have yet to unveil our own true light. Darkness is what we will continue to see as long as our own is not recognized as a cover for an underlying virtue that never was given a chance to shine within us.

Deciding to change our minds about what we believe is our truth is the first step in opening the door to what is, rather than what we remember or think this darkness represents. To get beyond limited-self's perceptions, we have to choose to know more than what we currently believe is the full truth for that part of us. Reaching into that drawer and pulling out that favorite shirt requires really looking at it objectively to see if it is actually in the same shape, color, and condition as the day we bought it, and whether or not it really suits us anymore. It may just need to be recycled, or worn lovingly with the knowledge that it contains the memory of many past experiences that give us character and depth.. In seeing it for what it is, we consciously decide how we wish to move forward with it. When another responds by commenting or remarking on our choice in wearing it, we already know how we feel about it and what we believe about it, so it is not received by us as a judgment or criticism, but rather a limited expression of what they don't relate to in us. Their opinion becomes just that and they miss who we are because they don't get past the shirt. Our innocence is retrieved once we begin thinking for ourselves about what is important to us. The outer world that keeps the victim intact begins to magically dissolve as we begin to unveil our inner light and begin to take it out into the world. We begin slowly shifting from worrying what other people think into honoring what we think, and with it we attract outer experience that further expand our awareness of who we are.

Initial negative impressions are like containers in us that hold different aspects of self that actually had a negative experience that was very real at the time. As long as we believe we are stuck with how to resolve or heal from these experiences, the emotions connected to them will be used to segregate and pack them away as they exist, to isolate these parts of self from being hurt further and from hurting others. We come to believe these parts of us are bad because we hate them. We associate these parts in us as the ones responsible for creating our discomfort, so we disassociate from them so they won't upset us anymore. What we cannot accept in ourselves consciously, becomes an unconscious projection on others. Our *Greater Other Dimensions* has relentless faith in us though, and supports us continually to recognize the value of what we have buried inside. We project our unrecognized beliefs onto others unknowingly. This is our *shadow*. But to our *Greater Other Dimensions* this shadow is an unrealized light that is there for us to learn to hold and work with. The clay that the victim and magician both work with is also our shadow when we are fearful to know how to approach it. At some unconscious level we are actually fearful of this part of us, and have severed ourselves from acknowledging that it exists at all, except in others whom we make a point of avoiding so they don't hurt us.

It is no wonder that these pockets of energy we hold contained inside us over time begin to contaminate our physical bodies because of this unconscious perception of being something *bad* being held there. Those perceptions influence the cells in that area, and before we know it there are actual diseases that emerge in pockets as blockages or tumors in our physical bodies, and they in turn terrify us because they threaten our sense of survival. What originates as a decision about us fueled by intense emotion, becomes a physically real demonstration of that belief. What begins as a loss of *feeling* of wellbeing becomes an actual loss of *physical* wellbeing. The magician is in all of us, but without knowing this, we create our experience of reality by default, rather than consciously. We live in a time when to fight disease is the norm when really we're fighting unrecognized parts of ourselves. This approach to disease may serve to strengthen our *warrior*, but with an unresolved *victim* active through us, the *martyr* takes the helm, and the *innocent child* and *magician* are left on the outside, looking to be accepted into our process. The child and magician appear to be wild conjurers of thoughtless fantasy when we are in this place of denial. The seven-year-old who misbehaves at the dinner table is looking for a way to be included in the process of being a family. Our personal process can be nurtured by engaging specific positive perceptions and backing them with positive emotional influence, but we have to recognize our ability to change our approach before we can consciously embrace a greater reality. To enter this as an intellectual exercise is to embark on a wild goose chase, because we are very clever at rewriting our history to suit our way of unconscious thinking and acting.

We love to take the clumps of clay in our life, categorize them into useful and useless and then either make something of them or stash them in the back of the cupboard hoping that some day we'll pull them out and know what to do with them. When our warrior becomes active, it is helpful to recognize just what it is that we are fighting. In continuing to keep the *clay of life*, or *the cancer*, separate from us, we are committed to slaying the dragon that confronts us. In holding the clay, we may come to recognize that the true dragon is within us, and is not threatening at all if we understand its true nature. When we commit to our own personal journey we are committing to taking the clay as it appears to us. In courageously holding it in our hands and, one step at a time, deciding what we experience of it as *we allow* the impressions we actually experience of it into us. We may choose to *honor our process* of learning to first hold our formless parts of self, and then summon the courage to know them for what they really are. If we become loving and accepting of our fears and insecurities, but carry on regardless to explore self's possibilities, we have the opportunity to become master potters.

I think that many of our autoimmune diseases and cancers are really just *abused-self*, that's been locked up in disdain for so long that we have unconsciously forgotten the *innocent-self* that suffered and finally decided to shut down to the light. Physical abuse is easily recognized, but emotional wounds are not so easily identified. The innocent child who gets shut down and locked up emotionally by an adult can get pretty ugly and cruel after being kept in the dark for so long. They outwardly become the *bully* when approached by others who threaten to expose them. As a person matures, their innocent child expression that has been locked away starts to look pretty ugly and scary to them too. As a society, we conquer and control the things that scare us, as a warrior would, and we approach disease that we do not understand in the same way. Cancer, as a disease, has been given great power as a result of the way it is viewed in popular culture. We are afraid to unleash it because we have convinced ourselves that it is the enemy and it must be conquered. Cancer is our teacher as well if we allow ourselves to explore its true nature.

Imagine cancer was an abused child who hadn't bathed or put on clean clothes in years, or even see the light of day for that matter, and you opened the doors wide to find this child there. Are you going to put the child out of its misery by poisoning and killing him because seeing past what initially confronts you would take great courage? Killing the abused child would be a crime but we do this to our bodies that exhibit disease, and society endorses it, even though the person undergoing the *treatment* continues to suffer. When we feel like we've been put in a closet and forgotten about as a child, we go on to develop compensations to forget about that part of ourselves because it is painful. When we notice dirt on the carpet outside the closet door, we quickly sweep it under the rug in an attempt to hide it. This is what we do with the unwanted parts of self. We tidy up quickly so that everything looks in order for others to see. We knowingly choose to keep this part separate from our experience and not let it out into the light where it can become a vital and healthy expression of who we choose to be. We know it's there, but we are attached to its identity as an unworthy part that is unable to stand scrutiny. This becomes our internal fight: To keep this inner-child contained and disdained so it doesn't infect the rest of us as an adult.

Look at where you stand now in your life.
Accept what you confront, and admit it is scary as it appears to you.
Recognize that in order for this to remain scary,
you are choosing not to investigate beyond
how it is has been presented to you.
Consciously make a choice to have this perception
illuminated to see the truth of it, and then after holding
it, decide to banish it from your experience for good,
or live in appreciation of its value to show the nature of your true power.

෴ ෴ ෴

To banish a part of self from our experience is to create an opponent within ourselves. We will encounter this quality and expression in others until we realize it is a part of us that we refuse to acknowledge and allow to mature more fully into a positive expression within us. We create discomfort to bring awareness to this unseen, unrecognized opponent we perceive that seeks liberation. We are not *just* victims in this world, but we may choose to remain in the experience of the victim to discover and exercise our *unrealized* resourcefulness and potential as a *liberator.* We learn about our strengths, our courage, and our ability to transcend suffering through our experience of self. As long as self sees its options and ability as a single expression of who we are, then seeking greater knowledge of our being is cut off from being explored. The body manifests disease when self forgets to support and nurture what our soul has chosen for us to experience as the magnificence of God. *Self has gotten caught up in conquering and obtaining what it desires* from our outer-world, and has stopped hearing the messages of the heart, where soul can lead us. Our soul is sending us messages every second of our lives but we don't stop to acknowledge them, or know how to engage our *magnificence* in order to realize them. What does come through our consciousness that is aligned with greater expressions possible for self, we ignore, thinking it may be a trick to catch us off guard. When we have not embraced our journey as one we alone have the choice to take, we may mistake these promptings as tests to our commitment to our community's faith. We may perceive these illuminations much like the forbidden apple appears to Adam and Eve in the Garden of Eden. There is great guilt and conflict in awakening to a greater reality when we believe it will dismiss what already exists for us. Honoring the process of self *expands* us and makes conscious our *capacity to hold* who we are as a greater expression of our *Greater Other Dimensions.*

When the integrity within is supported physically and energetically, we are capable of healing the body, the mind, and the relationship we have with life again. We begin following a different leader than self, and we become conscientious about our choices, as well as about the assumptions we make about things outside our own experience. The *warrior within us* that defends self is transformed into the *truth seeker* who possesses the skills of the warrior and is therefore prepared to defend its virtues if need be, but is secure enough to allow in greater perceptions. Self was just the player up to bat when the victim energy first entered our experience. We relive the initial experience again and again, even though it is in different circumstances, because self is determined to hold the perception of its experience in place until it somehow finds acknowledgement that justifies its existence. The emotional charge we've hidden from our awareness gets triggered by situations that are offering an opportunity for us to exercise self more fully, as a *truth seeker*, independent of the victim. It is calling on something positive we have yet to exercise constructively in us, and because we have judged and decided that self is the victim, and limited in its ability to meet challenge, we keep it disabled and separate so we can continue to function. We just keep going around the same block, reenacting the initial experience in different situations with different players, but all because we honestly don't recognize that there is *another alliance besides the victim,* for this part of us to choose. We don't realize that we have chosen this alliance, and to change our minds feels like it opposes everything that we believe in, and expose our already existing vulnerability to be hurt again. We may evoke the *martyr* in ourselves by holding our position at the expense of honoring our own innocence. We get really tired of ourselves, and discouraged, because as we consciously choose to expand who we are in our life, all we attract seems to magnify the frequency and intensity of the *victim-self's* experience. We tell ourselves that to open ourselves up to go beyond this we will threaten our ability to function, but if we are honest with ourselves, we will realize that how self currently functions leaves a lot to be desired.

We feel pushed and pulled and drawn towards a black hole that we must avoid falling into at all costs, because we believe that in that hole we will be consumed by the victim. It never occurs to us that the black hole is an illusion and that within it lies the truth of the victim and also the aspect of *magnificent-self*. Once our current perceptions are allowed in honestly, our self's alliance with the victim becomes clear, and when illuminated in truth we realize this aspect of self has *choice!* Seeing the whole picture *enables* us to choose the alliance with our *magnificent* expression of the aspect of self, instead of the victim. This aspect of self experienced the hurt, but got disabled there before it grew wings to experience the whole array of emotional experience that included happiness. The power to heal has been waiting patiently to be liberated from within what we perceived as darkness within ourselves.

After all, in this state, the hole represents the end of our sanity in coping with our life, as it currently exists. What we used to cling to for security no longer satisfies us, and what remains is the experience of being suspended, indefinitely in pain and solitude. This accepting of our discomfort, and acknowledging the beliefs we have about ourselves is heading in the direction of healing. We just don't recognize the signposts, as we have yet to open our eyes to what we have become and our personal responsibility to accept a different experience for ourselves. We have stepped past the threshold of our adopted identity into the unknown, and there doesn't seem to be a reception waiting for us on the other side. In shedding the ideas and thoughts we have about our roles, or who we are within those roles, we are accepting an invitation to grow wings. These symbolic wings will be the vehicle that will carry us through the life we had defined for ourselves and others have defined for us into a much fuller existence. In expanding our wings we open ourselves to our *Greater Other Dimensions*. We gain a new perspective on everyday problems and we are empowered. In awakening to our current identity we may begin to hold a greater capacity than the one we thought was possible. The *martyr* begins to work with the idea of being of an *altruist*. The *victim* begins to work with the idea of being a *liberator*. The *warrior* begins working with the idea of developing *presence*. The *child* recognizes its innocence and begins working with the idea of being a *magician*.

In realizing a greater capacity in which to experience our current circumstance, everything that has held us intact up to this point seems to fall away as if the glue that held us together has dissolved. As the glue dissolves, those wings begin to unfurl and we trust them to carry us to clarity. Unless we place faith in them to carry us through our challenges, confusion about who we are can set in and take up residence in that void we feel deep inside. We flap those wings around and we flounder about, making a lot of noise as a signal for others to recognize how fragile we are and how much we need help. We become complainers, or stoics, and then finally when others just fall away because they can't be seen or heard through our racket, we stand justified that indeed we are *the victim,* because the thought of the unknown is far more threatening to entertain. This is a lonely place where there is no one to comfort us. It feels like we have been banished from the kingdom to live in a remote cave, or chained up in captivity where we are of no threat to other's ideas about security. The harder we try to hang on to things the way they are, the wider the gate opens to self-judgment and self-loathing. There is a deep hopelessness and sense of defeat that cannot be consoled. It feels like it will pull us down so deep that we will run out of strength to struggle against it. We are terrified that we will be consumed, never to see the light of day again, so we *fight* these feelings, and anyone who evokes them in us. When we are exhausted from the fight we succumb to the feelings of defeat, isolation, and rejection. In this state we are separate from soul, completely immersed in the darkness of isolated-self, and cut off from soul's boundless potential. Isolated-self, separate from soul *is like the insatiable dragon in the fairy tale that is never satisfied.* We can never have enough, be worthy enough, satisfied with what we have, or who we are, as long as the criteria for experiencing ourselves is reliant on external validation. We don't even realize where we have landed because we are committed to identifying with limited-self, and other's ideas about what we are experiencing, without knowing it. Our outer world treats us like a *victim* who needs care, and we are encouraged to identify with the *warrior* to fight hard for our life, but in siding with any one of these identities, we miss where we are.

Our process of healing is to recognize that in attaching ourselves to a defined identity, we will indeed become what *we most fear*, to know it for what it is. We become consumed by our own power, *the dragon* in the fairy tale, without recognizing it. We awaken to find that we have become our shadow in order to understand our humanness, as well as to understand our ability to own our potential. In continuing to identify with the warrior, the victim, the martyr, or the abused and abandoned child, we miss the fact that we have indeed adopted the limited experience of each of these as a reflection of our deepest fear. It is difficult to recognize what we have become because few around us know how to support us holding the power of such a realization. That feeling of being swallowed up and suffocated is our *inner-dragon* seeking to be recognized! The self-judgment and self-loathing is also our *inner-dragon* feeling separate and alienated because of its inability to express compassionate expression for it's passions. Our feeling of isolation is our *inner-dragon* seeking acceptance. Our wounds of defeat are also our *inner-dragon* facing challenge that cannot be resolved through physical mastery. When we enlist *what we do know of ourselves in our innocence*, and give permission to ourselves to face our discomfort, we come to realize that we have choice and that duality is not the only solution, as conquering our fears is but one limited perception available to us.

Deeply ingrained unconscious energies within us about these various identities can keep the development of *our inner-dragon* a very limited and negative experience for us. Our passion for life and our creativity is a powerful force to reconcile when *we allow it* out of captivity and accept its current state of experience. Our passion is the fire within us. For women, when our dragon rears its head it evokes a fear so deeply engrained in us it is hard to own it. Our *masculine energy*, when not acknowledged as a valid part of us, keeps us from *allowing* expression from our inner dragon because we are so focused on the threat of the warrior. Expressing how we feel about things and what is important to us from a deeper level of our being is difficult if we are unconsciously influenced by the oppression and struggle in claiming our power in a patriarchal society. When we have not stood up for ourselves or our beliefs when confronted by outer-dragons, our passions build into an internal bonfire, that when released can be very threatening not only to us, but to others in its intensity. We don't have to deny the fire's expression altogether because others can't initially identify with it. We can learn to internally harness the fire's virtue of burning away illusion and revealing clarity, by *allowing ourselves* to own our own dragon in its shadow form, to know it for what it is beyond this.

In the modern day fairy tale men need not be the villains, for in changing our identification of the villain from the dragon to men, we still face the same fears within ourselves that seek transformation. Women need not be the heroine in the modern day fairy tale, for in changing our identification with the damsel-in-distress to the heroine, we still have the dragon to contend with that threatens our survival. In the midst of *a warrior* culture that sees the role of the warrior to conquer its fears, this is how the woman has *allowed* herself to compartmentalize it. In reframing the opponent from a mythical beast to the human form she is able to better relate to it, and move on from the idea of a man rescuing her, and harness the skills of the warrior for herself to enable her to develop her own passions. Rather than the dragon being held captive chained up in the dungeon, we now have a dragon that lives isolated from the kingdom, up in a cave where its expression doesn't pose problems for anyone, and yet it's vantage point is perceived as being superior. We still have to face the truth of the dragon if we are to be free to spread our wings, own our fire, and find meaningful relatedness to the kingdom. Transforming victimization into being a warrior is an important part of this process as it enables perceptions of dependence to become experiences of independence. It is in finding security with our independence that we have the courage to own the dragon, which is really our own power in disguise.

When we develop resourcefulness in ourselves by going through the feats of the warrior, we may take the sword that we have claimed mastery over, and use it as a spiritual tool to separate illusion from reality. We don't have to put down our swords and walk away from our own passions, as women have had to do in the past in order to survive. In facing our dragon consciously, which is really a synthesis of actualized self, we may hold our dragon, and in allowing it expression through us we find our true voice, our true nature, and honor our process of becoming who we are because we embrace our journey of becoming. The journey for most means finding out the truth about these identities for themselves, whether they think in terms of archetypes or not is not really the point. Recognizing ourselves in others and developing awareness of the unrealized potential with each of these qualities for ourselves, is really what the process is about. As we move from needing to claim our independence in order to anchor what we find in our hearts to who we are in the world, we become interdependent. In recognizing self's ability to be independent we may honor our personal journey as one needed by us to harness who we are and our interdependence with one another.

We are living in the age of the magician, the time of transformation that enables the union of higher truths with who we are as a shared humanity. The innocent child within us who has faith to look fear straight in the face and give it the best shot of *who they are,* learns the magician's skill of transforming the fight of the warrior into an experience of acceptance. They become allowing and accepting of greater expressions of reality and make something useful of their passion for life. We gain presence with every part of the dragon we actualize because we realize the mythical beast represents a power of true magnificence that only threatens self's idea of importance.

God is love,
and love is the essence of what we are experiencing
and evolving in our ability to be.
There is a divine plan,
and it envelopes and supports us all in realizing our true nature.

The dark night of the soul appears at significant times in our lives. It appears when we are called to mature in some way, or find a deeper meaning, and expression of who we are in our life. With this awakening of our deeper identity comes the growth of new awareness, where we expand and transcend what society has endorsed as real for us. In spiritual terms, it is as if we begin to grow wings; invisible to most, but very real in their ability to carry us to a greater experience of what is inherent in all life. Those wings can take us to where we see clearly that our problems are so much smaller than who we really are, and what emerges is our true majesty and grace. The limited-self, once realized for its alliance with a false understanding of itself, is awakened to grow and experience the brilliance and positive attributes that are inherent in aligning with our true nature.

Whatever path we choose to take on our personal journey, whether it is willingly, or kicking and screaming the whole way, we reach a point of solitude and silence that becomes our experience. Out of this stillness we begin to hear and feel guidance that is the most reassuring and moving experience of all because our soul has entered our awareness. Self realizes that the ultimate destination is beyond its comprehension or ability to control. We may choose any path, and in learning to work with our resistances, we truly *change our minds* to choose smoother more enjoyable routes to where the divine reveals itself to us. The destination is the illumination of *love's expressions*, and self's ability to consciously experience the journey towards its most pure state and make it manifest in physical form.

Self is the *vehicle* for recognizing who we are. Our physical bodies are the form, and our evolution shows us how that form has adapted and changed to become more and more intelligent and conscious of itself. The seed of genius is in us all, and in all life here, and unless it is supported by a sense of self that is aligned compassionately with a shared humanity, we may believe that self is the creator and that self is superior to other living organisms. Some would believe that self is powerful, but if you cut the cord that connects self to a greater dimension of intelligence beyond the physical form, it cannot survive.

It self-destructs. It is interesting to look at the similarities between this and the technology that has been experimenting with genetically modified organisms. New intelligence is being activated by self, from within the plants and animals, beyond our understanding or ability to control it. In not fully respecting the inherent and mystical dynamics involved, it is becoming evident in disastrous ways that we cannot deny. Animals, plants, and humans are part of this current experiment, and the individuals implementing such beliefs about their personal power, are operating without a conscience because self believes it is a god all on its own. This is our shared experience right now, and GOD is leading us compassionately to understand the consequences of our self-driven actions. And it is not only the actions of those playing god for us all that are leading us astray, but also of those who allow them to do so because we are not conscientiously exercising our choice not to follow. We are each a unique expression of god, but when we falsely believe that self has control over it all, we manifest a greater truth that reveals self's limited perceptions about its power and ability to create reality. Reality already exists, and we create our personal experience of any part of that reality by what we choose to think and believe exists for us.

Chapter 2

Integrating Self with the
Greater Dimensions of Our Being

Moving through emotions as we know them,
opens us to sensory awareness,
to discover what exists beyond self's current experience.

≈ ≈ ≈

When we have reached the limit of self within our experience, in order to broaden our capacity to experience more depth in our life, we have to expand beyond our current understanding of self. In many cases, actually recognizing the aspects of self in relation to the greater dimensions of our being is a major shift in awareness. Without this step of recognition, we have no idea what we are missing, but our discomfort keeps driving us towards unveiling this awareness. The Neanderthal was driven to *develop skills* in order to survive, but in order to have the confidence to be safe enough to venture outside his cave to explore the world around him, he needed to develop his emotional awareness to *feel secure* enough to go beyond what he instinctually perceived to be threatening to him. What occurs to me is that in our current state of awareness, we need that same emotional energy to *mature* into a state that supports the next threshold of perception we are being summoned to cross over, in order to evolve as a species. Our spiritual nature depends upon this emotional energy to be engaged constructively, beyond the expression of anger, frustration, fear, and grief, if we are to feel our connectedness to life.

The polarities of experience and physical realities that are so vividly demonstrated in our world are making this threshold more and more visible. How much of this diversity do we need to witness and experience in order to accept that our pain and discomfort are here for a reason, and that we need to pay attention to what we are stifling from growing, in ourselves?

Suppressed emotional energy drives people to do incredibly hostile and aggressive things to one another and yet they are completely unaware of this driving force. They have severed themselves from acknowledging its power and its ability to reveal greater awareness and resourcefulness. This same emotional energy is what gives our perceptions depth, intensity, color, and texture. The aspects of self, fueled by unrecognized emotion, can take over without our realizing it. Many limited collective illusions become personal reality when people are unaware of their attachment or belief in the power these perceptions have over them. It is important to remember that no one has the ability to choose how and what you think and believe, except you. It is not to say that some horrible and brutal acts of violence do not exist in our world, for they do, and they can hurt us, but there are also many compassionate acts of love demonstrated in our world as well. To which of these you resonate depends on what you choose to open your eyes to see and experience for yourself.

We must become blind to what we have been conditioned to see and believe physically appears before us, so that we may reach deeper to find clarity beyond our personal filters. We move beyond being the damsel-in-distress and the heroine to become the dragon to know true power for what it is. The dragon starts to take shape because we feel it, and we don't recognize how it has appeared because it has always been depicted as the biggest threat to the kingdom, and we have been conditioned to believe we are the victim. When we unknowingly listen to the intellect without emotionally filtering the information, and acknowledging its influence over us, we miss the truth of what is being expressed and demonstrated. Our clear inner vision is born out of chaos, but can just as easily, once obtained, become very colored by unrecognized emotional energy. It is often not until we are disoriented, confused, and hopeless that *self* relinquishes its authority, our assumptions are dismantled, and spirit is given space to enter. As self gives up control, a greater guide that sees the whole picture can enter our awareness, and those metaphorical wings further extend outward. When our assumed reality becomes so convoluted and disoriented that new depths of perception are given space to emerge, we open our minds beyond our personal experience. Awareness of our *Greater Other Dimensions* can lead us towards more fulfilling experiences for self. We *knowingly*, for the first time, embark on the journey of trusting a greater master than self, to lead us towards a soul-*fulfilling* prophecy that endorses an appreciation of all life forms, seen and unseen.

We don't move beyond who we think we are
until we choose to willingly explore where our depths can take us
beyond self's current identity.
Choosing Inner Alchemy is trusting energy to lead us towards clarity
and a greater knowledge of reality.

✐   ✐   ✐

In my book *Healing through the Eyes of a Woman,* I go into detail about the process of Inner Alchemy and explain the components thoroughly so you can take yourself through the process. It may not take you to the experience I'm sharing here, but it will surely take you to where you hold unconscious impressions of self that influence your perceptions and ability to function fluidly in your current life. When I do Inner Alchemy sessions with people who are in the midst of a depressed state of experience, there is a common period in time that has emerged for several of them. When we track the origins of the sensations they are currently experiencing in their body, it commonly takes them back to the experience of the Neanderthal. Even though there are specific personality traits, preferences, and unique perceptions with each person doing this Inner Alchemy work, there are collective similarities that I'll share here.

We begin with the patient setting the intent to have the *Greater Other Dimensions* of themselves guide them back to the incident or experience where this *stuck* sensation within their body first originated. In order to do this work they must be willing to enter what they think they recognize within themselves and discover where it can lead beyond their current conscious awareness. When they first enter the energy it takes a few moments to really accept and recognize how they are experiencing the energy in that moment. We are never sure ahead of time where and what exactly they are being led to, in the way of exact aspects of self, collective energies, or the situation in which the impression was made. Their posture, how they experience their hands and feet and their thoughts are usually the first indications that link them to recognizing the archetypal energy of the Neanderthal, and then the thinking and beliefs held there reveal their specific identity with their current self not recognized in its entirety. When they begin the process, all they know is the feeling of their discomfort, and when arriving at the place of its origin they look down to see in their minds eye, big and hairy feet.

Having said that, there is obviously a definite leap of faith required just to enter a process without trying to analyze or make sense of it ahead of time.

Let's just call it "imagination" for now, so we can let go of our conditioned ideas about reality. I'm not going to open a can of worms about whether reincarnation exists or not, or evolution as we know it exists or not, as it really isn't relevant in this context. The experience of consciously becoming energy is actually fascinating, although a little disconcerting for many the first time. This Neanderthal archetype that has emerged, although not recognized initially because it doesn't make sense intellectually at the outset, is possibly very revealing about our current experience in evolution. Many I've worked with have unknowingly resonated with this primitive energy.

Standing in the energy of the Neanderthal (even though they are lying on my table), they feel like their body posture is hunched over, the body feels heavy, and the mind flits from one thought to another unable to focus. Others have said it is difficult to think, as if they are under a cloud and can't wake up. When asked in this energy how they see their world, they respond similarly. Things often look murky. There is an absence of color. They feel alone and there are no emotions here. Some identify fear and the feeling that their life is very uncertain, as if it could end any moment. They are concerned with finding food, being safe and sheltered, and surviving another day. They feel very insecure. The feeling of being immobilized or unable to function because they are afraid is also a common experience in this energy. I confirm with them that in their experience of the Neanderthal there are no emotions, and all of them, without exception, have verified this is absolutely true beyond any doubt while *in* this energy. It is interesting that most people do not identify fear as an emotion and don't recognize the experience of it even in this pronounced state.

When we explore a bit further and travel back further in time, energetically we ask that any negative emotional energy be released from being contained in their physical body. This is easily accomplished because there is no sense of feeling it, only the heavy *sensation* of it. Consciously, the emotional energy is completely unrecognized, so attachment to it is completely unconscious, and easy to let go of on the conscious level. At this point, there is no relationship made by them to any similarity to their current life experience. The Neanderthal energy feels so fictional and is so out of context that there is very little resistance in just being in the process. After choosing to release the negative emotional energy, which they all think is very odd as they aren't aware of any, they return to the original Neanderthal. Upon returning to the Neanderthal after freeing up this unrecognized emotional energy, they feel much less burdened in their physical body, and the experience seems to be quite different from when they first experienced it moments earlier. Their common first impression is that they feel more awake, more alive. There are vibrant colors, textures, and smells, and they are curious to explore the world around them. Their body doesn't feel as heavy as it did before and they are no longer focused on survival. They actually feel like their body is able to stand more erect. They still don't feel any emotional energy, but they feel *engaged and in-tune* with their life and their environment. They are still standing alone, but they don't feel isolated or afraid, as there is a *sense of connectedness* and peace within themselves.

What is absolutely amazing to me is that no one that I have worked with who has gone to this energy has ever recognized this cohesiveness and sense of connectedness as emotional energy. It is possibly because initially there is no outward expression specifically to an emotion we recognize, it is just completely frozen. On returning to the energy after emotional release on the energetic level, there is such fluidity present, that many do not associate this with the expression of emotions because they have never experienced emotions in this same way. Emotional energy is defined by most as negative; crying, anger, irrational expression that is volatile and senseless; rather than an experience of fluid energetic frequencies that have sensation attached to them.

Everyone has had different personal impressions when entering this Neanderthal energy, but the common elements of awareness are identical. This raises questions for me. My patients are modern people encountering challenge, whether it is the experience of depression, anxiety, physical health challenges, or a general inability to focus and function effectively in their life. Most of the patients who have gone to this energy, whether they acknowledge it or not, are unable to emotionally relate to themselves. There is either a complete absence of emotion or they feel extreme discomfort with their internal world that makes it very difficult for them to verbalize or express their state of mind. Quieting their mind is very difficult for them, and remaining focused when not physically active creates great discomfort on the mental level for these people. Simply, they are not happy with themselves and being alone creates great discomfort that is difficult for them to be with.

After the Process of Inner Alchemy, when they bring their awareness into the present moment and they begin to *feel* again, they describe experiencing more color and depth in their actual physical perceptions. Their physical body feels lighter, and they are *more communicative and engaged in dialogue* with me following the session. The question it brings up for me is this: If the Neanderthal evolved from the *instinctual* mode of operating into a more emotional and intellectual species, then what threshold of perceptions are we currently crossing that is creating such challenge for so many people? Denied emotional energy has the ability to prevent us from accessing our innate ability to feel and experience the depth of perception that gives us a sense of connectedness to life. How many people are operating not too differently than that Neanderthal in modern society because they are unknowingly being emotionally influenced to believe their survival is at stake in every moment? Obviously, the people in my office are not Neanderthals, but where they are stuck in their emotional isolation isn't so different from the Neanderthal they experienced themselves to be during the session.

It is easy to be afraid and uncertain of one's safety in the world today. A few moments of listening to a news broadcast can confirm our vulnerability if one is subjected to facts without the emotional maturity to recognize the illusion of these limited perceptions. Of course, there are terrifying things going on in our world but this is only one end of the spectrum of our experience and it is tragic to realize that this exists when there is so much abundance, resourcefulness, and compassion equally present in our world. One of my patients, having previously gone through the Neanderthal exercise told me that the grass is greener, the sky is bluer, and her sense of taste and smell has never been keener then it is for her now. She feels life as a sensation in her body rather than experiencing life as an observer happening all around her. Her comment a few months following the session was "If the world is going to end, and we are all headed towards doom and gloom then why does everything look and seem so much more hopeful to me than ever before? I love my life."

Consciously allowing energy to lead
takes us to a level of awareness that experiences self relative to soul.

ﺧ ﺧ ﺧ

As we reach through our perceived internal darkness, we become aware there is so much more beyond what we currently recognize, and self is so much more than the enemy, or the victim, and is actually very valuable in enabling us to effectively function in our world. We can't see spirit, or explain it, but we *feel* something fill us, something that assures us we are going to be all right. It's been there all along, but we become so focused on the world of isolated-self, that the subtlety of spirit has been overshadowed by our drive to assert *self's will* in order to survive. Our emotional wisdom is not being successfully cultivated in modern times, because we have disowned the validity of emotions in relation to remaining functional. The number of people from the age of eight to eighty on anti-depressants is staggering. Ask most people and they will tell you that emotions get in the way of being clear, and are a good way to give away one's power. The idea that emotions are all about anger and sadness means there is nothing left that they can relate to as emotions. In order to evolve in the awareness of who we are, we must constructively reengage the emotional quality of our humanness to reveal the current illusion it is creating for us. Emotions recognized and accepted as they are, keep self fluid, and enable us to experience connectedness and sensitivity to who we are. Honoring our tears and laughter keeps us emotionally aware and fluid energetically. Spiritual awareness is claiming our ability to be fluid and adaptable and always open to learning more about who we are *through* self's experience. Self always maintains the ability to choose what and how it wishes to think about things, but such decisions when spirit is infusing greater knowledge and awareness beyond self's experience can be liberating and fulfilling beyond anything we can imagine.

In not recognizing self in relation to our *Greater Other Dimensions*, or *GOD*, we buy into the illusion that we are somehow inadequate or fall short of fulfilling our roles. We shortchange ourselves on fulfilling experiences every time we encounter another person and fail to extend ourselves outward for fear of revealing that we are human. We want everyone else to change and somehow *get us*. What we end up doing is testing the waters before we exercise our voice or hearts to be present with another as our authentic self. We ignore the prompting from spirit to extend beyond *limited-self's perceptions* to meet others. We may as well hide in our caves and only venture out for food and items needed for survival. We enter our relationships with others, having already decided to shield ourselves from a negative experience with them or avoid the possible threat they may pose to us if they *really* knew our vulnerability. (The *dragon* is beckoning our attention with these perceptions because in the dragon's shoes this is how we feel when we are reliant on our outer-world determining our worth) Today, the idea that others may experience us in our humility because we are *in the process of becoming,* and are not yet fully actualized, is not practiced in our competitive world.

In an expanded consciousness, if self integrates with spiritual awareness, fulfillment encompasses the courage to strive to become a truer likeness of a loving God in this existing reality. The soul-fulfilling prophecy becomes about realizing our divinity amidst a material culture that challenges us with *what's in it for me.* According to accepted social norms, hiding your true self is the only realistic way to survive. Self integrated with our *Greater Other Dimensions* brings us to the realization that we have everything we *need already,* and to actualize it requires participating in life experiences to fulfill our deepest desire to experience love.

Our world becomes a very dark place when we face in ourselves the challenge of stepping into the unknown, alone, if we haven't cultivated an inner knowledge that allows us to *feel* safe. The darkness to me is the experience of self, cut off and lost in the thick of the illusion that stifled emotion provides for us, completely alienated from the light of our Soul. Soul is never dark, but separated from the knowledge and experience of this truth, we stand lost in our self's darkness, unable to find an opening that shows us where we are. We can feel this darkness as children, as teenagers, in midlife, and also in old age. It commonly comes down around us when we are facing a new stage in our life or an unexpected trauma that we didn't have time to prepare for. It is in the face of these challenges that we fail to recognize that it is time for some part of us to grow in awareness of itself. But we often dismiss an important step when faced with challenge. We need to honor the part of us that emotionally *feels* the experience. The grief, the sorrow, the hurt, the jealousy, the disappointment are all valid feelings that make the experience personally real to us. We grow deeper in our knowledge and experience of self the more we acknowledge the emotions we feel, including the joy and gratitude that can emotionally move us. Once acknowledged, these emotions are no longer trapped and stifled within us. These emotions then freely move through us and bring us to greater realizations beyond what we believe they represent. We move through self into greater depths of knowledge when we feel life. Spirit becomes consciously with us, guiding, informing, and infusing vision beyond our own recognized experience.

Our life literally becomes more colorful and vibrant with every part of our emotional anatomy that we explore and experience. The many facets of love, both positive and negative, become honored and valid experiences to enrich us as individuals. In focusing on conquering our world and remaining functional, we become conditioned to disassociate from the emotional part of self as quickly as possible because effectiveness in the material world depends upon being emotionally detached. In dissociating from our emotional response to life we also stifle a part of self from becoming fully actualized. We may appear more effective and functional, when the emotional component is not part of the picture, but if we dissociate rather than accept and go through them, we depersonalize our experience, and miss the continual learning offered to us. We miss completely the power of presence and experience of compassion, as we rely upon thinking our way through challenge, not trusting what we feel in our heart to guide us toward truth. Personal experience is what allows us to hold and know our *Greater Other Dimensions* as a human being. When we bypass or shut off this internal acknowledgement, we become hardened and unable to really feel life and its many levels of experience. Should our own life appear to be crumbling around us, we have no internal barometer to guide us through our discomfort to a greater understanding of who we are, for our validation and acknowledgement for believing we are worthy rests solely on external criteria. If the situation that defines us as being worthy changes, or the people who are important to us *change their minds about us*, where does that leave us if we have not claimed responsibility for our own thoughts and beliefs about ourselves? How many people do you know who have a difficult time remaining vibrant and excited about their life once they retire? Men, more often than women find retirement very difficult, and their wives find it difficult because all of a sudden their husbands are at home without anything to do that feels rewarding to them.

If we remain honest with ourselves, and take the emphasis away from the external things affecting our ability to be happy or worthy, we end up face to face with our internal emotional world. When left unacknowledged for long periods of time, our internal world feels like a jungle that can't be tamed. It's been left consciously unattended for so long, that the beautiful garden of imagination that we played in as children has become a tangle of weeds. We don't remember the magical trees and vines that carried us to freedom when we spent time there everyday. We only associate discomfort and vulnerability within this realm of experience. The garden of daydreams takes us to places of experience that the real world has the ability to show us everyday, but we forget to slow down and *feel* life through the many aspects of self as we develop them. When imagination is engaged, we experience a release from the confines that limited-self likes to impose upon our experience. As limited-self, we don't trust how to relate to imagination, because we can't get past the internal dialogue that seems to be full of criticism and judgment about ourselves in relation to it. Self has limits, and depending upon our upbringing and influences during our life, we believe that we are able to do some things, but that others are out of our reach. Self would like us to believe it is in control but there is nothing further than the truth. Somewhere along the way we gave up our faith in imagination and our sensitivity to our emotional impressions, and bought into the reality of a self that stands alone against the world. Our sensitivity to feel life became a handicap and we learned to keep it hidden.

Some would say this is what it means to grow up and assume responsibility, but this definition of maturity is a sad one because it requires us to turn our backs on our dreams and of what could be, and accept what we have been conditioned to believe is possible for us. Life becomes completely personal and the realm of collective consciousness is dismissed as having no influence on us. After all, to stay safe, we believe self must maintain control. Emotions have the ability to take away our experience of control if we fail to ride the wave of them. Those waves end up taking us to the stillness of the open sea, where we gain perspective beyond the undertow of the waves crashing against the shore if we trust them to guide us towards clarity. If we dare to go through the threatening internal dialogue to the sensations within us, it often feels like a huge weight pushing down on a part of us that needs space. Those wings that can give us the sense of freedom are pulled in tight, held close and used to shield us. We forget how it *feels* to unfold them and let them spread out beyond our physical reality and conscious awareness, through our discomfort, to the truth of what is... magnificent.

To loosen ourselves from the grip of self-imposed limitations by denying our emotions is to further deny where they might lead us. That weight is self's illusion that it is alone to bear the burden of a world gone wrong. It feels like it's just too much to deal with, so we are frozen into complacency. We don't float here. We fight to stay above all that threatens to pull us under. The drama of compressed-self pulls up every doubt we've ever had about our ability to survive and be free of what is inflicted upon us. That garden of imagination, if visited only for a few moments, becomes a boundless reality, where the emotions and illusions that serve to keep isolated-self intact are transcended into the experience of creativity and innovation. If we could just find that one thread to begin unraveling the confusion we find inside ourselves we would have a place to start, but we cling to the belief that we are victims and at the mercy of things beyond of our control.

Those deep caverns inside us that can illuminate our true nature are well hidden, cleverly concealed under layers of imprinted beliefs and emotional energy that deter us from venturing near them. There is rarely a visible end that we can pull on to bring us closer to clarity. We often lose hope along the way that our true nature has any sort of expression of light left to it. Experience, void of emotional maturation, has colored our faith in our pureness and our innate greatness as loving beings. Moreover, there is much in our world to mirror this illusion of hopelessness right back to us, if we are determined to explore no further. To step clear of the fear we believe this inner journey represents means adopting a new perspective, one that is not endorsed as being real by separate-self's standards. This is a journey of faith, as is the experience of accepting the grace of our *Greater Other Dimensions* into our lives, through our humanness, which means it must include emotions. There is often a heavy ominous cloud of emotion that separates us from experiencing peace with our internal world. The entanglements become real to us as we develop the shell of ego to function in this world. Ego, in this stunted state, greets a world we must protect ourselves from. Self, or ego, as an honest expression of who we are, integrates self with the truth of our soul and serves as a vehicle to contribute to a world we know to be full of possibilities and hope.

Children naturally exhibit self expressively as it develops, without any concern about what others think of them. They just are, and the criteria for experiencing themselves hasn't become a list to satisfy before they can enter the '*what if*' realm of imagination. Children express emotions fluidly until they are conditioned otherwise. As adults, when we catch ourselves daydreaming, we put a halt to it. Daydreaming is unrealistic and unproductive, we are told. As we grow older, the internal list of self-imposed limitations lengthens, and before we know it, we have built the walls of our own personal prison. We keep a list of excuses in our heads and as time passes, the list becomes internalized. We don't even realize that we have a list. Our list becomes simply the way things are for us. If it's not our heritage, it's our skill level, our education, our income, our dependants, our responsibilities to others, our physical fitness and health, and anything else that serves to keep us accepting our limited-self's fate. The possibilities for happiness and freedom seem to diminish as the clouds of believed inability descend down around us. We are a culture plagued with undeveloped emotional wisdom, and it is catching up with us quickly. We are all praying so hard for the world to change, and our prayers are being answered tenfold. We just need to change our focus to realize that the change is here, within us, seeking our attention.

The darkness falls on us like a shadow when we are separate from our soul, and yet we can't seem to see the light that is within us. It isn't for lack of trying that we can't see this. We are trying so hard to find it, but we don't know how to read the roadmap we were given at the beginning of our existence. The way is in the whisper that is prompting us to unveil our core and reveal our authentic self. We insist upon seeing the problem in everyone and everything else. When we are pushed to own our part in it, we throw up our hands and blame the system. Our internal roadmap is encrypted in a language we haven't practiced using in a long time, so we have forgotten how to read its message. This encryption can be decoded by subtle energy, our fluid emotions, and sensory contact with life through feeling and experiencing the world. Developing our sensitivity enables this information to be accessed and integrated with our humanity. We completely miss this route if we remain attached to "what to do" about our discomfort, instead of integrating "what we choose to be" which naturally moves us step by step through our discomfort. The emphasis is taken off the discomfort onto who *we choose to be right now*, so discomfort may be present, but is in relation to *how* we are, not *what* we are. Focusing on *what we choose to be* reveals the path of least resistance to realizing our potential, here and now, and with this new focus, we transcend the limited-self that sees suffering as the only means of redemption.

Facing our shadow enables us to look it directly in the eyes,
accepting expression of it beyond our assumptions,
so we may know it differently,
than it is currently experienced by us.

≫ ≫ ≫

We stroll through life until we stumble or something 'trips us up' in our path. We look behind to see what it was that interrupted our stroll and see nothing. Our shadow seems to follow us always, but how often do we look around and take notice of it? On a bright sunny day, we turn and see it clearly, and as children, we often play at moving around to see how it dances right along with us. As children, the *Greater Other Dimensions* of our being leads self, and our shadow follows naturally, as the play of light is our experience. Our shadow is our friend when we are innocent. It's not a threat, because we see it clearly for what it is and continue on, knowing it is there but that it brings us no harm. Symbolically, our shadow acts just like an aspect of self, unrecognized for what it is. Self is not detrimental to us as beings, but because we buy into believing it is who we are, it becomes very restrictive and takes on greater proportions than necessary in order to keep itself feeling confident and in charge of things. Unrecognized self looms over us, and observes and monitors our every action as if it is something we account to. If we have forgotten the greater part of our being and have cut ourselves off from visiting and liberating our greater being regularly, we get lost in the illusion, and forget that self is actually just a player in the larger play of our life. As we grow in experience and those bleak overcast days roll in, one after another, we don't take notice of our own shadow anymore, and we certainly don't take time to dance in the sun with it and befriend it.

The more that *focused doing* enters our lives as we mature the more we are distracted from the blessings of each day. That same shadow appears to stalk us and the pull to feed its criteria, to keep us sidetracked from seeking guidance from our greater dimensions of awareness is very strong indeed. In this state, anything that challenges us to dig deeper and go below the surface, can send us into retreat. We disconnect from people, circumstances, and external stimulations that trigger our feelings of inadequacy, as if somehow in detaching from our emotions our shadow won't belong to us. We become busier and busier, consumed by the *doing* of each day, rather than integrating self with the being part of each day. The "I have to…", the " I need to…", and the "I should…" take over our internal dialogue. The doing is being driven by keeping at bay that voice that is afraid to stop and hear what is going on inside. There is no sense or rational explanation here because we don't recognize the thinking we have fallen into. We keep ourselves from listening to a deeper discontent beckoning our attention. When the rational *doing* ceases to exist, we further invest in dissociating from our discomfort. When those emotions enter the picture we experience further senselessness.

We don't hear our limited-selves because we are so busy distracting ourselves from the negativity we feel inside. But somewhere deep inside *we still know* that aligning with isolated-self isn't really taking us where we yearn to go. We are confronted by our choice, and don't realize it's never too late to change our minds! In choosing differently; a set of new options and ideas enter the picture that gives us faith in our ability to meet challenge effectively, with self being satisfied and fulfilled beyond anything we could imagine in the process. Our doing is not the problem, it is the thoughts and motivation *driving the doing* that create resistance, for without spirit consciously working through us we are limited in our resources, and self becomes exhausted.

We become attached to the illusion of our inadequacy to adapt when challenged, retreat, and hand over the authority to place our fate into the hands of others. We choose to be fooled by them instead of looking up at the sky knowing the sun is just as radiant as ever, just above the cloud cover we currently see. We begin to fight our way through our day, when we're actually fighting an illusion of who we believe we are; our own shadow that we don't recognize anymore. That overcast day symbolizes an invitation to be more inwardly reflective rather than outwardly engaged. Just like the weather, there are sunny days of rejoicing, and rainy days of self-discovery and self-development. Full experience requires embracing the full experience and integrating who we are at a deeper level within us, with the natural ebb and flow of emotions, which in turn sheds light on this external play between light and shadow. Without comparison, how do we know something to be what it is, except in relation to our personal experience of it? *To banish self from our experience is to deny the experience of soul to make its debut into the current realm of physical experience.*

Self is the vehicle that makes the connection between the essence of our soul, spirit, and our physical body. It's like a bridge, and once recognized as such, it can fulfill its role without feeling threatened by extinction. Self as a bridge doesn't have to carry the whole load because it is anchored and supported at both ends; one being heaven, the other earth. There is great assurance in this metaphor. The resources from the heavenly realm that sustain self's relationship to the earth are constantly being held up by a higher consciousness of the greater dimensions of itself. The grounding that enables self to fulfill its role and flow with emotional impressions is anchored by the proof that manifests as physical reality for our eyes to see. Through imagination, innovation, discoveries, illumination, adaptation, and flexibility, self is able to contribute to a greater experience of reality here on earth.

Often it isn't until we exhaust ourselves in the struggle to stay 'up', and separate from what we believe stalks us, that those clouds seem to swallow us up. Hopelessness sets in, as we exhaust all the avenues that we hoped would take us another way to that clear space of perception. Those clouds, no matter how hard we try to find another way, are the only things separating us from the clear sky above. These clouds of emotional energy left unattended create an illusion about who we are. Our doubts seem to make them grow even bigger and the illusion of our helplessness grows right along with them when left unacknowledged for long periods of time. We have to shed that heaviness within, just as the clouds release rain to nurture the earth below. To us, this release is an *idea* we hold about a part of self that needs to be relinquished in order to get our buoyancy back that allows us to rise up naturally. And some perspective is needed so the clouds don't just swallow us up, and spit us out to hit the ground hard. The sun is like the soul's deep call from within to be free, but there is so much emotional energy and collective illusion in the way that prevents us from hearing clearly what needs to be liberated, that all we see and experience is negativity. This too becomes a self-fulfilling prophecy because of what we unconsciously keep *choosing* along the way. Every time we have thoughts about what we don't want to happen, or don't want to experience, we are aligning with the negative instead of aligning with the positive realm of possibility. Fear is in the driver's seat and self feels like a helpless passenger. Spirit has the ability to take us there, but we have to consciously choose to align self with it and decide to grow wings to meet it half way.

Our identity, that part of self that can go no further in its current state without causing us pain and discomfort, gets stronger with each retreat away from accepting it until we are left alone. Then self-loathing seems to rear its ugly head. The part of self that stands separate from our innate nature is constantly talking negatively to us, but we don't listen! It's annoying. It's upsetting. We have been ignoring if for so long that it's become background noise. However, the tape is still running and it affects us deeply. We shove it deeper and deeper "out of sight" in hopes of sending it "out of mind", until it actually does leave conscious mind, and it becomes subconscious or completely unconscious. That inner dialogue that puts a negative slant on everything runs on autopilot. That discontented self is still with us, but we have separated from consciously having to deal with it, or acknowledge it as belonging with us. Our ability to nurture healthy relationship with our inner dreams and yearnings, our sadness, our joy, our humanness, is slowly concealed away in those dark caverns within us, and what we attract only reflects this bleakness back to us. It is so much easier to blame others for what we don't recognize within ourselves. With every utterance of blame, we feed the dragon of self-loathing and there is no lasting sweetness in this futile exercise.

Busy in our lives, it is easy for our adopted identity to feed on what it needs to keep things intact for self. We miss the gift of the rainy day, and continue as if each day was in full-blown sun and radiance. But take away the external acknowledgement of our place in life, and we are left with isolation. Unfortunately we are also left with all those caverns full of unresolved experiences that have built up over time. Being pushed to unveil these depths within us can happen through tragic events, a serious illness, or losing anything dear to us like a loved one, or a job or home. But tragedy is not the only fuel for growth, at least from obvious circumstances such as these. Losing anything that represents our ability to function effectively in our world can also plummet us into despair. The simple process of aging can have this effect. Anything that compromises our idea of who we are can be a threat to our sense of place in our current reality.

This feeling of isolation can creep in as we grow from one phase in our life into another, and need to clean up behind us, before moving on. And it can feel tragic because a part of us awakens to realize that we have forsaken a genuine need within our own being. For that matter, we can't even identify what this need may be anymore, because we have severed a conscious relationship to it for such a long time. All we often can identify is the feeling of being utterly alone in our suffering. This cycle of maturation, by its very nature, slowly releases us from being supported and nurtured by others to take the reigns of responsibility for caring for our selves. Caring for ourselves takes on deeper and more meaningful expressions as we age. Our purpose evolves as our *awareness expands* to include a larger circle of perception and more appreciation of what is outside of our self's immediate experience. Think back to the child drawing a dot on his page for his presentation to his classmates. The dot was great when it was just for him, but it limited his experience with others, so a new purpose became visible and the drawing grew to be inclusive of what he became aware of. If he hadn't first drawn the dot, he may never have come to realize its limitations. The dot lead to a fuller appreciation of the choices available to him and the effect those choices have on his personal experience and on the ability of others to relate to him. As choices are allowed to naturally play out, the opportunity is created to grow in awareness when making them, because connections are made through the experience.

Expanding beyond our comfort zone requires fostering the flexibility that we took for granted when we were young in body and open in mind. We first come to recognize self as children and, as far as we are concerned, all life revolves around us. We change our minds frequently, go with our instincts, and make decisions without being concerned about the long-term effects because emotionally we are fluid. Little thought is given to the consequences of our actions, not because we are thoughtless, but because our realm of awareness is still very focused on ourselves in our immediate experience. In our minds, life is forever, so there is lots of time to do things and nothing is predetermined. The emphasis is on the *me* in the now. The focus of awareness is about satisfying the desire to conquer and expand oneself in relation to everything outside of self. We could say that in this stage we appear to be quite selfish, but it is really just experience void of objectivity and is a necessary and healthy stage if we are to grow and learn about ourselves. As self assembles the skills to stand on its own, there comes a confidence and awareness that continues to expand to recognize and benefit from the great teacher of experience itself.

As self's awareness broadens,
it naturally takes us to the experience of spirit,
for self, when secure, is curious to experience more!

Just for fun, let's imagine the Neanderthal's life after he expands awareness beyond his instinctual nature, and begins working with the emotional component of his experience. There he stands, the masculine, outside his cave looking out from his terrace on the cliff to an incredible view all around him. He is inquisitive and *wonders if there is more to know* down below those cliff walls. His cavewoman is inside stoking a fire, and her man, having engaged his emotions, is secure enough to go out and explore the world. The cavewoman, in her instinctual awareness, has now taken to nesting and making the cave an environment to nurture and care for her mate, as her basic feminine energy acts through her. As she fulfills her role, bears children, and keeps the home fires burning, the clan grows. As the children get older and test their limits tension grows in the cave. The masculine energy has driven the man out each day to provide for the wife, knowing that the wife, completely aligned with her feminine energy has provided the sustenance and security on the emotional level to him and their children. It has become a comfortable routine, and as the children reach an age when they begin to seek a life outside the cave, things begin to stir inside the husband and wife.

The wife becomes aware of her discomfort first. She wants more out of life. She's tired of having her man show up looking for dinner and then eating it in silence. She seeks a further expansion of her feminine energy, a creative outlet for self expression and, in feeling satisfied that her role as wife and mother has been fulfilled, she draws on her unexplored inner resources. She decides to take up *art* and starts drawing on the walls of the cave. Upon arriving home to find this, the husband, although initially alarmed by this change, is fascinated by what she is doing. And since his masculine role of providing and being out in the world on their behalf is not threatened, he feels quite secure in *allowing* her this pleasure. Dinner is still ready on time and his needs are being met, so he thinks this is fine for her to amuse herself with. He doesn't spend any time giving it a second thought, for it doesn't interfere with his world. He begins arriving home to inform and share with her what he has discovered out in the big outer world. They both begin to experience each other in a new way. The first signs of the feminine energy, beyond birthing and nurturing family are taking form here. They begin relating to each other over *their* newfound passion. She is experiencing the ability to communicate creatively. He sees his conquests taking physical form on their cave walls for posterity. He no longer comes home just to grunt, eat, procreate and sleep. He begins to become interested in intimacy and developing a reciprocal relationship with her. She is feeling very validated and is becoming more secure in her newfound creative power. In those cave days, I imagine things were simple, but the dynamics of the interplay between the masculine and feminine, first as roles, and then, more subtly, as qualities of energy beyond gender were present then, though not realized.

After a time, as the children get older still, the girls are at home with the wife learning the cave duties, and the boys are going out to learn the skills of hunting and becoming worthy providers. But the wife begins to feel restless. The cave walls are full of intricate drawings and family history and she begins to wonder if she should go out and discover for herself what lies beyond the cave opening. She has the desire to experience this outer world for herself now. That feminine energy has pretty much exhausted itself within the walls of the cave and she is looking to exercise some of that masculine energy for herself. Her man is feeling secure these days and welcomes her company on his outing the next day. After all, the daughters can tend to the cave now. They venture out together. He is set on his path, but she wants to stop and smell the flowers and touch the rocks along the way. He becomes impatient with her. He has certain things he wants to accomplish today and she is holding him back, distracting him from his focus. He becomes annoyed with her while she is extending herself to come up with ways to communicate what she is experiencing with him. They are outside the cave now and on his territory. He is not looking for her input. What she is asking him to do is like asking him to reinvent the wheel and it's all gibberish to him. Her world is expanding but he doesn't want to take the time to hear about it. It has not yet occurred to him that listening to her may be useful beyond his immediate needs that day.

So off he goes ahead of her, focused completely on getting done what he has set out to do that day. The masculine energy sets goals and then pursues them with focus and precision. He has been coming home with food for many years, so he certainly knew what he was doing. She wasn't disputing his abilities, just seeking a deeper meaning. The cavewoman is quite content to let him go ahead in his chosen direction while she takes things at her own pace so she can observe the dynamics she's sees at play all around her. She realizes he isn't listening, so she stops trying to communicate what doesn't interest him as she continues to nurture her own desire to explore further. As he returns home to the cave she is more anxious than ever to talk about her experiences with him, but he is more interested in showing her what he has brought home. He doesn't realize that what she wishes to share is what she has brought home with her as well. Her treasures just aren't visible like the fish slung over his shoulder. She feels a little dismissed by him but she is very excited and moved inside herself by her outer experience that day and isn't going to allow him to determine its value to her.

She wakes up the next morning ready to express more on those cave walls! She now sees gaps in her drawings that can be filled in with the things she saw outside the cave that her husband had neglected to tell her about. She wonders if he simply didn't notice these aspects of the world outside the cave, or just didn't think they were important. But she has seen these things and is no longer concerned about how he sees things anymore. She does realize though, that she must now venture out into the world to see for herself, and she will need to develop some skills in order to make sure she can provide for herself should her husband not be around to protect her. She has a mind of her own. He may not agree with her or understand her completely. For him, at this time, there is only right and wrong. Nothing of value lies between setting the goal and then going after it. She loves him dearly and truly appreciates his ability to provide for her and the family. She knows that he will come to want to explore the in-between world that she knows if she allows him to find it for himself. In honoring this realization, she stops trying to get him to *get her*, and she carries on without him… at her own pace, honoring her own rhythm. He will be fine about this as long as when he gets home, she is there, ready to greet him with the home fires burning, his dinner ready, and available to procreate should his instincts require it. The rest he doesn't really notice, and has no desire to seek at this point. As far as he is concerned, his needs are being met, and he is content to know she is happy.

Little do they both know, that one day in the future they would meet other people similar to themselves and those feminine dreams that make no sense in the present, like learning to communicate, and ideas about making wheels, will lay a foundation for developments later on. The masculine, when it *serves a purpose* will use that information as a basis for what he becomes driven to accomplish. When that day comes upon them, and they meet others on their path, the man and woman will both be very grateful they took the time to share their strengths and innate qualities with one another.

Modern day or cave days, there are definite similarities in how we approach, avoid, and or choose to transcend confrontation in life.

Let's travel on through history, past the times when women were a pretty dress on the arm of a man, through the time when women were burned at the stake for openly expressing their ideas, through suffrage when women got the vote, through shock therapy treatments to make women compliant, to now. Women have endured many hardships in their struggle to have the same privileges that men have. Most importantly, we see women progressively taking their own ideas out into the world. The feminine energy has evolved considerably from those cave days, not only in the roles that women have today but in how women view themselves. And with all this progress comes the reality of being a woman in what has traditionally been a man's world. In honoring their own worth, women have taken their place alongside men in their world. Their internal rhythm in some cases has been altered considerably as a result of the stress of conforming to the pace of a man. We have developed synthetic interventions like Hormone Replacement Therapy to allow women to function the way a man does and maintain her grace while competing for her place. The inner rhythm that makes women female is suppressed so she can fit into the men's idea of value. The masculine energy, as a result, is rather stagnant in its expression in women rather than naturally adaptive to serve us all beyond gender. A woman's discomfort in recognizing the masculine energy as it is expressed by her has been camouflaged, or completely not acknowledged or experienced compassionately at all. Women have learned to express their masculine energy as men do in order to compete in the world as it is. This is as a valid indicator that we are out of sync with a deeper rhythm that seeks expression through us.

Many of us grew up with our mothers saying, "Wait till your father gets home." when there was something we did that required discipline or a big decision had to be made. We've avoided saying this as mother's ourselves because we handle things independently. We are beyond waiting for our husband's to get home to proclaim boundaries or decide how things are going to be handled in order for harmony to exist in the home. Are we as women inadvertently sending the same message of dominance in cutting the father out of the picture? As we further our awareness and our roles with children are less cut and dried than they were in the past, perhaps we could again use these same words, "Let's wait till your father gets home", or as the case may be, " Let's wait till your mother gets home". In using it with our youth, we would be demonstrating a compassionate masculine energy that honors the other parent's involvement and valued input in raising the child. A teenager may benefit from discussing the different approaches and viewpoints of their parents and reach an understanding with them together. Younger children need to be dealt with more immediately because they will have long forgotten the incident by the time everyone sits together to discuss it.

There is so much more to our own awareness now in recognizing the importance of respecting another's pace and rhythm as they learn to express their own masculine energy constructively. The words may remain the same, and carry a completely different meaning used consciously, because they become inclusive, not exclusive of a respected partnership in rearing children.

We have evolved considerably in many ways. Women and men both demonstrate the masculine and feminine traits within themselves, so they are not so reliant on the other, emotionally or intellectually. The feminine energy has advanced in its expression from just being a recognized emotion to the development of what we have come to acknowledge as intuition. Now we face the same need for the masculine energy to find comparable expression. Women seek to experience compassionate masculine energy, but what faces them daily in their outer world is in opposition to this model. As long as women continue to compete in what is perceived to be a man's world, there will remain the opposition of masculine energies. What we see in others, or run into continually in our experience of our outer world, is mirroring an expression of self we don't recognize as active within ourselves. Recognizing the impact of collective impressions on us enables self to move through the residue of these expressions. The masculine in women in many cases, is as stagnate as it is in men. As a woman writing this it breaks my heart to know we are doing this to ourselves without recognizing a constructive expression that now rests in our own hands to demonstrate. It's time for the masculine energy to become secure enough within us to open the door to compassion when men enter the picture. We control the ability to allow the feminine to receive within ourselves through the maturation of our own masculine energy regardless of what confronts us.

The patriarch as an archetype is as present in women as it is in men. The difference is that it has not been suppressed and oppressed in men in the same way. These same masculine expressions aren't creating the same discomfort in men. It has served them as it is for a very long time. Where women have *met their own discomfort* in relating to their masculine energy, it has sought expression in other forms to help build relatedness to their idea of a compassionate society. They have realized greater expressions of themselves in becoming the martyr, and accepting their suffering as a means to obtaining greater ideals. Currently, the *altruist* is the name many give this martyr archetype, as we seek to transcend the suffering and begin celebrating our independent thinking. The altruist becomes a transformative expression, as it allows women the experience of holding their own dreams and ideals, independently of others. As they gain comfort in holding their own passions, they naturally become more accepting of others being an integral part of them realizing them.

As the masculine energy of the warrior is transformed from a conquering expression into an *accepting* of ourselves, our need for duality to define our position relative to current reality is transcended. The martyr, or altruist if you prefer, is a valid part of our personal journey, as it allows us to step out of the warrior mentality to pioneer new vision that embraces new approaches to unveiling our shared humanity. Women have willingly taken birth control pills and used Hormone Replacement Therapy to force their own rhythm into alignment with their masculine energy. They have disabled their feminine energy from expressing its natural function in order to keep self functioning and in control in their lives according to society's standards of the masculine expression of competence. As women, we alone have the ability at this time to recognize this shadow that appears to stalk us and take inventory of where *we hold unconsciously* this very patriarchal expression that seeks liberation within us. In holding it consciously we may liberate it into authentic expression of our heart's ideals. The reward is realizing *a common passion* with others, and the ability to engage intuitively in existing masculine environments without feeling vulnerable. Competition ceases when the opponent no longer exists inside us, and a *common deeper rhythm* is realized that supports the different expressions of the masculine and feminine equally, beyond gender.

The women who have liberated the unconscious expression of the masculine have broken through the threshold of the illusion that materialism has dictated, to draw from the realm of greater knowledge that comes to us as ways to further ourselves *as a humanity*. With matured emotional energy the value of *intimacy* and equality has become a reality for many, and has taken relationships to a different level of experience. Self is evolving and finding integration with higher ideals on one end of the spectrum, but on the other end there is profound isolation being experienced by those missing the opportunity to willingly accept their discomfort and an indicator that the circumstance they now find themselves in is able to receive a more expansive expression of them. It feels like the unknown, but in holding back on being exposed we miss the prompt to step up to the plate and give others the best shot of who we are. The unknown will reveal itself if we reveal who we are. In holding back, we keep the dynamics of relationships like those of the Neanderthal enabled in a modern and more elaborate environment.

Today we have more amenities. Our caves have become considerably larger and we can buy our comforts instead of hunt and forage for them. On an emotional level, however, intimacy is often as it was back in the days of the Neanderthal. Men are still resisting the idea of shared communication unless it is on their terms. Women harbor resentment that exists only because they don't recognize their own developed expression and choice to exercise compassion. Men are feeling just as disempowered by women as women are by men instead of being empowered by shared knowledge and accepting the different *approaches, and qualities inherent in both.* Everything isn't black and white, right or wrong. In union they are empowered to seek something beyond what they both currently know is possible, but both need to be willing to embrace change.

Women have adopted this unconscious masculine energy, or have actually become it *at the expense* of their inherent feminine, instead of accepting and allowing it to evolve inside themselves cooperatively. As women, we judge and criticize, not only ourselves, but others, because we aren't being heard. Instead, we need to honor our own pace, align with our rhythm, and express ourselves freely, confident that it is safe to do so. Our newfound power may threaten others. They may leave us or attempt to silence us. Women have learned to suppress their masculine energy to appear less threatening when meeting the masculine energy of men. This approach simply discourages men from experiencing the discomfort that will drive them to develop the feminine virtues for themselves. If men leave, it is not always because they walk out on the relationship. Countries send their men to war to fight and die for a cause. It is the masculine energy that engages in war to focus on the task of conquering the enemy. Men have forgotten, as have women now, that without an internal sense of security it is difficult to be out in the world and not feel threatened and vulnerable unless you carry a weapon. The masculine energy is now ripe for change. The feminine energy has already found expression beyond duality through intuition, but in gaining mastery of self, we find ourselves standing face to face with our own dragon. The question becomes, how are we going to use our swords in hand?

If women continue to believe that they cannot survive without men they have greatly underestimated their true power. For with internal worth nurtured, one can learn how to do almost anything. The external world poses no threat to a woman's ability to adapt and develop her abilities to survive. If survival is what drives us, then the feminine power of creatively engaging and intuitively sensing becomes a lost art for which humanity suffers the consequences. Our sensitivity and ability to value and nurture life is compromised and as a race we become just like technology, devoid of experience and love for another. A compassionate masculine expression is what is being called for right now in all of us, one that allows the feminine within us to conceive and birth a fuller experience of reality. One that we may share through our relationships with one another and that also supports relationship with a deeper, common rhythm called life.

Chapter 3

Enabling Self to Discover New World's of Existence

Already In Our Midst

> *God is beyond the masculine and feminine.*
> *God's will becomes manifest through the creative energy*
> *of the feminine when the masculine is aligned with and*
> *allowing of greater consciousness through us.*

What if women and children, rather than men, had been sent to solve the first dispute in history? How would this have affected the evolution of the dynamics of power? This obviously would have completely dismissed the development necessary for us as a civilization. For the women to agree to go to battle the masculine within them would have been engaged and on side with the decision, for the masculine is what would have driven them with purpose to show up in the first place on that field. The choice to confront what threatened their families and sense of safety would have been the masculine energy.

Imagine the scene on the battlefield. The women and children would encounter the women and children from the other side of the dispute. All would be prepared to fight if necessary. But ensuring the safety of the children would likely be the primary concern on both sides. Immediately engaging in physical combat would mean putting the children at risk. As women, their feminine aspect would likely seek expression when confronted by the reality of the situation. The emotional charge of the situation would probably surface first. There would likely be lots of inappropriate yelling and screaming. Emotions vented, catharsis achieved, they might decide to pool their resources, put together a meal, and talk things over. Compassion for who they were as individuals with innocent children would have become blatantly visible for all with eyes to see. Weapons and personal differences aside, they could communicate while the children played with one another.

The feminine in general seeks the sameness, not the differences because it is a *blending* type of energy, not a switch *gears* and *pick a position that is most effective* type of energy. The feminine nurtures, so feeding the children would have been taken care of, and then nurturing an environment conducive to understanding another's position would have been taken care of, and the working out of the details would be taken care of together. In working together, cooperating for a common cause, blending perceptions and gaining better understanding, the women would establish harmony amongst themselves. The children would witness this example and gain a sense of security on the physical as well as spiritual level in the process.

Most of the time invested in resolving the dispute would have revolved around creating a environment conducive to the creative process. The least amount of time would have been invested in finalizing the details of the resolution, as creativity revealed their mutual resources, and faith in the others' contribution. Achieving this, they would efficiently implement their ideas into constructive actions from which everyone would benefit. They would resist being pulled back into figuring out how to justify their actions to the waiting men, and packaging their decisions into something the men would recognize and be proud of. The men would say on their return, "It would have been quicker to just blow the opponent away and do what is right for our own people". The women would respond, "What time it took to look at the strengths of everyone involved was worth investing, and we invested it gaining understanding, rather than cleaning up all the bodies and rebuilding what we would have destroyed in haste to get things done efficiently". They could both agree on one thing: "We are all free to move on now, and we are *all* better for it, as nothing has been lost, only gained." The masculine when utilized in awareness becomes an allowing energy that cooperates with birthing greater awareness of dimensions within our reality that are beyond our current ability to identify. Having the feminine unveiled on the battlefield would definitely cut down on the amount of time spent on defending one's position. The "battle" itself may take longer, in a completely different expression than brute force, but without the cleanup, they were all ready to embark on *living the new world*, not stuck on figuring out how to create what was already there.

Emotions can be messy, but they can dissolve quickly after they have been expressed. Often what remains is a clearer and more compassionate perspective on the situation. Past those messy emotions is clarity about what the heart values. As women we have already been pegged as the crazy ones when we have disagreement with our husbands. Many of us have actually become that crazy woman when we attempt to discuss things and meet resistance from the masculine energy, but it needn't be this way. As women, the masculine in us can become very critical of the rhythm and approach of the feminine inside ourselves. Those emotions, when left unacknowledged by us as valid guidance towards recognizing our unrealized heart ideals, can build into a forceful demonstration with a life of their own. In men that emotional force is often demonstrated physically, whereas women tend to express verbally. What we begin to experience in our husbands is our own unrecognized masculine energy blocking us from meeting them where they really are. Husband's and wives both demonstrate this, but recognizing our *capacity to meet another* transcends our need to change them in order to find agreement.

The feminine seems to do lot of nothing, at least in terms of outward accomplishments that others can always honor or acknowledge, but somehow things fall into place beautifully when we are allowed to do a lot of that outwardly apparent, nothing-type stuff. The feminine is a quieter energy that's blending nature often goes unnoticed, but this is also the nature of having our sensitivity engaged. A masculine that is allowing in us, is also there to protect the feminine in this state of acceptance. Without relying on another to do this for us, we become allowing of greater consciousness to be birthed through us, regardless of our partners participation. There just might be something to the masculine within becoming more allowing of the feminine for men and women. There lies great mystery in what cooperation and acknowledgment of these energies within us can birth beyond them both.

> *Blaming others for our problems*
> *is a reflection of our own undeveloped awareness*
> *of what is active within us.*
> *Our Spirit will manifest discomfort for us because we remain*
> *unconscious to the heart of humanity heralding us to change.*

❧ ❧ ❧

When we become frustrated and angry with others, it is often our own *vanity* that confronts us. We believe we know more than they do and we dismiss the fact that they know and experience things differently. We try and get the *gears* in their mind to work like the *blending* of ours, and it just isn't happening the way we think it should. This sounds rather patriarchal doesn't it? If those gears were to begin blending it would possibly leave us with a new dilemma we hadn't anticipated. The very things that get done to ensure daily life is supported is accomplished by the masculine energy, and women have become very good at disguising their own competence so as to not compete with their husbands in the home. In disowning our own masculine energy, we've placed expectations on men which are demeaning to their competence. We sit back quietly as if we are supporting them, when in reality we are silently criticizing their methods. We want to "teach them a lesson", and we think we are so clever to implement it. In the end, it does nothing to help them better appreciate us. We wait to see what they will do, rather than going ahead and doing what we are capable of ourselves. Are our husbands' egos so fragile that they would not love us even more if we exercised our true self with them? Or are our own egos so fragile we are afraid to exercise our power and work through the resistance with faith in finding resolution with them, because we believe equally in their power too?

We all do it. We maintain a silence until our pent up emotions erupt in a hysterical outburst. Tears don't have to be our way of appearing less threatening, but as long as we deny the existence of our emotions they are harbored until they fly up in anger when we least expect it - often over nothing. During a bout of hysteria is no time to deliver a clear message. If we focus solely on being right, there is no room to shift towards a resolution. We don't have to be submissive, but sometimes we're expecting our partners to hear and understand something they have no frame of reference for, or interest in hearing to begin with. Can you imagine the relief it would be for a man to know that his partner loves and believes in him, respects him and has faith in him and his abilities enough that she is not afraid to openly be herself with him? Her challenging his decisions is not because she can be right, or thinks she knows better, but because she is looking to engage his creative mind with her own to reach greater potentials for them both. Our own *blending nature* creates confusion because we often confuse being understood with voicing an opinion. We mix emotions with mental energy and weave in ideas that don't seem relevant to immediate issues except to us. This drives men crazy. They cannot follow the female logic in this way, for the emotional and mental capacity within them are often distinctively separate gears. They are quite capable of being competent with each, but *we don't allow them* to express it their own way, or move towards an understanding as a joint venture. We insist on extracting from them what we want to hear expressed from them at that moment based on our perceptions, and then get frustrated because they fail to do it the way we would like them to or assume it should be done. We want them to understand us, but we don't seek to understand them or accept them as they are.

As wives, we have learned through experience to appreciate the art of timing. We wait until the right moment to "bring things up". We do not honor our own timing but rather his because it is not our own we have learned to honor, it is the husband's, because for centuries our security has relied on the husband's providing. We keep dinner waiting for him, we keep the home cared for, we get our own work done so we are free to be with him when he is available, and then we get angry with him for not honoring our contribution to things running smoothly. Excuse me, but who set that up? It is our assumption that these things are ours to take care of, and often men are more than willing to share in the responsibilities of home life. These are learned roles and responses, and are not relevant anymore unless we allow them to dictate who we choose to be now as women in partnerships with men.

We look for acknowledgment and approval from our husbands, and then resent that we feel we need it to feel good about ourselves. Perhaps it is permission to be fully ourselves with them that we secretly seek. This gratification will never come to us from outside ourselves. Security in the relationship will always rely on trust and commitment, but to what do we trust and to what are we committing? Is it growth that we trust and commit to, or is it an outdated model of security that we've become unconsciously slave to? Men do leave and so do women when they don't know how to grow past the resistance they find with one another. Those who don't physically leave, check out emotionally and shut down to being present in the partnership. We get angry at our husbands but we also *wait* for them to change, and *hold back being who we are* with them. Maybe we're really angry at ourselves for underestimating their ability to adapt and grow with us.

Our partners may honor and value our input because we express and demonstrate our capacity to express compassion with them. They may allow their own feminine to receive us. If we develop a compassionate masculine energy within ourselves to be allowing, regardless of their receptivity to hearing us, then our feminine energy can be expressed with wisdom. Our husbands, if confronted by our immovable masculine energy, are put on the defensive. Rather than engage their sensitivity which would enable them to understand our needs relative to their own, they dig in their heels. To honor our own rhythm initially shows through our actions our capacity for compassion when our words meet their deaf ears. Often our husbands are not initially engaged in growing with us, as they don't recognize the need to develop their own feminine qualities. They will develop these qualities when the need arises for them, and when they consciously choose to do so because they appreciate the value of them. This may happen independent of us in a different situation, but how they choose to be is *independent* of how we choose to be. Back at the cave there may be new relationship territory forged because of the knowledge gathered outside the cave walls.

We don't change our minds about how we view another until we realize that we will suffer without developing awareness of these parts of ourselves. The responsibility of realizing the potential of the relationship rests upon both partners honoring the feminine and masculine qualities in themselves so that they can invest their energy in the joy of co-creatively living life, rather than spend energy protecting their vulnerability. Remaining sensitive to our partners enhances trust in our *Greater Other Dimensions* of consciousness. Through the increasing intimacy of the relationship we unveil greater depths of awareness to life. We must begin to recognize our own resistance to change in order to move to a higher level of union. We cannot disengage from our loved one in an effort to cope with our relationship difficulties. Our attempt to be complete on our own through isolation, in the midst of a relationship will only result in the worst kind of loneliness. In committing to growth within ourselves we are open to experience love's greater capacity through the relationship. Our sense of completeness becomes a feeling of union with all life, not a misplaced expectation on another to make our personal world right for us.

> *How can one honor in another*
> *that which they have yet to honor exists in themselves?*

≈　≈　≈

Clearly defined gender roles have all but disappeared in modern society. Gone are the days when women were reared to become wives and mothers. Our daughters are expected to pursue the ambition of their choosing and stand as equals with men. This is a recent development. Only a generation ago, most girls trained to be teachers, nurses, and secretaries, careers that capitalize on the feminine energy. Modern women have discovered their masculine energy, and through their experience of it have come to understand its value. The masculine is a recognized energy within us and it is being experienced freely. Problems arise, however, when the masculine energies are engaged on both sides. We must seek a more constructive expression when confronted by another's masculine energy. In the end, our partners benefit, as we can acknowledge and appreciate their masculine values more readily, and learn to meet them with our own without aggression or compromise to our own ideals. But where does this leave the power of the feminine? When the masculine confronts us, is backing down and becoming the submissive feminine really the way to go? On the battleground, what brought those women back to the power of the feminine? Primarily the instinctual part of them that knows continued life depends upon the survival of our children, but also at work was their innate faith in the *heart* of humanity to be a guiding force that leads to true power. The masculine energy for the women on the battlefield would have been engaged initially upon arriving, but it did not back down, bully or demand compliance in order to stay in the game. Instead, it expressed itself compassionately by finding out what the other side really wanted beyond the assumed threat, and allowed more to enter the picture *beyond their currently recognized position.* Inner security of the masculine ultimately allows the feminine to receive God within us, to cut through the illusion of separation from our perceived opponent, and find compassionate expression for the common values we both share, but that may be disguised by self's current perception. Our own masculine energy does not have to be disowned or disengaged in order to experience peace in our personal relationships with men. Our own masculine can be accepted as worthy and able to *meet them compassionately* as a partner engaged co-creatively with greater dimensions of who we both are, not our small selves trying to simply hold our ground.

There is innocence present always, but often the actual presence of children brings this truth into plain view. We don't have to actually birth children to be part of nurturing and growing these parts of self. The feminine, in its unique pace and rhythm creates a nurturing environment that receives spirit, but the masculine within us has to agree to open the gates to receive it in order for it to become manifest through us. Whether we have children or not we have within ourselves the innocent child ready and waiting for creative expression that meets another with inspiration to experience the possibilities present. Manifestation of the God energy relies on *self choosing* to expand its awareness, to include these higher ideals. The manifestation itself requires that we *allow*, and *accept* greater dimensions as our reality, as it is derived from something greater than both the feminine and masculine qualities, and *already exists* before we consciously recognize it. As long as we remain attached to self's idea of what is possible, we miss the opportunity to experience greater awareness that brings us into a fuller expression of our humanity.

Both the masculine and feminine are needed equally for us to be at peace with who we are and develop true compassion for others. We are co-creators of our earth *experience.* For any conflict to be resolved, a greater truth that transcends duality must be unveiled. Until we unveil the *underlying needs* in a situation whether it concerns the physical, psychological or the emotional, the spiritual will not be recognized. Our hearts must be open to accept a truth beyond that which we are comfortable. After some initial discomfort in shifting our positions, there emerges a rooted faith that we are a good and compassionate people. It doesn't matter how you measure the soundness of a good decision, it will satisfy everyone's needs, because it surpasses the confines of time and space and embraces a greater reality. As long as the decisions honor everyone involved and benefit self's knowledge of a whole humanity, does it really matter who makes them in the end?

The feminine can engage and communicate effectively when the masculine is not threatened and is aligned with a common focus. Both energies are needed equally and must coexist in harmony, to create a space for spirit to enter. While the functions and approaches of the masculine and feminine are different, each is limited, unless they are viewed in context and implemented constructively. We must look at a situation, recognize it for what it is and then draw on resourcefulness that exists outside self's current experience and knowledge. Self may integrate higher ideals with its current understanding and become more through this process. The minute the masculine traits of competition and aggression enter the picture it is very challenging for the feminine to remain receptive. When the feminine feels threatened, up comes our masculine protection that creates a barrier that prevents the possibility of resolution for us. The feminine gains faith in expressing true power when it is developed with a constructive masculine backbone that knows it can be resourceful and do what is necessary to stand alone if need be. The feminine can remain receptive because it is relying on a greater dimension of us for its sense of security. Our perception of being reliant on another can significantly color our expression of authentic self, and shortchange not only ourselves but those in close relationship to us from experiencing a greater expression of us. It comes back to being big enough, feeling secure enough, and competent enough, to be receptive to new and challenging ideas because we know who we are beyond what another can identify or recognize. We are free to grow in our awareness by accepting more of what is offered to us through experience.

You are the only one who can choose
what and how you think about yourself and your life.

≽ ≽ ≽

Opening ourselves up to the experience of co-creation challenges us to let go of our unconscious ways of relating to those closest to us. As we move into greater understanding of self, we must reconcile who we really are with who we appear to be or think we are. Sadly, we have allowed others to define us. People who haven't been to school in years often continue to measure their intelligence by the grades they got when they were teenagers in spite of their current successes. The little girl who was told she was fat still sees herself that way in spite of evidence to the contrary. The husband who is repeatedly told he will never amount to anything, not surprisingly, never strives for success. Somewhere in this stage of realizing self in relations to others, it seems we go amuck. We unknowingly adopt what is outside of ourselves to dictate what we believe is *supposed* to be inside of us. The illusion of inadequacy creeps in when we believe we have failed to meet the expectations of others. We become so busy doing what is expected that we forget that self *can be* an expression of our innermost essence.

When self gets a false sense of identity which is then reinforced with acknowledgement and praise from without, self begins to fear that others will discover the truth: that we are not what we appear to be. We begin to lose our ability to accept ourselves and others. As we venture less and less into the world of imagination and possibilities, and become more and more anchored in physical reality, we yearn for the *feeling* of freedom. We believe what we see, and we increasingly find ourselves identifying with and trying to fit into the flavor of the cultural movement. We see only what mirrors our own internal discord. Our internal world of imagination and potential is slowly left behind. We retreat into isolation separate from our *Greater Other Dimensions*, rather than venturing into solitude to meet our *Greater Other Dimensions*. We are expected to outgrow the world of imagination. And we do. With this sense of separation comes the illusion that we don't fit in. Solitude and inner reflection become the experience of isolation rather than a tool for maintaining objectivity. We find ourselves on the defensive, wanting to be right, wanting independence from the influence of others when in fact we feel vulnerable and not sure of our position at all.

When we were conceived, it took the *will* of two people to make the conditions right to receive the life force of who we are to enter into the human form. This is real, our body is real, and who we are as *essence*, or soul, is just as real even though it is beyond the physical manifestation of our form. So coming into this physical reality was our choice, and those that chose to receive, nurture and foster us. But that *essence* of us existed before we were exposed to this human condition, and like all other life *forms*, we exist beyond the parameters of thought and perception. So why do we buy into the illusion that others thoughts about us can somehow make or break us? Others may influence us, but *we alone can choose* to accept or reject their opinions. Self is the conduit for this interaction. If we learn to recognize self and integrate with our authentic nature then life will become exciting and we will constantly be amazed at the revelations and possibilities that are revealed to us.

Self, separate from the subtle realm of soul builds confidence, and soon believes it is in charge. Self becomes identified by its ambitions, achievements, and material wealth in its insatiable need to conquer and be in control of its reality. Of course buying into and striving toward someone else's idea of success does not satisfy us in any meaningful way. In a sense, we close our minds and hearts to feel and be in this world as we truly are, and we begin to seek a sense of power through material means because this is what we believe will bring us acknowledgement and security. Our perceptions of personal value and worth do not have to depend on how much money we have or on what we own. When we relinquish our belief in such a limited definition of success we can begin to experience the reality that we have everything we need at any given time, not only to survive, but to flourish both physically and spiritually. This abundance relies on cultivating our resourcefulness and growing in our ability to acknowledge what we do have, not what we don't have compared to others. Abundance may not come to us in a way we might expect, but there is great fulfillment in trusting this life process where self is the vehicle, not the master of our destiny.

We alone decide how much we choose to invest in the "appearance" of our lives, and how much we invest in the "meaning" of our lives. This balance is often lost when we overlook the one major component essential to the process. This one thing, when not acknowledged, creeps in just like dense cloud cover, and with it comes the illusion about who we are, and self becomes separate from our *Greater Other Dimensions.* This one thing is *emotion*, and it can be very deceiving because it feels powerful, and persuasive, but *it DOES serve to keep self real*, and reminds self that it isn't actually in control of anything, and most importantly it pushes self to recognize it's choice to grow and adapt. Acknowledged emotional energy gives humility a secure seat in our hearts. That same emotional energy when flowing and acknowledged is also the bridge that takes us to where our metaphorical wings can unfurl, giving us an authentic sense of freedom from *confined-self.* We move into the experience of our authentic and integrated self that chooses our *Greater Other Dimensions* to guide us, not intimidate us. Those same emotions are what allow us to sense and discern reality from self's limited perceptions. At this very moment, open your mind and heart to receive the possibilities already inherent in this world. This single shift in consciousness takes us immediately from *limited-self's* illusion of lack into the realm of abundance.

Chapter 4

↗︎⌒

*The Masculine Expression
finds Compassion*

---

*Make the most of what you have,
and your unrealized potential will be revealed to you.*

↗︎ ↗︎ ↗︎

Imagination is a great way to open the doors to possibility. Looking at situations that we aren't personally involved in, but are intrigued by, helps us build relationship to what we currently don't recognize as active in ourselves. Our masculine energy has a way of expressing itself without our realizing it in our personal relationships, but we witness and run into it continuously in our outer life. When the insecure masculine is unconsciously engaged, we perceive opposition, experience resistance, and feel alienated. We become defensive and seek justification for maintaining our position. We rationalize our point of view. We feel as if the door has been slammed shut. We close down and fail to see the opportunity that exists if we would only see the circumstances in a different way. In fact, we slammed the door shut all by ourselves because we decided ahead of time that our contribution wasn't honored or appreciated. We miss the chance to see ourselves as generous and compassionate in the face of adversity. Our experience becomes one of feeling isolated when the immature masculine energy is engaged. We mistakenly think that our vulnerable feminine energy has been exposed. This active and unrecognized immature masculine energy in us seeks someone or something other than self to blame for its discomfort. Tremendous emotion is present, but *we don't allow* it acknowledgement or expression. These emotions hold us hostage to self's position, and keep our perceptions intact that everything and everyone around us is separate from us and even worse, in opposition to us. We take theses experiences personally. Life is against us. To protect ourselves, we pretend we are indifferent to what confronts us. In denying our emotional attachment to the situation we can't see the door being held open by another to receive us. It is the *will* of our masculine energy that chooses our focus and our intent, and when backed by the feminine energy of suppressed emotion we can become immovable. Only when *we choose to allow emotion* to enter the equation can we move beyond its influence to see an outcome to benefit all concerned.

Where we perceive another inflicting their will on us, and we don't realize the power we have to choose a broader appreciation of their expression, we can be pretty sure our own masculine energy is the roadblock, not our feminine expression or another's approach specifically. Although another may very well be unreasonable and inappropriate in their approach and expression of their will, we may transcend receiving them at this limited level by knowingly accepting them through our own recognized and secure masculine energy. Sometimes this means walking away from a "closed door" and being grateful to be able to walk away emotionally intact. We know our own worth and align with a perception of ourselves that goes beyond the fact that they have rejected us. Forfeiting, or even disowning our masculine to avoid confrontation, or the experience of opposition or rejection, does nothing but keep us validated as the *victim*. As long as our masculine energy is engaged *unknowingly with limited-self*, we will be unable to interact from a higher level of understanding. Through our own developed masculine energy and our own developed feminine energy, we can create a greater consciousness. The clearer vision born from this co-operation between our masculine and feminine energies transcends the old feeling of permanent separateness. By engaging the higher forms of the masculine and feminine energies, *a compassionate response* which illuminates the common values held by both is possible.

In the face of conflict with another, most of us either walk away or try harder to please. It isn't easy to move beyond a conditioned response to conflict. Someone pushes our buttons, old tapes start to run in our heads and before we know it we are engaged in the same old patterns of behavior that have dictated our response to conflict in the past. We must reach beyond self and find compassion by allowing our Greater Dimension to broaden our understanding of the situation. The dictionary defines compassion as: "sympathy for the suffering of others, often including a desire to help." I'd like to suggest that we expand on this definition to include a broader, more inclusive meaning of the word. What if to be compassionate also meant to find a *common passion* with others? What if this common passion transcended suffering and allowed the experience of *Greater Other Dimensions* to influence an outcome? Sharing this common passion with others opens us to work together, bringing all of who we are in our totality to the table. A greater collective consciousness is born through the experience. In taking our focus off of the suffering, and putting our focus on a common passion, we liberate the light in us all. The masculine and feminine energies are honored and although the common passion is the focus, everyone experiences a shared humanity.

Spirit infuses us with ideas and inspiration when we find this *common passion* with others! Let's say you are a school teacher. After six years of teaching, you become discouraged with the school system and the parents lack of involvement, the children's lack of respect, the lack of government funding, and the number of hours you work without a sense of fulfillment or reward. The list goes on, but each item focuses on being consumed with *the lack* you experience in your current situation. You look around you each day in the classroom and talk with the other teachers and begin to see that you alone can do nothing to change things, as the problem is too far reaching and is essentially out of your hands. You do your job, and begin to wish that you could change your career, and do something more spiritual, more healing!

You enroll in yoga classes and take a Reiki course to develop your sense of wellbeing, but you still view your day job as one of limited spiritual expression. Your spirituality and your teaching career seem to have nothing to do with each other. You are deeply conflicted. Soul knows that this perception of conflict in your life is just an illusion. Your soul has limitless faith in the human spirit, but to hear what soul has to say means allowing yourself to dream. Do you spend anytime envisioning what your classroom would look like, feel like, sound like, if everyone was inspired and excited about what they could express and do there, including you? What if you imagined the experience of being free to express yourself without being worried that you might upset someone or that you might jeopardize your job? What if you changed your mind about what you were willing to accept as *lacking* and decided that even though the situation *may* be lacking, you were going to enter it from a personal perspective of *abundance.* Right away, your resistance rears its ugly head. This is the power of unrecognized emotional energy *disabling your masculine energy* from being constructively focused and exercised! You are personally attached to seeing your situation in a certain way. To change your mind means giving up the pain you have suffered under this unjust system. To change your mind means to give up believing you are powerless and to take responsibility for the way you are going to experience life. To enter the world of imagination would mean you would have to give up the notion that your influence is limited and go out on a limb to imagine what could be possible *if* you were free to do something about it.

If you allowed yourself to imagine being in the situation without limits of any kind, you might be surprised at what happens to your thinking. That desire to develop awareness and experience of spirit is showing up in your life, but not where or how you thought it might! Masculine energy doesn't have a reputation for being constructive. In fact, the masculine has gained a reputation for being dogmatic, stubborn, and downright insensitive, and rightly so, for much of the masculine energy exercised is at the expense of emotional expression. We have learned to compartmentalize emotions and focused intent. That blending between emotion and intent that co-operates with the greater dimensions of who we are has been lost and in its place is self's desire to stay in control. We compare ourselves with one another instead of imagining how we can increase our capacity to be a truer likeness of God. Our *own masculine energy* is what closes the doors to greater experience of self, and chooses which ones to open. Our own masculine energy is the one that stands on the other side of the door trying to figure out how to get the person on the other side to change his mind. The masculine sets our intent and our feminine receives and births awareness that supports that chosen intent. If the intent is to get another to come around to our way of thinking, the feminine will manipulate, or more subtly, engage the fine art of orchestration to accomplish its masculine will. Our feminine receives whatever our masculine sets its focus on, and sets its will towards experiencing it. Given the choice between self's idea of what is possible, and God's idea of what is possible, to which one are you going to listen?

Women have a reputation for becoming the *orchestrators* and the *manipulators* in response to their own masculine energy wanting to satisfy self's desired outcome. Men do this too, but differently. Men are more likely to say what the other person wants to hear and then proceed according to their own plan. When confronted they will claim that the other must be mistaken. They are sure they didn't say that, and that they must have been heard incorrectly. If as women we are conditioned to believe that the masculine energy is the opponent, and we see men exclusively in this context, we miss exercising our own masculine energy constructively, and developing our own compassionate capacity that *we alone can choose* to exercise for ourselves. We miss the best part of men in general, and of ourselves for that matter, for we all hold the capacity to receive and birth greater consciousness through building integrity between our own masculine and feminine qualities. Emotional maturity allows a spiritual expression to surface in us that respects and honors others. We no longer need to be coy or flattering to get what we want. If as women, our own masculine energy is inflexible, how are we to receive and nurture the inherent goodness and potential in another beyond our limited-self's experience and idea of who we are? We remain co-dependant in our partnerships by refusing to relinquish our own dualistic positions of superiority and vulnerability. We completely miss the potential of co-creation with others, and our own *Greater Other Dimensions* because we get in our own way. We unconsciously protect our vulnerability with our disowned masculine energy, rather than develop our capacity to receive compassion from God and be led towards our potential as loving beings. Instead, we spend our time and untold energy seeking acceptance from others whom we believe define our worth.

By recognizing our feeling of resistance, and bringing ownership back to self for insisting on holding onto our current perception of what is best, we may honor our emotional reactions, and move beyond them, rather than deny their influence. We may very well encounter dogmatic, rude and self-centered people who are hurtful and inconsiderate, but we alone choose who we wish to be in response to them. In honoring our hurts and our wounds as valid feelings, but not as indications of our identity or worth, *just our developed capacity to feel*, we are moved quickly past them to a clarity that empowers self to be compassionately enabled by our *Greater Other Dimensions*. We are able to see beyond the immediate situation. Backing down, or heading in the other direction when the masculine in another attempts to define our place relative to them, are indications that we have denied our own masculine qualities, and left our feminine strengths unrealized in their ability to grow and birth greater awareness of self relative to our own *Greater Other Dimensions*. In expanding our awareness into the world of imagination, we are able to untangle our assumptions about others, the situation, and ourselves, and be free from the grip self has on us to maintain composure and control. We open the door for imagination to lift us up and away from the illusion of being *the victim*, and set us back into the seat of the *student of possibility*, aligned with the art of creative thinking.

Every generation is given this challenge; ours is no different. So why are we folding under pressure at this time? Children are flexible. As adults we forget how to be flexible. As adults, we adopt the idea of powerlessness whenever we are challenged instead of embracing challenge as a chance to test our limits and see what is possible if we bring new ideas into the mix. You're thinking to yourself right now, "But I'm so tired and I feel drained. I don't have the energy to spend on this". If indeed you see your work as a job that you have to go to each day to meet your obligations, then you are already spending time there. Why not decide *who you choose to be* and what inspires and energizes you? You're already showing up at work. What if you really *showed up?* Instead of simply spending time, *invest time* by turning your thoughts towards what *you'd like to be* in that situation? When we change our perception from one of *spending time* to one of *investing time* the process of blending self with higher ideals follows naturally. What if you *invested* the same amount of energy on openly being who you are and trusting it to lead you to a greater experience of others as you currently *spend* on hiding the real you.

Suppressed emotional energy weighs down on self and takes so much of our internal resources to keep in check. We don't even recognize what is influencing us, but we feel repressed, tired, and defeated, and our situation mirrors this perception to us. It isn't the whole truth though, for there are endless possibilities present as well. We are just fixed on seeing only repression and the things that have the ability to take away from our fuller experience, so nothing else enters our awareness. Those same emotions, however, once accepted within us as valid, can fuel us to become involved and enable us to *invest* ourselves in a better outcome. We can express our dreams and ideals because there is passion present in what we are moved to experience. We believe that Spirit is something that is far out of our reach and separate from anything we know. This is not true. Spirit has been with us since birth, always infusing and attempting to illuminate a greater understanding to us. Being capable of free will, it is completely up to us to choose whether or not to utilize spirit's realm of knowledge to expand our consciousness to a greater understanding of ourselves and the world around us. Sometimes we have to sit with our discontent and really feel it in order to access the dreams and ideals that we buried long ago. Our discontent relies on our remaining in the realm of comparison to others, whereas our dreams and ideals are aligned with spirit's full range of possibilities. In consciously choosing to change our mind, we open the doors for expanded awareness of our situation because spirit is always waiting for an invitation from us. We sometimes have to give up the idea of being right to become receptive to other options. There are always plenty of jobs and ways to earn money. They may not be what we think we would like to do or believe we are capable of doing, but they are all opportunities to contribute and become more through the experience.

Spirituality is not yoga, qigong or meditation. Spirituality is a way of thinking that takes us beyond our current understanding of our personal experience. Yoga, qigong and meditation are but ways in which to cultivate the tools with which to work with our minds, to expand our awareness of self, and all that exists beyond self, in the realm of the unseen. Often where our own perceptions don't fit in with those of others, we fuel the expression of our denied masculine energy and begin to doubt ourselves. We blame others rather than develop a greater understanding of where we need to expand and grow to become more tolerant of those who are different from us. The more we accept and love what we find in ourselves, the more tolerant we become of others. And where we find our limited perceptions endorsed, we can also buy into collective illusions that serve maintaining our decision not to get involved or extending ourselves beyond our comfort zone. Spirit can't do anything to elevate us if we choose to stay where we are. We tend to group with other like-minded people to gain a sense of security, when security can never truly be obtained from being like others. What happens if we change our mind and those same people don't agree with us? How will they give us a sense of security then? Developing awareness of our internal world can open us up to identify and understand our spiritual needs in relation to the needs of self. Otherwise, we rely on others to tell us who we are.

Navigating through life's challenges requires us to consciously align with our *greater-self* rather than with limited-self. When we align with limited-self, there is a perception that we stand alone against the world. Integration with our *Greater Other Dimensions* allows boundless opportunities to be part of that which enriches and inspires, not just self's agenda to be recognized and admired. Our focus on acquiring material things has overshadowed the development of relationship *within* us. We are unable to perceive externally what we have no reference for internally. We *spend our energy* seeking validation that is impossible to find. Our soul searching is diverted by a mental exercise of acquiring the *me's* desires. The *me* engages self in a quest for empowerment in relation to and at the expense of our *Greater Other Dimensions*. Waiting patiently inside us all, are the undeveloped parts of self. Practicing Yoga, Qigong, or Meditation helps us to cultivate awareness of who we currently are and who we have the ability to become. These practices are some of the ways in which we can begin the experience the world in a spiritual way. But the spiritual is present in every waking moment, not just in these classes! Learning to recognize our own spirituality and how it expresses itself allows us to recognize spirituality in the many forms it takes in others, including in those who don't know the meaning of the word.

Let's go back to the example of the disgruntled teacher. She goes home at the end of the day to cook dinner, clean up, and get the kids to bed, fulfilling the parent role and the housekeeper role. She discusses' the following day's schedule with her mate, fulfilling the partner role. She calls a friend to confirm an appointment, and catches the late news before going to bed. She has successfully completed her duties of the day. She goes to bed exhausted, wondering how she'll have the energy to do it all over again tomorrow. All of these activities are the expression of limited-self. And within each of these expressions of limited-self is the seed of spiritual awakening. We perform our roles without being aware that there is a whole lot more, spiritually dormant, in each of these tasks. The victim, the martyr, the prostitute, the silent child, the rebel, and many, many more archetypes, are the various aspects of self, and of everyone else for that matter, waiting to be awakened into something meaningful from which to learn and grow. As long as we remain in the unconscious *doing* mode, we can often keep self and its unrecognized need to continue to learn and grow, occupied. On a conscious level we begin to be aware that we feel unsatisfied, but the unconscious masculine energy of *doing* drives us to adopt behavior that keeps us seeking validation from others, rather than enriching our experience of self and understanding of others. As long as we are *doing*, limited-self is kept occupied, and at a safe distance from any discontent we may feel on a deeper, feeling and *being* level. We systemize our lives into two camps: *What we believe we have to do*, or *are supposed to do;*

and *what we place faith in* and *choose to do*. Going off to meditation class can remain a compartmentalized expression of us, and feel completely separate from what we experience of ourselves in our day-to-day routine.

The illusion that we are alone emerges whenever we pass through a new threshold into greater awareness of our self in relation to who we are on a deeper level, and in relation to our current life. Feeling alone is not a bad thing, as it is different from feeling lonely. But it can be disconcerting, as we may initially feel exposed and vulnerable. We haven't yet developed a reference for how to be in this experience of expanded awareness comfortably. The yoga classes can help us to learn the art of aligning with who we are, but to take these skills out into the world, we have to take who we are with us. How do we translate what we have realized in the Yoga studio into the language of our everyday lives? This is where our perceptions of spirituality can blind us to recognizing the spiritual in what we experience each day. It's like arriving in Germany and not speaking German. We assume others will not understand us because we don't speak the same language. We assume we'll be misunderstood before we even attempt to communicate. The opportunity to communicate through discovering a commonly understood expression beyond the two identified languages is completely missed because of our assumptions about what confronts us. Self takes us into various situations in which we can learn to integrate who we are in awareness with who we were before. We must have faith and allow our heart to lead, trusting that our mind will follow with the right words and actions. The more centered and the more rooted we become, the fewer assumptions we make about new situations. The fewer assumptions we make, the greater the challenges presented to us will be. Every situation has spiritual capacity. The challenge is in recognizing our part in unveiling it. With an open heart we will find the way to express and receive a greater reality. Once we become more aware of our own spiritual capacity, our awareness of it in others becomes apparent. Knowing how to proceed will come naturally to us, supported by our faith in human nature.

When our spirituality goes unrecognized, self believes it is in the driver's seat. Merrily barreling along set on its destination, it is oblivious to soul's master plan. The discomfort that takes over is self alright, feeling threatened by our soul's attempt to break free of constraint. Imagine a suspension bridge with Soul on one side and self on the other. If self has filled the bridge with its accumulated stuff, Soul can't cross over and be recognized. As self clings to its possessions, its backlogged emotions, and its ideas about how influential and important it has become, the bridge becomes heavier and heavier and increasingly difficult to hold up. In a larger context, earth, at one end of the bridge is becoming depleted, and heaven has been held back from making passage because self has become so involved in accumulating stuff to help keep the illusion of its current existence and security intact. Our role in this scenario evades our awareness completely. Take away the possessions that validate self's existence, and we stand transparent in our humanness. If there is integrity and humility there, then the riches of heaven and manifestation on earth are both at self's disposal in abundance, but self knows it owns none of it. Self becomes the vehicle in which soul finds expression. Soul's passage through self into the realm of realization reveals just how fulfilling our lives can be. Others may still identify us by our role, but it is of little consequence as our focus is no longer on seeking external validation or confirmation of who we are from others. That same masculine energy that unknowingly chose isolation in order to preserve self and keep the illusion of its ability to control life intact, matures into a co-operative energy within us, that taps into our feminine responsiveness and is allowing of the experience brought by spirit's boundless potential.

With the bridge intact, that same schoolteacher who is feeling powerless to change the *system* becomes empowered to recognize the components of strength inherent in the system. It's no longer about the teacher against a system. It's about the teacher within a system in which she holds the power to change who she chooses to be, and the influence she has over inspiring a greater vision. Trying to change the system is self-defeating, like banging one's head against a brick wall. As long as one insists on trying to change the system, the steps necessary as part of the process of change remain invisible. What happens if that same teacher stops and *feels* inside the true need as a soul within that situation and allows her individualism to shine? The teacher becomes the vehicle for change by tapping into her inspiration and the response she elicits from her students. The fire is lit and profound change is the result. Imagination, play, and creative problem solving come naturally to children, and as adults we have the capacity to imagine right along with them, to help them harness these skills into something of value for us all. We are all constantly changing. The world we are functioning in is ever-changing, so it is natural that the system will adapt to serve these changes if the people within it remain adaptive, flexible, and willing to learn. It starts within us as an awareness that drives us to adapt our thinking to follow where our heart is leading us. This is how we illuminate what has always been there but was obscured by our self-importance.

Our attempts to control our children, to fit them into the old model of order, are well intentioned but possibly misplaced. We want them to succeed so we try to prepare them for the world we know. We are overwhelmed by the speed at which the world is changing even while we are trying to prepare our children for it. We are so focused on life outside our front door, that we are missing what our children are showing us. Our children are stressed both physically and emotionally. Their bodies are being fueled by processed, chemically contaminated food, vaccines, and drugs that numb them. They are trying desperately to find their place in the world, wanting at once to please their parents and to fit into a world their parents know very little about. We all hold the power to be part of a vital system, and with adults who recognize and support children's potential, the system adapts naturally to fill the needs of those that enable it. As long as our children are emotionally fluid their energy will be boundless, and their attempts to wake us up will be relentless. There seem to be two extremes among our young people, and the teachers are the common thread that connects them. On one end of the spectrum are the kids who are speaking and acting from a place of unity and hope for humanity. On the other end are the kids who have shut down and are struggling to get by in our fast-paced world. They slip into complacency because they don't realize they have the choice to change the way they see themselves. They don't realize that they alone hold the power to choose their alliance: with *the victim* or *their magnificence*, it rests completely in their hands. I can't imagine a more fulfilling role than to be in a position to cultivate and influence that kind of enthusiasm and genius in our future generation. It requires great security in our masculine energy to allow others to exercise their own choices, and learn to harness greatness with compassion and appreciation for others. The disenchanted teacher has found the spirituality and healing that she thought was lacking in her job.

I am very fortunate to live in a community that has crossed this threshold from an outdated model of personal success into one that supports humanity's success. All three of my children are in publicly funded schools. Each of them has had exceptional teachers who have gone out on a limb, successfully influenced the system, and brought compassion and enthusiasm to my children's learning experiences. There will always be those who justify our trust in compassionate authority outside the home. Everyone can think of a teacher or role model who had a positive influence on us or our children. Unfortunately, there are also those in positions of influence who have told our children that they don't measure up. These people have not only abused the privilege of their positions of authority over our children, but they have betrayed themselves. By failing to see the potential in *everyone,* they have denied themselves the experience of living life to the best of their ability.

In knowingly engaging our own compassionate masculine energy, we demonstrate our ability to be conscious adults, parents, and teachers in support of our children's magnificence and potential for resourcefulness. Our children learn the art of discerning the difference between aligning themselves with magnificence or with the victim through our modeling. We implement clear boundaries even when it is not popular, and we encourage them to go beyond their comfort level to find experience greater limits. Children have their moments of frustration, but we are given the gift of growing with them when we constructively meet our own resistance in receiving them as they are. Children learn to trust this process.

And although there is discomfort at times, children may learn to recognize their discomfort, not become disabled by it. They are encouraged to make the decision to take constructive action, rather than assume defeat. In all honesty, I think children grow with us as much as we grow with them.

I have had several people comment to me about what a conservative, and very unspiritual community we live in, and it completely baffles me whenever I hear this. My children are in three different schools, all public, and I see those environments as extremely progressive and spiritual. I have a hard time believing that all the other schools are so different. Then I realized, that the criteria these people are using as far as spirituality is concerned is not based on the human condition, but an ideal about how spirituality is presented. You don't have to do yoga or meditate in order to be spiritual. There are no yoga classes in my own kids' schools, but they have moved towards endorsing healthy food, and implementing the community's resources to support greater learning experiences for our children. I believe that when our children are treated as incredible young minds, and able bodies, they are influenced by the support and encouragement within that community. If the school has water and juice available, instead of pop, then that school, in its capacity as a respected place of knowledge, is endorsing these as supportive of their students potential. Making choices available that support students in being their best lays the groundwork for the habits they will choose throughout their lives. What child under the age of ten knows what is best for them to eat? They know what tastes good based on what they have been exposed to, what is popular with their peers, and commercially supported, but do they actually make the connection between adequate nutrition and their ability to think clearly and be physically healthy?

To educate our children today to cultivate resourcefulness from what exists inside them, and around them, is more important than ever. If we are looking for validation to stay where we are, and continue doing what we're doing, as unfulfilling as it may be, then we will find justification all around us that enables the *victim-self* to manifest full expression within us. If we lose our job, we will see it as proof that we are the victim and miss the door that opened for self to walk through. The job may be lost, but what opportunities have arisen as a result? Self has been handed the opportunity to shed the victim mentality and stop seeking only *what's in it for me*, and begin to experience a shared and vital community where we become a valued contributor because we are *willing to invest* who we are. We learn and grow through our discomfort. We can be sure that we will be presented with the lessons in whatever form they need to take to wake us up to our own dormant possibilities. To consciously align with people who are involved in keeping the heart alive in a community through the nurturing of one another's potential is to become a valued and appreciated contributor. Self is satisfied beyond its wildest dreams, and our spirit is elated to be included in making it happen.

If the school teacher rises to the challenge and recognizes her own spiritual capacity, within her existing environment, she becomes the valued and trusted teacher of possibility. *Teachers of possibility* encourage their students to seek solutions in creative ways, and not be afraid to make mistakes, or explore other options when problem solving. *Teachers of possibility* help the students develop meaningful and useful skills, and give them the opportunity to exercise them within the school curriculum. *Teachers of possibility* inform parents, and those with the desire and ability to invest in their efforts, about *what they do need* to be supported in their roles, and they place faith in eliciting co-operation and support for growing our children together. In my own community, I don't hear the children or teachers talking about spirituality, I see them demonstrating it.

We each have the ability to become teachers of possibility when we knowingly begin living our own life as a student. Those who have rigid views about what spirituality is and how it is expressed may be missing it popping up under their feet and between their toes! The ground beneath our feet is shifting, but *are we willing* to give up our current experience of spiritual lack and invest in abundance? Spirit is waiting for an invitation to infuse us with new ideas through our imagination if we are willing to expand our capacity to receive it.

You must be the change you want to see in the world.

Mahatma Gandhi

🖎 🖎 🖎

We have many schools in Ontario that give their students the opportunity to travel to other parts of the world and help communities to build homes, or get water to their village, or learn to read and write. They experience life in different communities where privilege doesn't mean borrowing the car on Friday night or upgrading a cell phone. Students are not going to these places to fix or change things, but because they share *a common passion* to make a difference. They bring themselves and their abilities and use local resources. The everyday amenities that we take for granted are non-existent in many other places in the world, and even though we know these places exist, have even seen pictures, nothing can prepare us for actually going there. We experience a whole new level of understanding and appreciation for a place when we live in it and meet its people. Before going, these kids are blind to those in their own community that are struggling for basic rights and amenities because they are focused on themselves. When these kids come home from helping , they see their own lives differently. They appreciate that they personally can make a difference.

One such program, "Developing Skills for Tolerance" in one of our local high schools, has proven to have profound influence on the students. When the kids return from these experiences, they are encouraged to explore what they realized about themselves when they were there, and how their understanding changed what they recognize existing within their own community. The Principal at my daughter's high school, Ian Jones, who initiated implementing this program into the high school, inspired the kids and came up with a way to make it happen that did not involve the monetary support of the system, but rather the resourcefulness of the kids, teachers, and parents, and members of our community. Once the ball got rolling, it took on a momentum that influenced the existing school curriculum to include a class that explores cultural influences such as these. Implementing this vision at the student level originated with the Principal, but as a parent, to look at how it has evolved, it is hard to tell the teachers, the students and the principals' individual influences as it is reflecting a true blending of our community's abilities.

Take away all the contraptions of the average North American kid's life, and humility about *life* itself being a privilege enters the picture in powerful ways that penetrate the heart and influence the mind to open wide! Actions seem to come naturally once this bridge of realization is crossed. The *we* these kids use when telling of their experiences is not because they are talking for one another, but because the experiences have brought them to a common understanding, and they see themselves unified, not separate any longer. The *me* thinking is replaced by a *we* that is united by compassion. The levels of achievement in school grades, sports, music, and community involvement that many of these kids experience as a result of this immersion approach, is quite remarkable. In *not taking on the system*, there are many, many examples of teachers, parents and students who are *demonstrating a healthy and vital system* that integrates the principles of our day, with new ways… that reflect a cohesive global community with common values. If you ask these kids if they are spiritual, they'll more than likely roll their eyes at you, because their incentive, their motivation, their inspiration, is not coming from *trying to fit in*, and do what's popular. They're teenagers after all, so they're interested in getting *out of the box*, not fitting into one. Their sense of adventure and desire to be part of change was a common passion that led them to commit to these immersions into other communities.

If as adults we give them the freedom to explore, providing safe boundaries that honor their choices, some unexpected outcomes emerge that benefit us all. Children influenced by secure adults who respect them, learn to harness their expression of rebellion into constructive experiences that open their minds to perceive beyond self, and allow in a vision that shapes a healthy humanity. Our role, if we are secure enough to trust them, is to create a safe environment in which to discover themselves and truly know one another. To hear the kids talk about their individual and group experiences to an auditorium full of their peers, parents, representatives from the Board of Education and teachers, was inspiring. The influence the kids have had within their own school community has resulted in an addition to their school's curriculum to include a "Interdisciplinary Culture Studies" course. Who wouldn't support an approach that proved to have such a positive impact on the kids achievements, both personally and academically, as well as their sense of power to be the change they wish to see in their world.

One day, the father of a very wealthy family took his son on a trip to the country with the express purpose of showing him how poor people live. They spent a couple of days and nights on the farm of what would be considered a very poor family. On their return from their trip, the father asked his son, 'How was the trip?' 'It was great, Dad.' 'Did you see how poor people live?' the father asked. 'Oh yeah,' said the son. 'So, tell me, what did you learn from the trip?' asked the father. The son answered: 'I saw that we have one dog and they had four. We have a pool that reaches to the middle of our garden and they have a creek that has no end. We have imported lanterns in our garden and they have the stars at night. Our patio reaches to the front yard and they have the whole horizon. We have a small piece of land to live on and they have fields that go beyond our sight. We have servants who serve us, but they serve others. We buy our food, but they grow theirs. We have walls around our property to protect us, they have friends to protect them.' The boy's father was speechless. Then his son added, 'Thanks Dad for showing me how poor we are.'

Author Unknown

≈   ≈   ≈

When we are inspired to follow our interests, we are led past our assumptions about what and how something outside of us exists, and led into the realm of possibilities within us. We open to our capacity to make a difference. Often the end result is beyond our ability to fully imagine ahead of time. The system isn't the problem. The system is the symptom of an underlying problem we don't like to admit begins with us. To blame the system is convenient and gives us permission to do nothing. It gives us a valid excuse not to extend our understanding of a situation through compassion. Our masculine energy has become skilled at remaining on task and filtering out anything that might disturb our personal reality. When we feel emotionally moved, we "snap out of it" and redirect our efforts to avoid unleashing all that feels out of control within us. When we do recognize that a shift is needed within us, we may become allowing through focusing our masculine energy to courageously venture into the unknown. We acknowledge our ability to dismantle what we believe to be right for us, in order to expand our understanding of what might be right for others as well. The doing is effortless and rewarding when the decision is derived from compassion, but we have to reach beyond the borders of what we believe, to empathize with another's experience, and then take a further step to a vantage point beyond the assumed duality we see as an outsider evaluating another. Looking from the outside, into the situation, shows us what we expect to find, or what we assume things mean from what we see and know of ourselves. But we must see without prejudice beyond our own experience and knowledge. Our lens is tinted by who we currently are and by what we know of ourselves. We must shift our perspective to further our understanding. To walk in the shoes of another gives us the opportunity to alter our perceptions of what really exists there. We need to resist the temptation to judge and label, and let go of the preconceived notions that keep our own sense of order in tact within us.

To step outside our own illusion and into another's reality may mean we see how far we have strayed from living as a unified world. As long as we are against another, a system, a culture, or a nation, we remain committed to keeping our illusion of what is our *idea of order* in tact for us. Anything else must be wrong, because it's not what we're experiencing, and it may dismantle our perception of being in control. The teenagers on returning from Africa after living with a local family for the duration of their stay, shared stories of what hopeful, trusting, and loving people hosted them. Mother's are dying of aids, and people are struggling to put foods in their bodies, but many children in these circumstances are out laughing and playing in the streets because they know no different. They opened their homes and their hearts without hesitation to welcome their new friends from Canada. Those who entered the situation whole-heartedly, experienced generosity and hospitality only an open heart recognizes. It can be tragic for us here to realize that they are without what we take for granted, such as running water in the home, or a home at all, more than a bowl of rice to eat each day; but many of them have never known anything else. To transcend our own victim perception by believing we are helping others who are less than we are is to miss the gift of the shared experience. Poor and helpless is a perception, of one side looking at the other from a perspective of being superior. When I observed the kids come back from Ghana, it became obvious that the children and people of Ghana helped them as much as they were helped, and it became obvious to them too when they returned to what they had always thought of as their regular lives. They shared with one another in completely different ways, but to each equally valuable. The principal, and teachers at my daughters' high school have fueled this change through inspiring the kids with what they can relate to through first hand experience. There are no *choose your alliance talk*s, or *think about the starving children in Africa talks*, but rather explorations into the human condition, and sociology studies that help bridge current accepted concepts with the knowledge of their actual experience.

Here's another example of a different approach to recognizing the thoughts we have about ourselves that determine what we experience of reality. We had a lot of fun with this at our dinner table- and to hear my children's idea's about this was fascinating to me. In the grade ten Sociology class, students were given an exercise to help them recognize who they believe they are, and the effect their thinking has on creating their experiences throughout their lives. The students were asked to pick a number between one and ten that they honestly thought reflected their worth most accurately. In the exercise, the number reflects the unconscious personal assessment we have of ourselves and our worth; one being the lowest. Even if we have never considered this consciously, within us, we have a definite idea of where we rank on the value scale. The study demonstrates that we pursue experiences which, and relate to people who, we unconsciously recognize as equivalent to our number. Our resulting choices reflect our unconscious beliefs about our personal power. The people with whom we choose to associate and the occupations we decide to engage in will reflect the number we identify as best describing ourselves. Water seeks its own level.

When conscious about what number we choose for ourselves and how it affects our circumstances, we can then strive to change this perception. We recognize it is our choice to decide our value for ourselves. While it would be great if we all decided we were a ten and then behaved accordingly, the reality is that unless we internalize this new belief, no change will take place. This is a very revealing exercise, and evokes many questions about why we think we are a certain number, and what we can change within ourselves to hold our number high, whatever it is, for others to respond to. It reveals the potential, as well as the responsibility, of becoming a ten. We alone decide this for ourselves, and at critical times in our lives it comes up for renewal without our realizing the significance of the choice we make, or rather the judgment we make on ourselves. Aligning with our magnificence is often an unconscious challenge when we are faced with uncertainty, doubt, or disappointment that if unknowingly allowed, can define us and limit our perceptions about self.

Whether we approach growth with a number study, or walk in another's shoes to understand their challenges, and learn to recognize our own in the process, we are led to become more conscious of what exists beyond the borders of the *me* mentality. Our masculine energy, if denied expression, becomes allowing of influences that we mistakenly believe are beyond our control. Growing wings of awareness expands our ability to remain vital and healthy as part of our changing world. Our masculine energy, if given constructive exercise, may become secure enough to be aware when we are summoned to channel in a *greater dimension* than what we may currently recognize. No matter what our circumstances, we share common beliefs with others that resonate with us. The more conscious we become of what we attract, the more empowered we become to choose change within ourselves. Self is no longer isolated, but rather integrated with *Greater Other Dimensions* that become real to us, through the acceptance and understanding of others, whose experience and perceptions enrich who we have the ability to be with them. We don't need to be a number ten to be happy! Self integrated with God, opens our eyes to perceive our wholeness, and fosters faith in being led to fulfill the truth of who we are. Aligning our masculine energy with *Greater Other Dimensions* brings compassion into our experience and we become the change we want to see in the world because we accept and appreciate the experience of sharing a *common passion* and *faith in humanity.*

You may very well be a victim today,
but depending on how you choose to respond,
and accept your ability to make aware choices,
your courage exercised today,
may change your experience,
and the experience for another tomorrow.

❧   ❧   ❧

There is a force at work that is fueling big changes. As s a global community we pray for change. We pray that conflict and economic struggle will cease, yet we continue to be the same people in response to what is happening in our *own* lives. Have we become so entrenched in the *victim* role that we have forgotten that change comes from within ourselves first, and then naturally extends into our surroundings? Contagious diseases could just as easily be contagious easiness. We must embrace our emotional upheaval, acknowledge it, and decide that we have the power to change. This irrepressible force is exposing our resentments, our hurts, and our misunderstandings of other's actions towards us. Emotionally recognizing ourselves exposes our arrogance and takes us to a place of humility that restores our faith in the inherent goodness of humanity. Humility can go a long way in changing that threatening force into a power that transcends our discomfort. Do you feel like a good person? If you don't, then what changes are you willing to make in order to become a better person? The power to choose to be who you are lies in your hands alone. As we become goodness, we see the goodness in others, and respond to that vision because *no other reality exists for us.*

Many would say that civilization is headed for disaster, but take notice who is saying this and to what purpose. Whether we are talking about today, or we are talking about centuries past, there have always been forecasts of doom and gloom. If we have any sort of materially based wealth, and our identity rests on believing that this wealth defines us, then what is happening in our world can be quite threatening to our idea of security. If we are experiencing discomfort, materially or otherwise, then we may recognize the need to personally grow beyond our current perceptions and allow in greater perceptions of reality. As long as there is discomfort, there is motivation, and it will not cease until our awareness recognizes what needs to change for us. As a society, we equate power, success, and accumulated wealth with personal value. We like to *say* that the class system doesn't have influence over us in North America, that all people have a voice, and that we are all equal. We take great pride in our talk, but our walk tells a different story.

We stumble when it comes to finding the courage to walk the talk when our creature comforts are threatened. When things outside of our control threaten us, we forget what matters and go into damage control mode to protect what we feel may be jeopardized. It's not only about our monetary wealth, it's about the foundation upon which it sits. When we wake up in the morning, do we feel truly blessed by the health and happiness of ourselves and our loved ones, or do we simply pay lip service to these feelings and spend the rest of the day consumed with mental lists? Any one of us could lose everything we think we are and everything we think we have in a moment and all that has existed outside our realm of awareness might be forced into clear view. The unconscious can come knocking on our door in many unlikely forms; a cancer, a serious illness, a divorce, or the loss of a job. We view these varying degrees of bad news as portents of disaster. Open the door, invite it in, and listen! There may be a whole other dimension that exists in our lives to which we have been oblivious. Our fear is a fear of what we have lost or might lose and is based upon accumulated assumptions about what the bad news could mean. These assumptions of impending gloom and doom are based upon our current set of paradigms. Cancer victims get very sick and die. Divorce is emotionally painful and scarring. Getting the pink slip is a lethal blow to self esteem. Assumptions such as these are disempowering and can become self-fulfilling prophecies. We need a new set of paradigms that will allow for the unveiling of the truth underlying our life challenges.

We spend our lives doing what we believe we are supposed to do, without questioning the source of these ideas, and when the rug is pulled out from under our feet we wonder how this could happen to us so suddenly, out of nowhere. Illness develops when we fail to recognize the voice inside that beckons us to change a way of *thinking about ourselves* that is hurting us or limiting us. That voice initially tries to get our attention in small ways that we often ignore. Next it gathers momentum in emotions in an attempt to express the underlying discord. Finally, an outward physical symptom appears which we cannot deny. We lose our jobs and our close relationships disintegrate when we have failed to listen to the promptings inside that urge us to move beyond our perceived idea of security into the unknown. We allow fear to isolate us from revealing ourselves to what we think we know in others, and wonder why a good experience of others seem to evade us. If we fail to exercise consciously what our heart knows to be the goodness within us, then disease and loss appear as symptoms of deeper unrecognized and unmet needs within us. As long as we look for others to honor our needs we miss our ability to reach for a reality that can understand, respond and fulfill them.

Self integrated with *Greater Other Dimensions* can expand our capacity to experience greater dimensions of our self, and in turn it is what we begin perceiving and experiencing with others. Tell this to someone who is *attached to placing responsibility* for their experience on another, and they will more than likely feel judged and deeply wounded by this insinuation because they want to remain as far as possible away from allowing their own inner discomfort and fear to surface. The fear of addressing what we often deny as belonging within us, and project onto others, keeps us safeguarding our feelings, and experiencing only the worse in others. When the masculine energy is at work without the influence of the feminine, it acts in defense of its perceived vulnerability. The masculine believes that if its vulnerability is exposed, it will be completely disabled or even killed if exposed. Our feminine energy is held hostage, isolated from its ability to be fluid and nurturing, preventing it from birthing greater consciousness. When we cease investing in unveiling our own magnificence, we become blind to what our outer world can reflect of it back to us. Emotions are running the show here, and accepting anything beyond what they support is difficult for us because there is no satisfying or understanding emotional energy. Only we can acknowledge our emotions as valid for self as it is, and choose to open ourselves to receive more than what we assume they represent. We *reengage* our ability to *feel beyond our emotions* which allows us to perceive a greater reality for ourselves..

Emotions exist whether we acknowledge them or not. When we deny the existence of our emotions we are unable to feel the subtle sensations beyond them. The sensation we do feel is physical pain, as the emotions we deny are attached to a part of self seeking to be realized more fully. These two together create resistance within us, and depending on the magnitude of them, the greater the discomfort we become physically aware of. We fail to see the magnificent part of self that lies beyond our suppressed emotions. Our true self remains hidden from us. Those who do manage to *transcend their challenges* will tell you how their disease, relationship loss, or job loss turned out to be the greatest gift in their life. Those who are disabled by challenge will avoid any other reality than the one they are unknowingly committed to, as they are set on holding this disabled perception of themselves relative to the challenge. No one has the ability to choose what we think about ourselves but us. When we completely disown our masculine energy, we *disable our ability to make choice* that empowers us to reach beyond our current perceptions to greater dimensions that enhance our wellbeing and understanding of who we are beyond our current experience.

Those who transcend their challenge *will tell you* that they emerged from the experience realizing how they had shortchanged themselves for so long without knowing it. Their masculine energy has been re-enabled, where before it had been unconsciously directed against self. They sent feelers out beyond self's perceptions to find a greater truth beyond the one they found themselves experiencing, and unknowingly committed to. In re-enabling a constructive masculine energy, rather than unconsciously engaging it destructively, they allowed greater potential to enter self's experience. These people respond by *telling you* their belief and position with complete security in revealing it, as their masculine energy is confident and competent in its ability to direct their personal experience. For many women because of harmful experience with men, the masculine is a distained energy that they sever from acknowledging exists within themselves in any form, positive or negative. It does exist, whether we like it or not, and in disowning it, because of limited perceptions about it, we engage in self-destructive behavior without any knowledge or awareness of our part in allowing it.

Many will tell you how they invested their full attention on the desired outcome of wholeness and fulfillment, and placed faith in their ability to transcend challenge, with or without validation from others. After transcending the struggle, these people recognize that they had reached the threshold of awakening to a richer reality. They are able to see that while contemplating the pro's and con's of actually crossing into it a new awareness and experience for self, life plunged them head first into the unknown. They will recount for you how they found themselves realizing their worse fear: Isolation. Without the comfort of any security they could relate to, they were forced to recognize the aspect of self they had left undeveloped. There is a confidence in their telling because they are speaking a new and sure truth. Their words are not rehearsed or guarded. They know that their newfound perceptions are the real deal to them. The masculine and feminine energies within them have become a co-creative force that expresses their spirit without inhibition. One's heart opens to receive their message of hope and possibility because there is such clarity and presence with them. Their words are spoken with authenticity and compassion. They have grown in their capacity to embrace compassion for self.

When we seek more understanding of our *Greater Other Dimensions* we open the door to awareness. The masculine energy can engage from a place of security to be infused by knowledge beyond self's current perception and experience. For some the experience is like growing wings. It is as if, for the first time, they are expressing their truth to others without assumptions about how they are received. For others it is like having the courage to unfurl their wings and allow them to spread out again with trust that they will support self in more expansive ways than previously experienced by them. With self extending outward to embody spirit, we transcend the illusion of a self that is isolated by externally imposed limitations, to a reality in which self is the only one capable of imposing false limitations when it is threatened to grow in awareness. Those who successfully meet their challenge, and heal self's perceptions as a result, birth freedom from the inner duality that unconsciously tormented them.

It is very painful to accept that we have to grow beyond protecting the *victim-self's* boundaries. Our repressed duality percolates into our daily life without our knowing it. We continue to ignore its source as being within our control. We ignore it, and we believe that by withholding our expression of it to others it will cease to exist or influence us. Our own unacknowledged duality becomes what we experience in others in close relationship to us. The masculine energy holds the power of exerting its will to *allow* the seed for healing, and inviting in our *Greater Other Dimensions* to illuminate where we may currently see only darkness. In aligning with spirit, the floodgates will open, releasing the backlog of emotion, and in its wake comes humility and gratitude. We become real with ourselves and authentic with others again. There is great internal integrity established when we reveal our inner fears and beliefs about who we believe ourselves to be.

The *victim-self* can always find justification for remaining intact when the compassionate aspect of our masculine energy is not honored. It is the compassionate masculine that can discern truth from illusion. We live in a world that has let us down. Our world includes deceivers, leaders in government and industry in whom we have placed trust. The deceivers knowingly market products that are harmful to our health and wellbeing. There are products on the market that the manufacturers and the producers know contain harmful substances that have been scientifically proven to cause cancer, autoimmune disorders, and death. Some of us are aware of the dangers inherent in these products and become advocates for our own health by buying healthy alternatives. But even foods labeled organic and natural are not always what they seem. Many plastics, cosmetics, building materials, and cleaning products contain toxic chemicals that could seriously harm us, even kill us, yet they remain in the marketplace. Not all labels tell the whole truth, and there are producers and manufacturers who are intentionally misguiding consumers. The unaware consumer becomes the innocent victim. There is no question that the victim archetype exists here, but *choosing to remain the victim* once recognizing it, gives those in these positions of responsibility further power to determine our fate. We choose, through our attentiveness, the ideals and reality we are committed to supporting.

In aligning with the *liberator*, our victim sheds its belief that it is disabled from making constructive choices. With this shift in awareness we are able to choose which products we are willing to support. If we all decide to invest ourselves in only what is good for us, the market that supplies the less-than-desirable products also shifts to support healthy and safe consumer goods. We empower self to make choices with awareness. By openly demonstrating conscientious values, we in turn bring awareness to others to do the same. People often recognize their own common sense when they witness another move through challenging situations with faith in the difference their choices make. In aligning with our liberator we *become the liberator* without taking on the deceivers directly. No organized boycott or other form of protest is necessary.

In disowning who we have the ability to be consciously, we too become a deceiver of a different, but just as dangerous, nature. The deceiver, both our internal deceiver and the ones in our external world, depend upon the victim for survival. When we decide that we are powerless to effect change, we resign ourselves to the status quo. We willingly become the victim. Our *Materialism* is fertile soil for the deceivers who thrive on our belief that we need *things* to show the world who we are. Our accumulation of stuff makes us feel secure. Our *Fear* speaks to our internal deceiver. That part of us which believes there is nothing we can do about our discomfort, affects the people in our life who place their trust in our ability to guide with good conscience. The realization that we don't need a Gucci handbag or a Porsche sports car to define us can come as quite a shock. The corporate deceiver is revealed. Like Dorothy, we realize that the wizard is nothing more than the man behind the curtain. And like Dorothy, we learn that it is up to us to find our own way home. Our personal journey, just like Dorothy's, is about becoming aware of our inner resources which have been there all along that support us claiming our true power. We return home whenever we choose, but we don't know it's a possibility until we recognize who we are. When the only criteria behind the choices we make is how we will be seen and judged by others, we are for sale. We become the deceiver of our own true self. When we are rejected by others we are shocked and become lost. Who are we without the approval of others? Driving a lovely car is fun, but it need not define us.

Deception is a dangerous game that hurts innocent people and preys on the conscience of those who play it. When we transcend *buying* into this role of the victim, and *invest* in opening our eyes to perceive greater dimensions of what exists, we find the places, people and products that support our liberation. They have been there all along, but we often don't notice the significance of their message until it affects us and those we love and directly threatens our own sense of security. We can *spend* our energy and resources in seeking justice and restitution, or we can *invest* in cultivating our awareness *because we are secure enough to exercise our choices conscientiously.* We begin to invest in our relationships and in the choices we make as consumers as a reflection of a mentality in which we have chosen to engage.

When we choose to grow and heal,
we consciously shift our alliance into the realm of possibility
and out of the ream of victimization.

≥o ≥o ≥o

The *liberator* resides right along side the victim within us, and all we have to do is choose to open our eyes to see it and make friends with it. When we identify with the victim and become entrenched in the experience of the victim, the liberator becomes an annoyance. Viewing the liberator from this vantage point just plants our feet more firmly in our chosen reality because we are determined to hold onto the idea that another doesn't understand our suffering. We would rather go down with a sinking ship than grab the lifeline held out by the hand of another. Choosing to change our alliance from the *victim* to the *liberator* in ourselves is to invite in a whole new realm of possibilities. The choice will always remain ours as to how to use the information offered by the liberator in us.

Who we are is not reliant on what our external world can always acknowledge as valuable. When hypothetically asked what is most important to us, most, or more than likely all, will say that it is our loved ones. But when we look at people's behavior, we see something quite different. When we face a major life challenge and do not explore it for its value in showing us where we have been unconscious, remains our loss. The darkness we perceive out there is a reflection of our fears, and as long as they remain out there and are not allowed in, we shall never know them for what they truly are. In our focus on keeping out what we believe threatens us, we close ourselves off from all the good feelings that can enrich our relationships with others as well. When our own shadow shows up, and we mistake it as something or someone else, it remains a threat, and we miss the gift of pure knowledge that knows its home in our hearts depths. We are the goodness, but we have forgotten through our pain and suffering to place faith in it and *exercise it* because it seems to be an overwhelming task to remain faithful to such a reality when facing adversity in our outer world.

Those who struggle and manipulate in an effort to outsmart the system are losing their influence, because hording does nothing but build bigger walls that separate people, and sabotage human and material resources that synergistically work together. Those walls they have erected are crumbling, as are their illusions of security. Those who are living consciously, and expanding who they are within the system are flourishing, even though they may be experiencing some material discomfort, they are knowingly using it to further expand their awareness of an unrealized spiritual dimension. Compassion is powerful, and often gets overlooked when we find ourselves in perceived crisis. Money itself is not the criteria. Rather it is the foundation upon which wealth rests that is becoming a very real criterion, one that can make or break our illusion of security. Our houses can become a fortress, an illusion of protection. Everything appears to be in order from the outside, but no one really knows what is on the inside because no one is allowed through the door. Or our houses can be *homes* in which people who love dwell and where the gates remain approachable and open always. Regardless of the size of the house or the furnishings within, the choice is completely ours as to which way we choose to live. Home invites others into the experience of love, whereas a fortress intimidates and evokes resentment from those left unintentionally outside the door. It may appear to be the exact same structure, but the energetic foundation upon which it rests attracts completely different experiences. Only we can choose what kind of dwelling we wish to inhabit.

Our physical bodies and what dwells within us is no different than how our place of residence is perceived. If we operate in openness and extend ourselves to meet the world because love dwells within us, we experience more loving and expansive aspects of ourselves and others in our life. Discomfort is part of the process, but it leads us to greater realms of experience, with more understanding, and appreciation of love and life as expansive experiences. If we choose to go through life wearing heavy armor for protection against perceived threats from the outside world then we miss recognizing the role of self to expose us to the experience of life that can give us meaning as soul. We alone choose with which image we are aligned. Our life experience will reflect back to us what can bring illumination to who we really are. Investing in magnificence, greatness, love, and compassion, can align us with so much more that is fulfilling and enriching beyond what any walls we can physically construct could possibly contain.

Listening to people express their perceptions and ideas about life often triggers questions within us. It is in this resistance to accept their beliefs as our own that we find the most enlightening realizations about our own limited beliefs. In another's openness, we are opened to realize some of our assumptions about them, or people like them, that we didn't realize we had until we allowed ourselves to really know them. We are not all so different in what we hold in our hearts, and when life isn't reflecting love back to us, it is difficult to accept we are the ones creating separation from receiving it. We feel that to change our minds means admitting we are wrong, when this is not really true at all! We can be right because of what we know at the time, but others can be right as well, especially if their knowledge expands our own appreciation and understanding of a greater truth. *Meeting them* with our own thinking, to blend and co-operatively influence us to question how we can expand our understanding can be mutually empowering. Becoming aware of aligning with our own spirit shows us more clearly when others are separate from theirs when we are met with harsh words and hurtful judgments. Although another is *not aligned* with their spirit, *if we are aligned with ours*, we relate to them at the level of theirs, and their inconsiderate behavior goes unacknowledged by us. We are given the opportunity to be their spirit's mirror, and reflect back to them their own unrealized capacity for generosity and compassion. They may just demonstrate the greatness that we now just assume is there if we allow them space to express it!

> *One who demonstrates compassionate masculine*
> *energy has faith in human nature,*
> *and is secure in their own ability to engage the*
> *receptivity of their feminine energy*
> *without fear of losing who they are,*
> *and what is important to them,*
> *by extending themselves beyond their currently recognized identity.*

✿   ✿   ✿

In a chapter entitled, *The Masculine Expression Finds Compassion,* one might expect that it will illuminate our ability to change our husbands into the incredible compassionate men we married. They may become this way if we allow them to meet us. As long as we hold onto the idea that we actually have the ability to change them, we miss recognizing where we sold out our own magnificence in relating to them on another level. We often hand over the power of our magnificence, without even knowing it, the moment we marry them. The masculine energy is a volatile demon to slay within us if we insist on giving away our power to our husbands in hopes of creating harmony in the home. It is worth revisiting for a moment the notion that compassion is currently defined as being sympathetic to the suffering, and a desire to help, instead of a consciousness that reveals *sharing a common passion.*

Traditionally men are given the role of the masculine, and women the feminine, and as much as times have changed, it is understood that, once we cross that threshold into the home, a woman relinquishes her otherwise exercised authority in the presence of her honored husband. Exactly when did we decide that our husband's were not strong, intelligent and courageous men who could take up the challenge of our own masculine energy? Why can't men and women create a partnership that inspires greater things beyond their separate sexes. As women, we step back and let them take over, or we learn to work around them rather than face possible discord. We then harbor our resentment and anger about how they handle things. Those of us who genuinely love our husbands and often think they don't get us, or hear us, or value and honor just what we do when they are not around may find what I am suggesting here in complete contradiction to what we currently are conditioned to believe. The fact that there is love between the partners is important, love that allows another to reach for their ability to be compassionate and let down their guard. We can remove our adopted masks and stop playing the games that protect us from revealing unrecognized needs. This kind of love extends beyond one that simply holds the marriage together.

Having the courage to be who we are and express ourselves honestly to one another builds integrity. Unfortunately, we often keep silent in an effort to bolster our husband's self esteem because we buy into believing that he is fragile. Why else would he behave like such a Neanderthal? We steer clear of his emotions because we think the lid will blow off of his carefully-bottled feelings and complete irrational behavior will follow… which it can without question. We suppress who we have the ability to be in hopes of not competing or challenging his authority. Sounds like a child doesn't it? And now, as females, we are being called upon to grow up and be adult women and become magnificent and challenging partners again. We are by nature blenders and harmonizers, but we can grow a very strong spine that honors and recognizes our own masculine energy as a force within us to be exercised with compassion- towards ourselves, and them. Unless we know what we need and what is important to us, our husbands are never going to "get" us. We don't "get" ourselves. They are not going to respond to our game of silence because they really just don't understand it. We cannot just expect them to figure us out on their own.

When we are healthy and vibrant does love remain as a spark that ignites *a common passion* with our partner? Women aren't being fulfilled by supporting what their husbands place their focus on, be it their careers, their accomplishments or their idea of posterity. Striking out on our own brings initial satisfaction, but the heart's desire to be aligned with a common passion with them makes independence feel like a step away from what we yearn to share with them. Often one partner gets ill in order to illicit the desired response wanted from the other, and keep unrecognized needs met. Everyday dynamics push us to see our own shadow reflected in our spouses without realizing it, and that spark within us becomes disguised by our fears of what we assume confronts us. I can think of no better way to end a chapter on the masculine energy finding compassion than to share with you the dynamics I witnessed between a husband and wife who are a beautiful example of what can play out in the lives of so many of us. Gwen and Sam have been married for over fifty years. They are not old by any stretch of the imagination for inside them they may as well be still thirty in how they see themselves. Gwen has an advanced degenerative nervous disorder and was in a lot of pain when Sam escorted her in to see me. He presented me with a four page, chronologically ordered list that he had meticulously hand written up of symptoms, diagnosis dates, surgeries, and medications she has taken over the past several years and her current regime prescribed by her Medical Doctor.

Nothing was managing the pain for her, and functioning was very difficult. Sam was concerned, charming, devoted, and very sincere in his explanations of her health history. We both helped her get onto the treatment table and he asked if he might stay for the appointment. She agreed to have him present.

Gwen is one of those women who you know from the first moment of meeting her that she is not afraid to speak her mind, claim her space, or decide how and what she thinks about things. Outwardly she didn't seem to be upset, just in extreme discomfort and pain. I loved her directness, but within moments I realized she was angry and resentful towards her husband, not life in general, or her state of health. She and I had a dialogue about this, and her husband sat up straight in his chair and leaned forward to catch every word of what was being said across the room while she lay on the treatment table. He was surprised by what I was suggesting, and definitely perplexed. He was expecting to hear how he was the problem and what he could do to fix it. Our body is a very intelligent organism, and although we may be consciously aligned with healing, if our body is engaged in holding on to its discomfort, the best intentioned help is not going to shift a darn thing for us. No amount of sympathy, empathy or understanding from another is going to reach what we no longer recognize or believe is within our power to accept or change within ourselves.

Our own masculine energy controls the part of self buried deep within us, and we become unconsciously consumed by the emotional energy surrounding it without even knowing it. Gwen's spirit could not get anywhere near this part of herself as long as her masculine energy was unknowingly focused on containing and keeping this part of self separate from anything beyond its perception. As we spoke, her field began to open, and she could feel the pain dispersing. There was a great deal of emotion she had been suppressing. Underlying this suppressed emotion was a part of her that felt there was injustice and vulnerability. I knew the treatment wouldn't hold unless she consciously became aware of her part in choosing to keep this part of self from realizing anything more than what existed beyond its perceptions. Sam interjected at this point because he wanted to know what, intuitively, I could tell him about his part in creating the whole thing. He was intrigued, whereas she was calm and very pensive, not sure exactly why what we spoke about resonated with her so strongly.

After she got off the treatment table there was relief from her pain and the three of us talked about how her own masculine energy was keeping her isolated and experiencing pain. They both shared with me the story of how they met in their youth while he was training at his local community pool and she and her girlfriends were there all dressed up to watch the swimmers. He began the story by telling me what an outstanding athlete he was in his youth and how confident he was that he could win her over. He told of how he couldn't take his eyes off of her and knew she was the one for him at first glance. That very first day, he walked over to her, picked her up and threw her in the pool, dress, jewelry and all. Then he jumped in to save her. They married and had a family together. As he told me about how she had captured his heart, she smiled and thoroughly enjoyed hearing him relay the events of their courtship. She also added that she could swim, but he was very gallant in jumping in after her. It was not difficult to see that there was still a spark alive between them as they sat there with me. Throwing her in the pool was the deal closer for her, and she even chuckled at remembering the event. During the marriage he traveled a great deal and she was left to manage her career, the home, and children. When the children became adults and left home, and she retired, she began to experience health problems.

When they first entered my office there was a distinct friction between them, and although he presented himself so generously, his energetic history told of a man who didn't always show his appreciation for his wife. He had a history of a temper, and was not always the receptive man I was conversing with. When I asked him about this he admitted this was true, but that since retiring this was no longer the case. When he told of his gesture of throwing her in the pool to show his affections, it is easy to see where this continued way of expressing his affections might spur her resentment and anger over the years. Those initial cute and bold flirtations can easily lose their charm when the long haul of dealing with diapers, dishes, laundry and entertaining enter the picture. Years later, still bickering back and forth to get a reaction from one another, it was obvious they loved each other. They wouldn't bother taking each other on if they didn't care so much! He absolutely adores her, and is doing everything in his power to help her, but she has to allow him to grow without becoming ill in order to illicit his receptiveness to honoring her needs. She allows him to care for her now, and because of her recognized physical fragility he is not going to be throwing her into any pools to show his feeling for her anytime soon. How did such an independent, capable and forthright woman become so ill? One wonders if it is because he wasn't home a lot of the time, and her masculine energy was able to be expressed without being challenged or shut down by his aggressive behavior. He failed to acknowledge and appreciate her capabilities. He failed to validate her contribution to the family. This wears down the spirit and eventually, the body.

The masculine and feminine when engaged as a co-operative synergy within us, opens us to our spiritual capacity. Gwen truly loves Sam, but her need over the years for his attention and appreciation to be expressed to her constructively with tenderness went unnoticed by him. He thought he was giving her his best. He was a good provider and he was doing it all for her. As her personal needs changed, her need for gentleness and a rapport on a deeper level emerged. He didn't know how to grow into appreciating this in her. She didn't know how to convey this need to him, either, or if she did, he didn't understand or hear what she was saying. He provided a good life, and the best of creature comforts he thought she wanted and deserved. Nothing was too good for her in his eyes, but this wasn't what she really wanted from him. When the children left home, Sam was ready to pick up where they'd left off in those early days. He was left wondering why she wasn't responding to the change the way he was. Sam genuinely tried to understand what it was she needed from him. He was working hard to be compassionate but it was up to her masculine energy to allow him to meet her. She holds the power to heal from her illness, not him. As long as she is ill, and not constructively expressing her masculine energy, he will be attentive, gentle, and appreciative of her. He will actively seek to help and understand her because he is not threatened by her strength to challenge him to grow. Her masculine energy remains unexpressed and his masculine energy remains unchallenged. His masculine energy is expressed as compassion as long as she is fragile and needy. Where her masculine energy was expressed outwardly before, and met resistance, it turned inward to control her own discord for the part of self hurt by not being honored for who she was. Until she decides to attempt to meet him where he is right now, and give up trying to illicit what she believes he is withholding from her, her resistance in opening herself to accept her perceived emotional vulnerability will create pain.

Somewhere within Gwen is a belief that Sam has the ability to define her should she reveal her sensitivity to him. In becoming ill, and allowing him to define who she is based on his understanding, *she gives her power away* to him. This can be a very difficult thing for an independent and resourceful woman to admit, for there is a great deal of stigma attached to such a confession, especially when surrounded by his incredible gifts of adornment that can't be denied as valid proof he has loved and cared for her by traditional standards. Why do we feel guilty for desiring our husband's interest, attention, respect, and gentle affection outside the bedroom? For her to trust to *be everything she is with him, with her own masculine owned and expressed,* creates a new challenge that has never been explored in all the years between them. She developed this with her children and in her friendships when he wasn't around. This means *being her all* when he is around, and not giving her power away in order to maintain the false pretense of peace and unity between them.

In honoring her capacity to exercise compassion with her own masculine energy *she could be allowing of herself, and in turn allowing of him* to develop emotionally on this new level and *meet her* if he so chooses. When she decides she is willing to risk becoming healthy and vibrant again, it will be a challenge to know how to relate to him constructively, as he too will be challenged to know how to constructively relate to her. In her illness, her masculine energy is secure, but not about exposing herself. Instead her masculine is engaged in protecting and controlling the *part of her self that she feels is vulnerable with him*. As soon as she deems herself worthy to be true to herself, regardless of him, she will move past pain into a reality that supports growing her self, independent of his ability to grow with her. Does she recognize her ability to change her relationship *with her self* rather than rely on Sam to understand and appreciate her? She can choose to *align with spirit* rather than unconsciously turn against herself and create dis*ease* in order to justify the validity of her suffering. When we fail to express our true needs, our body will express them for us in a way that will allow us to associate discomfort with our way of coping with life. She is the one who continues to suffer by severing herself from the anger and betrayal she feels in the relationship with him. Through her suffering, he is able to experience a *limited* expression of compassion because she is fragile. He in turns suffers because he is unable to alleviate her discomfort by simply providing for her. Although he is sympathetic and has a desire to help her, it isn't an empowering demonstration of intimacy that she receives from him. In denying our feelings, and refusing to honor that they are personal and valid regardless of another's perception of them, we never move beyond our feelings to reveal where there is discord in ourselves and in our relationships with others.

Sam, and others just like him, cannot appreciate everything their partners are, as they have yet to honor and develop their own sensitivity to the feminine qualities of receptivity. The very skills that enable them to be the good providers often keep their own inner depths from being explored except relative to an efficient and competitive world. This is true of many women as well as men, as it is not always the wife who becomes ill. The masculine and feminine qualities share the very same dynamics regardless of the gender, although they may be expressed and demonstrated very differently.

Sam genuinely appreciates Gwen to the best of his ability right now. Is she secure enough to be healthy and maintain her integrity regardless of his ability to appreciate her? Emotionally, he admittedly is still showing his affection by metaphorically throwing her in the pool, but he is *willing to learn* to express it more constructively to engage in *a common passion* that leads them both to fulfillment and experience of wellbeing. He is *willing to grow*, and develop a sensitivity that honors her emotional responses, but he honestly doesn't understand what she needs because he thought he had provided what was expected of him all along. It hadn't occurred to him that he was missing really receiving her, until her illness brought him into the experience of being out of control to truly provide what she needed to be well. He may not be able to manage the change. It is impossible to give someone everything that they believe they need without losing true self in the process. She will perpetuate her anguish and pain waiting for the change to take place. Gwen's pain returned two days after treatment. The challenge for Gwen and Sam is to become all that they can be *independent of the others approval and understanding.* Is illness required to meet her unrecognized need to be cherished and treated gently by the man she loves when exercising her own free will independent of his?

In her current pain, isolated from spirit, Gwen does not see the man Sam is today reaching with all his might to meet her needs to the best of his ability. Her masculine energy aligned with spirit could show her *how to constructively allow him* to grow in his ability, to know and appreciate more fully the woman she is today, as she embraces the woman she has the ability to be. In remaining enabled in her own ability to be *who she is* independent of him, *even when he is home,* he is left to be resourceful within himself, to develop more fully his abilities to nurture intimacy within the relationship. Taking on the commitment to grow with another takes great courage. Our traditional roles fall away to make room for a new kind of relationship in which we meet the challenges we encounter together. When the masculine energy finds a common passion with *our self,* we transcend the need for our partners to understand us as we are enabled to grow beyond the current experience with them that we believe defines our relationship. We develop a common passion *with* our partners and restore our faith in their ability *to grow and learn with us* regardless of our gender, age, experience, or stage in life. In aligning with our spirit we allow in an awareness of *Greater Other Dimensions* already present in the relationship, and the co-creative potential is ignited from the spark we cherish and keep kindled within ourselves that we see mirrored in them.

The last time I saw Gwen and Sam, he told me how when her pain is gone he is so happy, and everything is back to normal because the stress and the tension disappear for him. When the pain is gone, she claims the stress and tension surfaces because emotionally she is hurt by his need to have his way of doing things honored. He says he just wants to know what he has to do, and he'll do it! Unfortunately caring, and sharing, and communicating honestly is a learned skill one does because they cherish their relationship with the other, and he wants a check list of things to say and do that will work at keeping her happy. Where Gwen has reconnected to her spirit now and is freely expressing herself without physical pain, Sam is struggling to find ways to deal with his own discomfort. Growth is a huge commitment to faith in what we will find with our partners!

As women, all the things we believe our husbands are not capable of, become our excuse for not further developing our own potential. We don't allow them to face the challenge of reaching for the greater depths of their awareness when we try to compensate for what we think they lack. We compensate for them at our own expense. It is our own emotional anatomy and spiritual dimensions from which we are severed. We often explain what *they're feeling* to help others appreciate what we know to be in them but in doing so we prevent them from developing the ability to recognize and express these emotions for themselves in a way that we can understand. We miss what they are expressing because it isn't being expressed the way we would like it to be. When our masculine energy takes on our husband's masculine energy in an effort to stand our ground, we miss aligning with spirit and we demonstrate the immaturity of our own emotional expression. Both partners can be unknowingly equally invested in keeping these dynamics alive in the relationship, albeit differently. Until women and men take ownership of what they believe is missing in their partner, there can be no new territory discovered, or co-creative capacity nurtured. The resistance and tension will continue to highlight what needs to change. No one can change another. We can only change ourselves.

Our capacity to love expands when we find *a common passion* that fuels growing and learning together. Actualizing *Greater Other Dimensions* reveals the *common passion* when we put our focus on gratitude toward and appreciation of another as they are. The perceived risk in relinquishing our ideas about security for something that spirit encourages us to follow pales when compared with the fulfillment we experience in reaching for dreams and ideals that we thought exist only in fairy tales.

Chapter 5

The Feminine Experiences a Common Passion

An open mind and heart ideal becomes the shared experience,
instead of remaining a limited experience,
where the will of one person is imposed upon another.

We all have favorite stories, fairy tales, and legends we enjoyed as children. As we grow older, these stories take on new meaning on another level. I always loved the story of Cinderella when I was a child. I don't remember it being too much more than a story about a girl who is rescued from a horrible existence with her wicked stepmother, by a handsome Prince. Because Cinderella was a good girl with a kind heart, good things came to her. Cinderella's fairy godmother took her away from her life in the cinders to become the Queen she deserved to be. When I read it now I understand the story as it relates to the idea of the masculine and feminine energies within us. It reminds me that good things happen to people who remain faithful to their goodness. Those who are mean and hurtful will meet their own destinies without anyone actually "taking them on". If we believe we are goodness, we will see goodness and experience goodness in our lives no matter where we are or what happens to us. Whether we see ourselves and our circumstances as the glass half full or the glass half empty depends on this premise. I must admit, that Cinderella and Pollyanna have always been favorites of mine. Although I know they are fictional, they demonstrate the inherent goodness of keeping one's faith in where an open heart leads us. Being goodness shows us goodness and keeps our challenges in perspective. As long as the glass is half full, we have resources with which to meet the challenges that life presents to us. These stories end with, "And they all lived happily ever after", but one wonders just how these young women went on to live the rest of their lives…

We are led to believe that once Prince Charming appears and we marry, what follows is not really important relative to this. I suppose that if one has the experience of love in their life, then the rest is really just icing on the cake. But love shows up in many ways, and waiting for Prince Charming can keep us blind to the experience of love right here, right now, already with us. What happens if Prince Charming doesn't show up early in life? Or worse yet, we mistake another for Prince Charming because we are desperately seeking love and we *want* him to fit the bill. If we seek to obtain love as an object of our desires, we miss the experience of love that expands our appreciation and experience of life. What if we believed what others told us about ourselves and our worth? What if we believed we were a "four" or a "six" out of ten without question? What if we had no idea that we could think differently of ourselves, for ourselves? In the story of Cinderella, true love finds her because she embodies love already within her life as it is. When the stepmother and stepsisters told her she was a number three, she didn't believe it! Amidst the cinders, she found love in nature, and in everyone and everything around her. Because she found love within herself, she shared it with others, regardless of their willingness to accept it. The stepsisters and stepmother stayed clear of her, and kept her hidden away. After all, their darkness was made obviously ugly when exposed in her light. Because of Cinderella's faith in love and goodness, she recognized her fairy godmother when she appeared in her life. Cinderella believed in the magic of life and this belief was manifested in the person of the fairy godmother. Love was her experience, even while she toiled in the ashes. She could have chosen to live life in the darkness as a victim. Instead, she chose to live in the light. Her story ended well.

Cinderella went from virtual slavery in the ash heap straight to life on a throne. I wonder if she felt like she had to grow wings in order to remain true to the virtues she had cultivated in her youth once she was placed on a throne. Although she stops to ponder her worthiness, and her ability to shine against the darkness of the cinders, she doesn't set her sights set there. She maintains her optimism and finds meaning in her servitude. She placed her faith in love, and a fairy godmother arrived with a plan. She recognized the fairy godmother because, in her chosen reality, magic was a real possibility. Cinderella sees all the good there is to see and the bad just seems to brush past her, leaving her innocence untarnished. There are many parts of that fairy tale that, although fictional, are symbolic of the maturation of the emotional feminine energy, because the masculine is secure in choosing its alignment with *Greater Other Dimensions,* beyond the physically recognized reality.

In being our goodness, our heart is open to
receive the blessing in every situation,
because our resourcefulness is illuminated by
Spirit to recognize the blessing.

⁂

The feminine energy in its innate power to birth greater consciousness doesn't maintain the silent grace and voice of humanity behind closed doors very long if it finds meaningful expression through the secure back bone of the masculine energy. Cinderella embodied beauty and compassion even though her rightful place in her father's home had been usurped by her wicked stepmother and stepsisters. She lost everything she knew overnight; her status, her things, and her beloved father. But she never forgot who she was. She had a presence, an inner strength and faith in her ability to rise above her circumstances. It takes a real Prince to recognize the real thing when he finds it, because only a man secure enough in his own masculinity is able to open the door to the feminine without feeling threatened. Our prayers for our world are being answered. The doors to our closed hearts are being opened and the feminine is being asked to come forward without being intimidated or bullied into submission. As the feminine energy emerges in its power, it remains as the feminine, and gives birth to the presence of spirit that transcends duality. The feminine no longer needs to adopt the mask of the masculine in order to have spirit heard and received, for it naturally becomes manifest once accepted and acknowledged for what it is.

While there appears to be a force gathering momentum that many assume will bring further conflict and discord in the world, the power of the feminine energy is right there in its midst. It knows its value and will not wait patiently until the world is ready to receive it. If that force is met with feminine *responsiveness* rather than with the masculine *reactivity*, there will be a sufficient pause for people to embrace the power of the masculine energy to focus and allow the power of the feminine energy to nurture what is inherent in all our hearts, constructively for humanity. Perhaps men need to become more secure and accepting of the expression of their emotions if they are to recognize the true power of the feminine within themselves. And women have got to recognize when *their own masculine energy* stands in the way of their feminine being constructively utilized. We must all be this change within ourselves to have the confidence to hold true to the faith in what we know is possible in the face of our circumstances. If we are to develop the ability to be present, then the masculine and feminine have got to give up the idea of one being superior to the other. If we continue to get caught up in the pull of circumstance, and our own identity, then we will continue to miss the inherent power of a love that transcends all fear and doubt. There is always a positive and negative aspect coexisting in every situation, but to see the interplay between the two, we have to be responsive with open minds and open hearts. With a responsive attitude we will no longer see only the threatening aspect of a situation but will see things as they really are.

Humanity has come far enough along its journey to realize that men and women both have within them the expression of the feminine and masculine. As more individuals openly demonstrate these qualities and have the courage to walk what appears to be to the beat of a different drummer, we are moved as a society to awaken to expecting greater possibilities within our relationships. Women who choose to stand alone rather than marry to gain acceptance, *can* do so without being exiled. They can fulfill their purpose with or without children and enjoy loving relationships with or without taking on a partner or provider. Likewise, men can stand alone and be seen as responsive, responsible and generous individuals, rather than entering relationships that are not challenging for the sake of appearances. Society is adapting and changing its ways as people are released from the illusion that their worth is based on another choosing to marry them. People who are demonstrating the truth that lies behind this illusion have kept faith in their freedom to be themselves because they hold true to the virtues of an open heart. These men and women, married and single, young and old, accept their truth and have courage to walk it with integrity, even if it means walking independently of another's interpretation of traditional values. They love who they are and accept others for who they are, without seeking someone or something to validate, or acknowledge their value.

Somehow, these pioneers have been able to go deep enough within themselves to find true acceptance and love for who they are, as they are, regardless of other influences that might tell them otherwise. They have tapped into the potential that their *Greater Other Dimensions* has blessed them with, and they have had the courage to pass through their discomfort in order to accept greater knowledge from it. They have transcended conditioning that would lead them to believe they have no place because they are different, and they have kept faith in their power to adapt and flow with high ideals. In exercising their free will to choose the experience of deeper and more meaningful relationships, they are revealing the limitations many have unknowingly committed to because it never occurred to them there was more beyond it that could be their reality.

Like Cinderella and Pollyanna, these people have ideas that challenge social norms. They look within for their guidance and inspiration. They choose to support and *be* the goodness they seek to experience in the world, regardless of their circumstance. Until they find it, they make the absolute most of what they have, and continue to cultivate it with conscientiousness. They believe in themselves, and those that have the privilege of experiencing relationship with them are inspired to live more richly and authentically because they learn to open their hearts to receive the magic that is inherent in all life. People like Pollyanna and Cinderella are memorable because in meeting them, we began to think differently about things, and enthusiasm and passion for life began to creep into our experience, rather magically, even after they are gone. These people have *presence* that permeates everyone and everything around them.

People who are experiencing fulfilling partnerships feel complete on their own. They have assumed responsibility for their own happiness and in turn can receive and share with another openly. What is happening right now in our world is truly inspiring, because in our increased awareness we are better able to recognize the wisdom of those who carry this presence. With this acknowledgement is born the opportunity to develop our own ability to hold such presence. Becoming a likeness of God as our own individual expression becomes our reality. The illusions of humanity are falling away to reveal our potential to be loving beings. If our own lives are similar to fairy tales at all, then the walls are crumbling around the remote castles we've been living in. This can only mean one thing: The masculine has recognized its feminine qualities, and the feminine its masculine qualities. Along with the knowledge of these inherent qualities comes the presence of our other dimensions with the great reminder of a common passion we all long to experience together. What good is a castle if the kingdom is starving, resentful, and hostile, and through manipulation and deception remains controlled? To continue to approach another as opposition is to remain separate and isolated in our suffering. Instead we must plant the seeds of compassion that will grow to nourish us all.

Now is the time for the integration of our masculine and feminine energies in order to move beyond them as polarities. The Cinderella's and Pollyanna's of the world may transcend the archetype of the victim at the mercy of the evil stepmother, or the system, or the horrible upbringing, to step into that magical glass slipper, gaze up at the crystal chandelier and experience the magic of the life around them. Maybe the symbolism of the glass slipper and crystal chandelier is akin to that of *growing wings*. Cinderella and Pollyanna allowed their natural expression of compassion to be taken to a new level where the challenges of a trusted relationship with a man brings further realization of her inherent strengths as a woman.

Cinderella held true to herself even though she did not have the acceptance or validation from her stepmother or sisters. Having transcended this challenge, she was ready for the worthy Prince to arrive, even though she wasn't holding her breath in anticipation. His world was the world of illusion of a different kind, and she would have to be very sure of her strengths and abilities in order to transcend yet another challenge, once brought to live in his reality. The Prince will come seeking her always, but if she fails to recognize her own worth, she will miss the call to authentically stand in her power when he does show up on her doorstep. Women have forgotten a natural law of energy in our struggle to be seen as equals. *Equal does not mean the same.* Masculine energy is attracted to feminine energy; the man goes to the woman. These days, women exercising their masculine at the exclusion of an honored feminine, pursue the man that interests her, and then gets upset because her feminine nature isn't honored by him once they start dating. She wants to dictate how the relationship will proceed on her terms, to the exclusion of honoring his. The masculine is the *doing* energy, the feminine is the *receiving and nurturing* energy. This truth is physically visible in our anatomy. In energetic terms *the man's spirit goes to the woman's spirit.* Masculine energy *goes* to the *receptiveness* of the feminine, as this is nature's way. This energetic dynamic is within us, and as our consciousness increases, we move towards experiencing this in relationship with another, beyond gender. When these two qualities are functioning co-operatively, the unseen presence of spirit manifests through us into something we consciously experience.

A woman who knows her worth is secure on her own until a man who can truly appreciate what she stands for recognizes her. She's not moping around waiting for him to show up, making a list of what she wants to attract, and silently hoping he will take her away to a better life. She is living a meaningful life already within her realm of experience. When that man does appear, and he will if she is living fully, and she somehow believes he has the ability to make her whole or give her something she doesn't already have, she has abandoned her power and sold out to a false understanding of love. She misses the gift of the relationship's ability to reveal greater depths of experience to her and her partner. If he is the true Prince for her, her eyes will be bright and sparkling. No jewelry will ever compare to the natural glow she wears because she is loved for who she is. She knows she is worthy of this love, as is he, and worthy of the life they choose to share together.

Maintaining her values while adapting to her new situation may be quite challenging to say the least. If she didn't know her worth before the Prince came along, nothing will fill the hole she will find inside her if she expects him to make her feel complete. If she becomes confused about who she is in her new surroundings, if wholeness was never experienced before, it is more difficult to find that security within again. When entering a relationship, the blending nature of the feminine that nurtures and makes manifest her heart's ideals, can make recognizing her own needs more difficult in relation to her mate. The fairy tale of Cinderella is as much a story about a woman rescuing a man, as it is about a man rescuing a woman. Spiritually, Cinderella represents the values that the Prince is seeking to keep him real, and the Prince can offer her the comfort of a home and the honor that allows her to give freely of her virtues. If Cinderella failed to honor her own power, she could never be an equal and challenging partner to the Prince. Upon recognizing love in one another, they embark on a journey that will challenge them to continue spreading their wings as individuals and soar to greater heights together.

Robert Munsch writes a wonderful modern day rendition of this classic called "The Paper Bag Princess". I love it when the Prince shows up and is upset because the Princess doesn't look the part of the Princess. The Princess has outsmarted the dragon and endured his fire in order to rescue the Prince. Her clothes have been incinerated by the dragon's breath, and her hair is a disheveled mess, but she remains herself. Standing there in her paper bag, hearing his disdained reaction to her appearance, she realizes he's not worthy of her after all because he doesn't see who she really is. To his dismay, she tells the Prince to take a hike. He is left bewildered. He thinks she has changed, and he is correct based on what he knows. She has not changed who she is but she has indeed changed her mind about him!

King and Queen, Prince and Princess, Father and Mother, Masculine and Feminine, as polarities, can go only so far separately, before acknowledging the presence and value of each other to keep them authentically aligned with their true power. We are on the threshold of accepting and honoring the power that is inherent in each of us, beyond the duality, beyond the polarity of the perceived nature of the masculine and feminine energies towards integration with our *Greater Other Dimensions*.

In inviting our Greater Other Dimensions to integrate with self,
our path here on earth is illuminated
by the experience of life, love, learning and laughter with others.

⚘ ⚘ ⚘

The Princess is now living in the castle. She's become a Queen overnight, and she wakes up to her beloved partner each morning. She has great admiration for him, and is very happy supporting him because she is cherished and he listens to her. The cinder pile is history. She has entered a relationship unconditionally with another. The times when she was alone to reflect on what was important to her have been replaced by her new duties and responsibilities that she believes she has to the partnership because she loves him. After all, the castle is new territory for her, and when she doubts herself, she finds comfort in what she believes is expected of her. She spends her time and energy fulfilling the role she has adopted. Cinderella enters freely and knowingly into the role of the Queen, and doesn't have time to realize what she's left behind until a couple of years later, when they decide to go for a carriage ride into the kingdom together.

Every wife in the world knows what it's like to be in the passenger seat of a car with their husband, the King, at the wheel and he gets lost. The situation is similar to that of Cinderella who one day wakes up to the fact that she has bought into the *illusion of the castle*. Somewhere along the way she adopted the belief that she had to be in agreement, and in support of the King at all times. She believes that this is her end of the bargain. She works to keep the relationship intact and outward appearances in order. Self goes unrecognized in the process of adapting to her role as Queen. Cinderella may have been quite clear about who she was before she moved into the castle, or built the castle, or renovated the castle, or had children, but once immersed in life at the castle and in her role as Queen, she loses perspective about who she is aside from these roles.

As much as times have changed, on a family car trip the husband usually drives. There are definite benefits to going along for the ride without feeling responsible for getting everyone there! When the husband makes a wrong turn and ends up off course, who does this compassionate King become? Does he pull over, pause, reassess, or better yet, ask for directions at the next gas station? Oh no. He drives faster, harder, determined to solve the problem on his own. He refuses to admit that he is lost. He knows where he's going, and he is going to get there all by himself! The Queen sitting beside him, after pointing out that they off track and is ignored, becomes silent. She quietly worries and tries to appease him. The King's behavior, reckless, plowing ahead, deaf to guidance, is the very hallmark of ingrained masculine energy functioning separate from *Greater Other Dimensions* or integrated with the power inherent in the feminine and masculine energy. He is lost on many levels.

Often in stressful situations we side with the masculine energy in ourselves, whether we realize it or not. The King takes over, and sadly, the Queen allows it because she has forgotten her innate power in the situation. Before we laugh too hard as women, let's take a good look at the significance of what this is showing us about ourselves and our own feminine expression. I have heard women joke with other women in the presence of their husbands about getting lost more times than I care to admit. The woman who was the silent, appeasing wife in the car revels in sharing the story with her comrades at a dinner party at the expense of her mate. The righteous voice of the Queen emerges once she has a sympathetic audience. There is often a slew of *how stupid men are* anecdotes added to the story just to add color and humor in an effort to entertain her subjects. If there is an underlying truth about the origins of men's behavior in these stories, there is also another valuable truth we often fail to recognize in ourselves in the telling of them. There is a demonstration of superiority, that rears its head *in us as women* towards men, and it does nothing to serve the union we committed to upholding with them. We tend to *speak* from our masculine authority *about* them, just as they tend to *act* from their masculine authority *towards* us. Women vocalize these unrecognized energies within themselves that have been denied expression in the past. The Patriarchal expression in society that we struggle with each day is endorsed by women as much as it is by men. The difference is most men have been raised accepting it because they are anchored on the side that believes in this as an expression of power. As women we have resented it and severed ourselves from acknowledging it exists also within us!

Let's go back for a moment to before the King and Queen were married. The same gathering of women from the dinner party would be commenting on what a nice catch the Prince would be, what potential he holds, and quietly hope he will notice them and choose the one who is most worthy of him. (That's not you, right- it's just other women.) Then once married to his Princess, his less than virtuous qualities can be revealed to his Queen because he trusts her to accept who he is. These are the same Princesses who claimed they weren't looking for a man to make them whole... or were they, and just didn't realize it? We don't know what we don't know, so life brings it to our experience through relationship and situations that involve others, so we come to recognize ourselves. You have to wonder, when years later at a dinner party we gloat about our superiority because we sat through yet another example of the King's immaturity. It's as if the Queens gather and compare how stupid the King they are partnered with has turned out to be, as if we didn't know what he was mirroring about our own immaturity in committing to partnership with him!

As women, we would laugh at ourselves if we could see what our gossiping revealed about us. It's not just about men being lost and refusing to take direction. It's about women being losing who they are, and looking for another to blame. It's about how the masculine energy within us all behaves. We aren't satisfied with being in control of ourselves; we want to control everyone and everything around us in order to feel comfortable with who we have unknowingly become. When we unconsciously adopt a role, whether it is the role of Queen, Mother, Prostitute, Martyr, or Maid, *we draw upon what we know of our power within that role.* We fail to take advantage of the opportunity to blend who we are with the role. Unless we have spent time sitting in the cinders on a cold concrete floor where we had a chance to harness and own our innate goodness and worth, most of us don't realize what power we have inadvertently given away to another.

The feminine energy on the part of both the man and the woman in that car is not being acknowledged or recognized for its ability to birth a greater consciousness. And it certainly can't do that if it is reduced to a display of unleashed pent-up emotion. Generally, women are conditioned to hide their emotions. Women may appear to be composed and unmoved by aggression. Tears in the boardroom will not win respect or gain another's confidence in our abilities. There is a great price to be paid for containing these emotions and failing to acknowledge them. More and more of our energy is consumed in controlling our emotions and keeping them hidden from others in an effort to protect our credibility. A display of emotion can compromise us in many situations, but when we are alone in our *internal* workspace, no one needs to be there to place judgment on our behavior. Sadly, we learn to dissociate from feeling our emotions altogether. We no longer express our emotions or even admit them to ourselves. We don't realize their influence on us and on our ability to be authentic with one another. We have become the judge and critic all on our own. We feel stuck and suffocated. We are no longer able to express our feelings honestly because we don't know anymore what we're aligning with.

The masculine energy becomes our foe because we attach to how we have seen it destructively exercised. As women, we exercise it alright, but not directly or compassionately. The King is not doing it to us all the time anymore. We're doing it to ourselves without him now. Obstacles don't move under these circumstances, nor does anything or anyone else for that matter. Those emotions, if denied, are harbored in resentment and we cannot access clarity. We become the voice of the King in our own heads when we internally turn our masculine energy against our own feminine. With Self at the wheel, deaf to soul, there can be no integrated energy that has both the focused intent and direction of the masculine, and the receptiveness of the feminine working together cooperatively. For the wife sitting by in silence as she worries and tries to diffuse the situation, her feminine energy is not responding receptively, but rather it is emotionally influencing the ability of her own masculine energy to feel secure and allow a greater expression to be birthed. The receptivity that opens her to her *Greater Other Dimensions* where she can be objective and resourceful, is prevented by her own masculine energy that wants to be acknowledged for being right and wiser.

We unknowingly choose *the victim* over *our magnificence* without even realizing it and to keep it alive someone else has to be perceived as the bully or the prosecutor. There's only one other person in that car, so we assume it's him! The unrecognized emotional influence on self may be outwardly demonstrated by the husband in his agitation, but just as active within the woman, is her own undeveloped emotional anatomy, disabling her confidence in her own masculine nature. In response to being dismissed by him as she perceives it, she becomes defensive, and takes on the role of the *validated-victim*, in the form of the martyr. Her feminine falls silently into submission, while the masculine holds firm to its position to remain in control, enabled by both the husband and wife. She's becomes the bully in her own quiet way. In her upset she resorts to getting her needs met using another less direct route. We know how well that works. Remember they are lost, and the masculine does not want to admit that it cannot solve the situation on its own! The feminine energies expression for both the husband and wife in this scenario has been diminished to a completely emotional response, the man in his agitation, the woman in her silent protest. The masculine energies are in a headlock, so silence and furious driving ensues. The feminine energy's ability to be receptive to input and guidance from beyond self's experience has unfortunately been disabled by both parties. Both the masculine and the feminine remain separate and immersed in their coping modes. This relatedness plays itself out in so many ways, everyday, waiting to be experienced more constructively.

The journey of growing closer to an understanding of one another, and *seeing self* in the situation, not the situation or another having the power to *define* self, has been forfeited in lieu of being right at the expense of the other. In the car, when they finally get to their destination, the wife quickly dismisses any satisfaction the husband may feel, for her masculine also needs to exercise its competence to stay intact. She may utter under her breath as she gets out of the car, "We could have been here an hour ago if you'd have listened to me to begin with". Now, just imagine, for one moment, if the husband and wife had not seen getting lost as a personal experience just between them, and it wasn't perceived as someone's fault? If it's no longer personally reflecting ones' competence or authority or control, the door is open to what their *Greater Other Dimensions* of being is leading them towards. They could end up on a detour from their desired destination, and find themselves where they least expected, but had unknowingly been seeking, as an experience in reaching an appreciation for the journey together.

We are so anxious to take sides with our unrecognized limited masculine because self is looking to exert its will, to be validated, accepted, and remain in control in its current position. It's about control, and when we are most threatened, and feeling most lost, we seek control to make our own world secure again. The feminine energy within the woman in that car is stuck in emotion, and hands over the reigns to her masculine energy that seeks to defend and validate her position. As long as we look to our partners to validate us, we will feel compromised. The power to validate and acknowledge comes from within us, through recognizing what is in play within our own drama.

Heaven forbid we change our stance, or be moved to expose our sensitivity. By sensitivity, I mean the part of us that is *receptive* to more than how the surface of something first appears to us, not emotional reaction. The role of the feminine is dismissed as having an integral part in birthing illumination about self's current experience. In not recognizing the source of the emotions, both the husband and the wife are reliving every personal injustice they have ever experienced as a child, as a victim, as the one that felt blamed, and the list goes on. We swallow our pride in the moment, and send it down into the chambers were we store our injustices, until we are in situations that we will find support for validating they exist for us. The masculine will continue to seek validation through evening the score until it is satisfied that it is secure enough to allow the expression of the feminine.

Women save up their stories of ill treatment at the hands of their husbands until they are at the dinner party with their Queen comrades. Then, every so cleverly, as if it is a private joke that her partner can't possibly understand, she exposes his irrational behavior. She feels justice has been served because the others, having had similar experiences with their husbands, validate her feelings of having been unfairly treated. Women earn their reputation as manipulators. The very masculine energy that women disdain in their husbands is the same energy that surfaces in them when they are pushed to the limit. The masculine energy in the woman meets the masculine energy of the man on the emotional battlefield. Each *needs* to be right. Each *needs* to win. Each needs to have the other validate their personal vision about the ideal union. Until we recognize our response to confrontation with the masculine in others for what it is, we will continue to butt heads to no avail. Spirit has a part in this, and the more evolved, dimensional part of us is influencing us too, to come to realize this about our self. Men aren't as stupid as women would like to believe them to be.

The ride home from the dinner party is more than likely in uncomfortable silence while the battle rages on inside their heads. A new awareness, that transcends the personal idea of union, is needed to end the stalemate. Humiliating our partner does nothing for the relationship. Prevailing in an argument, and being right, feels good until the initial euphoria wears off. The sensitive among us soon realize that we have done more harm than good. Our behavior was unflattering and unattractive. We feel sorry that we managed our self in the situation so poorly. We missed the opportunity to build the relationship, tearing it down instead. The truth is that we have humiliated ourselves, and exercising humility is going to help rebuild the bridge with our greater dimensions and our husbands again.

In that moment, lost on their path, the couple in the car are everywhere but in that car. *Each is* reacting to a part of self, *within themselves*, that they don't even recognize. They will get worked around, back and forth until that part of self is either dismissed by the other, or shut down because it can't find resolution. The need to keep the established self secure and intact is overwhelmingly strong. Self wants desperately to survive, even at the expense of the relationship. The bridge between who we are in relation to the big picture gets pretty clogged up with self's ideas about its importance.

We all get stuck on having to be right and protect self from being exposed for what it is. I am not just referring to the husband's lack of communication and receptiveness to the input of his wife, but also to the husband's inability to recognize he feels threatened by not knowing what to do. And in all fairness to him, *he is not being given the space* to acknowledge the need to go deeper within himself before his wife jumps in to remind him of his inadequacies. The wife, in her vanity, is right there on his case, with a whole list of ways she feels *he has betrayed her worth*, because he wouldn't listen to her.

The wife is not behind the wheel. She must be secure in the knowledge that they will arrive at their destination safely with her husband in charge and doing the driving his way. She can drive next time if she feels that strongly about doing things her way instead of just getting into the passenger seat complacently. In these circumstances, it all depends on who backs down first, and whose inner child is feeling most vulnerable. I suppose it can also come down to who drove there and who is driving home, because the potential for seeking awareness, is sealed up tightly along with anything that might expose the vulnerability of self. We remain de-sensitized and isolated in self's experience as long as we don't realize that change rests in our own hands.

Silence of the feminine is not a powerful thing when it is full of unexpressed emotion, nor is the bulldozing of the masculine a powerful thing when it is at the expense of unrecognized ego. Both the husband and the wife have these polarities within themselves. They both love to accept an invitation to play out the drama of their injustices, with their partner's participation. What better way to keep things in check than to blame the other party? Neither of them realizes that they are witnessing the worst of themselves mirrored in the other's behavior. In this scenario, there is no question that the husband and wife are both lost. They have unknowingly become each other in behavioral terms.

Both parties have the opportunity to honor the relationship and play an integral role for each other here. They could recognize the part of self that is expressing itself, and meet one another with humility. Together they might laugh, and rekindle the love and compassion they feel for one another's humanness. Their perceived vulnerability is shared openly with each other, and together they grow wings and invite in their shared union with God. Another possibility is that they both retreat from communicating honestly all together, and pretend everything is just fine. In this scenario they lose something dear to them both; trust and openness to be who they are with one another. The better or worse they both committed to way back before they built the castle, is forgotten in each one's effort to maintain their illusion of power. Through *self-serving choice*, the walls around their castle are reinforced to keep God's likeness from disturbing their self's illusion of stature.

This is a story about much more than simply losing one's way in the car. We can all identify with this common pattern acting out. There is something to be said for recognizing self when we engage in a power struggle with someone we love. There is great opportunity here for communication and integration of these parts of self when we summon the courage to reach beyond what we perceive to be within our grasp. The desired destination may be reached but the gift of the journey is seldom recognized, let alone realized, when self is functioning separately from awareness. A trip taken together as a couple, under these conditions, can deliver us to our destination as polar opposites instead of to a common trusted bond that enables us to grow closer in union.

> *It is amusing to observe our behavior when we*
> *allow ourselves to be guided by limited-self.*
> *It's like taking a trip without a roadmap.*

Our wounded child loves to get involved when the controlling part of self takes over. The dear husband at the wheel becomes the frustrated little boy. The dear wife becomes the mother to his fragile ego to keep the peace. Reacting to her, the husband turns on a dime into the role of the father in control. The wife reacts to this, and spins into the dismissed little girl, or the overbearing mother sending her son into retreat. The friction, or rather *fiction*, in that car ignites in a matter of seconds when we go off track and lose our bearings. Silence usually prevails, at least until the wife finds the sympathetic ear at the dinner party.

You know you are maturing and exercising your wings when this scenario evokes humor shared in mutual appreciation and understanding of our human qualities rather than the power struggle that neither party can win. Do any of us really know where we're going? We think we know, but we don't know what we don't know, and we'll never learn more if we don't open ourselves to the experience of others who can broaden our awareness. In exposing ourselves to those we love and in being prepared to listen to them, we bring *Greater Other Dimensions* and the light of our soul to the fore. Self preservation can take a back seat to compassion. We learn to listen to a greater guide than the one we often side with inside. Self heard and accepted for what it is, can be given a constructive outlet to evolve so it reflects who we really are, not what we think we should be to be in control. The next time you find yourself making a joke about your mate at his or her expense, consider honoring the *power of the masculine and feminine energy* to reveal a truth beyond your current expression. Or are you afraid to admit your vulnerability? Do you need to feel empowered by disempowering that which threatens to expose you; the confrontation of the masculine energy, and the emotion of the feminine energy.

If we think the masculine is so ridiculous, then why do we as women insist on expressing it ourselves so ineffectively whenever we are challenged to draw upon the sensitive resourcefulness of the feminine? Is self's need so great that it must remain superior for all to see? Is being right so important that we will unknowingly betray *our own ability to be integrated with greater awareness?* Unrecognized self functions separately from awareness. When we operate only on this level, we alienate ourselves from being honestly received by our partners. There is so much more to the feminine than emotion, and there is so much more to the masculine than dominance and superiority, but rarely are they recognized or exercised constructively as the *sensitivity* that receives illumination from *Greater Other Dimensions*.

If you love your husband, is it not worth learning to be in your power with him, possibly creating challenge for him, but possibly just allowing space for him to constructively exercise his own power with you? We get lost in our illusion of a personal power that is completely self-reliant! There is no room for God's input if we believe we already know everything.

Our shadow follows us,
Our light leads us,
Our heart guides us,
Our conscience governs us,
Our world mirrors us,
Our experiences teach us,
Our soul reminds us…
who we really are… beyond duality,
as students of Life itself.

                             ✍   ✍   ✍

When the Prince and Princess, or Adam and Eve for that matter, first looked into each other's eyes, they saw a reflection of themselves. Though they didn't recognize it then, it was a good reflection. When the romance was fresh, it was easy to be carefree and comfortable with one another because they were united by a presence beyond both of their experience. The *Greater Other Dimensions* were present, grace and compassion was infused into both of them, and they were both open to receive it. They weren't analyzing parts of self, or delving into self knowledge, as self was secure, satisfied, and not looking to assert itself. There was no threat being posed. Innocence is an open threshold to receive the goodness and grace of Love, and greater awareness naturally evolves through us when the door is open and we feel this love being expressed and received. It is easy to love and be loved when we are innocent because we don't know any different.

As we mature within the relationship and begin to spread our respective "wings", the inevitable happens. We get tangled up from time to time in situations such as the those we have already discussed. Those wings are hard to get used to because as high as we soar when we stretch them out, the further the fall when we run into challenges along the way. It sometimes requires plummeting to earth, then taking time to heal before we can trust them again. This process usually requires that we develop new skills, humble ourselves, and let self become the student again. When we begin flying again we have a greater understanding of the responsibility we have to ourselves in caring for our wings and being careful of how we spread them, so we honor the wings of others that share the heaven's equally with us. The maturing of self can be a very rewarding and fulfilling process if we let our *Greater Other Dimensions* influence and integrate with self. We reach for higher ideals and see possibilities that will create a peaceful kingdom, one built on the respect and honor of everyone's contribution instead of our own self-serving agenda. We open the door to growth and renewal of our innocent nature and faith in a shared humanity when we appreciate the privilege of cultivating consciousness, and its infinite possibilities, hand in hand with those around us.

Chapter 6

Growing Wings to Move Beyond Our Identity with the Masculine & Feminine

---

*How we unveil the knowledge of our own divinity
happens through choosing to experience life,
and allowing it expression through all that currently exists.*

Maturing brings us to new levels of awareness within ourselves where there is often a period of not recognizing how the lens of our perceptions have changed. If we dare look at our actions though, it becomes clear how limited-self has been driving us, beyond what we may have justified, or mentally told ourselves. When we remove the lens of what we believe things to be, it's like going to bed as usual, and waking up on a mountaintop on foreign soil. The bed may look the same, we *think* we are the same, but everything else has changed, and we have no idea how we got there! We instinctively turn our focus to looking for someone or something outside ourselves to blame. It seems that just when we begin to experience the various parts of self stretch their wings, and become who we choose to be independent of others; we walk through another threshold of consciousness without realizing it. That familiar rhythm and experience we identified with, is out-of-sync with what we are being drawn towards to know of ourselves. At certain points through life, for some it is very young, some very old, we seek greater meaning, and it takes us beyond self, to the realm of *Greater Other Dimensions* of reality.

To be in this world today and not be overtaken with the pain and suffering of our own creation, we need to integrate self with the *Greater Other Dimensions* of our being. Pain and suffering are symptoms of our unrecognized perceptions, colored by our own accumulations, and are subjective, not objective. Sooner or later, peace needs to be made with *God*, and the aspects of self we have come to experience. These thresholds we cross in spiritual development are not restricted to the stages experienced through our physical maturation. I think many of us have had the experience of waking up in the morning in what suddenly appears to be foreign soil, and wonder just how it is we managed to get there without realizing what we were doing or where we were headed. Be it waking up to a personal relationship or business relationship, the veil of illusion has been lifted, and we stand naked of our identity for a bit. Our comrades become strangers because we don't recognize ourselves anymore, and what they have mirrored to us about ourselves, we don't respond to the same way anymore. We don't feel validated by the *limited-self* as we once did when acknowledged by others who agreed with us.

A pull to the depths of our being, a deep grief that feels overwhelming that can't be consoled by our sense of accomplishment, or sense of power in the world, is not recognized as personally belonging to us. This spiritual crisis is not restricted to adolescence, midlife, or old age, as it is being revealed to us in very young people today! The need to expand beyond what is endorsed externally creeps in from the day we are born, and now many of us raising these youngsters don't recognize this mentality as reaching out from within ourselves, yearning to be recognized and healed within our own psyche. Our adopted sense of identity as we mature becomes more fragile because we have left behind the unresolved, unexpressed child in ourselves that didn't have a stage to play itself out on, amidst our world's drive and focus on progress. When that dark hole appears to us, it is possibly just a glimpse of our own reflection, as we are plummeted from our existing experience of self, into new territory, in order to learn about who we really are, in relation to limited-self. Could it be that we are the very shadow that we are so anxious to severe ourselves from in others?

Many of the children coming in to this world are having a hard time expressing themselves in this time of transition. In their innocent attempts to extend outward, they are meeting even greater resistance with people that are trying to control and keep them contained, in a way that will not be accepted by them at this time. Those leaps in progress and material gain that the current generation of adults has taken to avoid delving within, is showing up as a deep crevice in the psyche of our children. Where we are completely oblivious to our own misunderstood, wounded child, we have created a blank spot for our innocent children to have themselves recognized when they are struggling. We want to fix them, divert their focus away from the experience of discomfort, as we have attempted to fix and occupy ourselves. The children in our world have always brought with them the gift of awareness for those already rooted with greater experience here in this reality, but at this time it doesn't seem to be able to be managed with sheer discipline or easing their discomfort and shielding them from experiences that can hurt them.

With every generation the veil that separates our humanness from the *Greater Other Dimensions* of our being, has become thinner. In praying for higher consciousness for our planet, we have unknowingly beckoned awareness to self, and it has been revealed, but we are possibly expecting it to appear differently than what appears to confront us. It has possibly surfaced more like a cloud cover, bringing with it confusion and uncertainty in what we see going on around us. This confusion is what we have to go through in order to gain clarity. We keep looking externally for things to change, when it is through our discomfort that we find our answers for awareness for personal change. That state of GOD that we are all born knowing, is not diminished to the same extent in today's children, as self-awareness enters their experience, so the children in our midst are giving us the clearest picture of what we need to change in ourselves. Their lack of experience, and unconscious behavior is a very true indicator and miraculous gift to us in answer to our prayers. They show us, innocently, where true imbalance exists for us as a humanity. If we can't receive from them without threat to our own importance, the delivery of heaven's message, than we are sunk. The experience of GOD and the experience of self are not at opposite ends of *experience* when we are in the early years of life. I imagine this world, and its current system of operating, must appear quite disturbing to a child, who believes there are no limits, and that it is safe to be who you are openly. Self to them is not experienced as something separate from their magnificent sense of being.

It takes time and an environment that supports integrating their awareness into our current lifestyle, rather than time and *conditioning* to get them to fit in to our current understanding of how things should remain to be effective. The meaning of God, our faith in God, our trust in God, has remained subconsciously compartmentalized into religious sects for many adults. The *Greater Other Dimensions* of our being has been dismissed as a collective experience and unless you belong to a particular belief system you are left hanging to redefine God in an acceptable manner so as not to offend anyone. Many spiritually oriented groups hesitate to mention or talk about God less someone think they are religious. We talk of acceptance of one another's beliefs, but do we keep our hearts and minds open to receive how people choose to express those beliefs? One would think that spirituality by its very nature would be inclusive, not exclusive of man's history and routes for relating to the divine. Many spiritualists', at least the North American brand of this name, don't talk about God, or make reference to God specifically, but instead politically dodge the discomfort it raises in people and talk about *the Light, the Source, or Spirit*, as if there is no relatedness to God, or religion at all. Just as we have slotted our understanding of the masculine energy into one of control and dominance, we have also often slated God into camps of religious dogma.

Religion has played a very valuable role throughout history in enabling many to bring understanding to their relationship with God. It has served us very well in making God accessible in terms that make people comfortable, or as time as gone on, uncomfortable, as our awareness has revealed our own ability to choose the foundation in which our faith rests. As we have developed greater awareness and consciousness has increased, we have gained insight into the meaning and experience of God right along with our expanded understanding. The church that once provided walls that contained God in terms that help people feel protected by others who are responsible for guiding them, have swung in the opposite direction over time to provide limitations for how people were able to openly express their own understanding and experience of God. As those doors have swung open wider, the threshold of understanding our personal responsibility in accepting the truth for ourselves about God, has been delivered into our awareness. God has not changed, we have, and relating to God has become even more important than ever, because self isolated from God is afraid, and limited, and threatened by others who think differently. Self integrated with God, transcends the perceptions of fear and doubt, and illuminates a world of hope, faith, and trust that we can learn how to serve and support through our collective experience.

Religion in itself is not the problem. The problem is how we have chosen to compartmentalize religion and dissociate from acknowledging our part in allowing it to stagnate, possibly is. The Church may have ideas that no longer serve us personally, but for many, that faith, and sense of community experienced in their church gives them strength and courage to reach for something beyond what they will on their own. With or without a church, a guru, a temple, or shrine, there exists a loving God that is available to everyone, anytime, anywhere. If the church can create a sense of safety for people to accept and embrace forgiveness for themselves, and others, then they are one step closer to cultivating awareness of their inherent goodness. The church can serve as one of many valuable sanctuaries that create security for people, to learn to trust themselves and to gain faith in life again. With the admission of faith in something beyond self, God enters our awareness, where only darkness resided before. We are negating the value of our own free will, if we judge these sanctuaries as anything but the divine utilizing all existing ways to reach us, where we currently are in our ability to accept greater consciousness of who we are.

Open hearts and open minds, need healthy and
vital bodies to be enabled and engaged
in implementing a better today, for our shared tomorrow.

≀≈≈ ≀≈≈ ≀≈≈

Where our children are asking for us to attend to what they need on a deeper level, beyond the necessities for survival, we often hear only how they aren't fitting into our routine and placing demands on our time. They require our patience, and *our own resourcefulness* to be engaged in order for us to embrace their reminder of our own true nature to be lovingly attentive to who they really are. I think God has a place in this, as the very mystery of life within us that gives us breath, and mindfulness to better understand ourselves. Meeting our children's need to feel love isn't about *time* for them; it's about *presence*. How does a child communicate this need for us to hear them on a deeper level in a language we recognize, if we are void of feeling within ourselves? Presence requires cultivating an appreciation for it, by practicing it. Many children are flatly refusing to develop an external dialogue that fits our criteria of acceptance. We don't talk about the experience of God, and much of what they ask us to explain, we are not able to neatly compartmentalize into rational explanation. We can demonstrate faith, and we can demonstrate trust, and we can demonstrate love through allowing ourselves to show them the values *we hold in our heart* for our humanity.

Through the development of vocabulary, and the ways we demonstrate to our children about how to communicate, it is no wonder they meet resistance with us as they reach their third birthday. When they seek our attention we often respond with "wait just a minute!". Many of us give our children things to keep them occupied until that minute, or more like fifteen minutes, comes where we give them our attention. Even then, we have one eye on what we are doing, and half an ear to what they are saying. It is rarely a complete pause in our own agenda, direct eye contact and all ears and listening hearts, on what they are expressing to us. Do our actions demonstrate a pulling away on our part from their need to make connections with something that they don't understand? Maybe they already are naturally internally awake, but it is not endorsed, or encouraged, so the stability and confidence to build relationship to it, and their ability to relate to the world around them is left unrealized. We possibly mistake this need, as a desire to interrupt us, when inside they feel interrupted from knowing what to do with what they feel.

In those moments of waiting for us, we automatically fill in the gap for them with external stimulation. We're focused on setting them up with everything they will need to be properly equipped for the competition they will encounter in the 'real world' as we often remind them. Idol time is a *gap* to be filled in most people's eyes. We are anxious to fill this gap because left open, there is often discomfort expressed, and it is resolved faster, or so we rationalize to ourselves, if we add a distraction. The time and presence on our part to allow the discomfort, and patience to allow them to find constructive ways to work through it in a safe environment, allows new perceptions from within them to enter their awareness. They are able to make connections between their internal sensing and their outer experience with others. If we don't allow our children the opportunity to experience their discomfort, they don't learn from it. Confidence comes with this development because they begin comprehending how they relate to things versus how others do, knowing they can trust themselves to think and feel differently then others.

This same gap, if perceived differently is also a pause, that when nurtured, and given room to expand, is the door in which imagination flourishes. Ideas and contemplations take shape in this space, and draw on our innate internal fountain of potential. We want our children to have every advantage possible in our world today, but our measuring stick for what is needed, is what we are conditioned to believe is endorsed externally, not what is inherent within us as beings. If we can honestly say that the world is working well for us all, and we are feeling fulfilled and comfortable and healthy with what exists then using this rational would be great. Unfortunately, most are experiencing a portion of reality that creates the experience of discomfort, anxiety, stress, and uncertainty. Do we really want to condition our children to step into our perceived reality with the things that are being endorsed right now? Our needs and wants are not working together! It's the video games, the cell phones, and all the electronic gadgets that everyone is carrying around that are creating this stress, not only because of the electromagnetic fields they have that affect our nervous systems, and brain specifically, but also because of the *importance* we have placed on them. What seems so chaotic and competitive in our outer world we don't recognize as mirroring what internally has gone unrecognized within. Our own body's wiring is not being supported physically, and is being further stressed by this added external electrical stimulation.

Those external walls we erect to protect our fortresses, are representative of the walls we have resurrected internally to detach ourselves from feeling the discomfort inside, so we can successfully severe ourselves from the experience of silence. There's a buzzing that has taken over. Walking around the grocery store, one just has to look around and it is hard to find anyone not talking on a cell phone as they roam the isles shopping for food. Technology is wonderful in so many ways, but it is often a tool for self to remain occupied, and connected to others, not a way of being or feeling. Are we missing developing a rapport that doesn't involve constant contact with another person? Is our insecurity so great at this time that we need constant reassurance of another's familiar voice to keep us from being out in the world alone? Where's the *pause* because we apparently don't have too many gaps in our schedules? We are so caught up in protecting our feelings, defending our borders and boundaries, and ways of thinking, and defining our roles to feel secure, we have isolated ourselves from our true nature as loving, and sharing creative beings. We are at a loss as to how to integrate our personal desires with the needs of others anymore, because many of us have never matured beyond the *what's in it for me* stage of development.

We are stuck on siding with one side of the gap or the other, because to integrate the concept of pausing to reflect on what we're doing, doesn't jive with our idea of efficiency or productivity. We are so caught up in engaging our children with stimulation to make them into everything we believe they should be, that we take them away from developing relationship with their internal resources. We are inadvertently feeding our children mechanisms on the energetic level that align with overcoming our own perceived inadequacies. Before we know it, they are aligned with their own inadequacies, and the outer world feels too much for them to deal with, because their nervous systems aren't supported or strengthened on many levels from a very early age.

The seeds of inadequacy have been planted by us, and from within them a drive to excel starts to grow. We spend the next stage of their development trying to encourage them to overcome these feelings of anxiety and *just do it*, and we tell them how wonderful, bright, and courageous they are. Our words are not enough, as those seeds we planted without even realizing it came from our example. In getting caught up in our own functioning, and accomplishing, the inner environment that shapes *how* we do what we do, and *what* importance we place on things in our lives, has been driving us unknowingly. These same children are the ones hanging out at the grocery store, in the shopping cart, rifling through mom's purse, or playing a handheld game, so she can talk on the phone without interruption. Mom's cruising the isles, putting food in the cart, without too much thought about what nutritional value is in it, because the children are drawn to what they've seen on television, and mom's are not up for saying "no", creating a commotion, while on their cell phone.

On the unseen level, this energy has been giving a clear and consistent message that has been impressed upon our children. What we *say* doesn't really matter in comparison to the example we *demonstrate* to them. We dismiss the value of the feminine and unconsciously express the undeveloped masculine, charging ahead without notice of anything beyond our own agenda to stay on task. Days can go by without us giving our children true moments of our complete presence, and we don't recognize this need in them, because we have betrayed this need within ourselves. When we do attempt to communicate meaningfully with them, they are so engrossed in the substitutions we have given them that they can no longer recognize their need for love or interaction with attentive people. Through our actions, they come to associate *presents*, with a promise of our *presence* when we're finished what we're doing.

By our demonstrated model, what we do, and what we accomplish, is more important than *what we are* to our children, or they to us. We talk this, but we don't walk it, so our words become empty promises and this is becoming their reality. It's a confusing world for sensitive children to function in when feeling must be translated into words, and the words they're taught don't *feel* right. As adults we have failed to model the *experience* of presence, and now we are paying the price for it. Not only are we paying the price in not being able to manage the stress of our own hectic lifestyles, but also many of us are void of the skills to delve into our own depths to recognize when something is bothering us, or hurting us physically. We wait for outward symptoms to show themselves before we acknowledge it is real.

Our depths are so unexplored that we are miles apart from experiencing the joy of creativity, the fulfillment of contemplation, the liberation experienced from freeform expression. By freeform expression I'm not referring to kids running around being destructive and inconsiderate of other people, although this is often how it first shows up when it hasn't been nurtured constructively all along. The carefree expression of spirit if not connected to the development of self to learn care, becomes a demonstrated carelessness. To learn to be full of care, is to bring consciousness to the relationship between spirit and self so we become a compassionate blend of careful and carefree. It is impossible for many to sit quietly in a chair in a quiet room without feeling anxious or uneasy because their mind is going a million miles an hour and they have nothing to distract themselves from hearing it. This is not just children, but many adults as well. There are few places that a model has been endorsed to know that this inner dialogue is part of us, not to be feared, or in control of us, when we are aware of it. When we listen, this is often what we are hearing, and there is no reference to put it into context for us. Our bodies and our minds have been taken hostage by a force that doesn't even make sense, and yet we persist in holding dear to it, not because we consciously choose it, but because we don't *recognize* it for what it is, and we are afraid to unleash it. This force is the subconscious drive of *limited-self* to survive, and it's built a momentum all its own, separate and untouchable by anything that can move us closer to the peace in our hearts that assures us we are not alone.

Relationship to our *Greater Other Dimensions* is important because we need to begin a dialogue somewhere that is accepting and loving for who we are now. To open ourselves up to others is difficult when we are afraid it will further compromise what others think and feel about us. Self can be a vehicle, that helps spirit impart thoughts and feelings that can help guide us through what we find so confusing within us. Once we recognize these thoughts and beliefs we have the ability to choose differently, but it is difficult to realign with positive hopes and dreams for ourselves when we are discouraged, and feeling helpless. Prayer is powerful; as it allows us to engage consciously in that *gap* we resist acknowledging. Allowing the *pause to take dimension within us* is engaging our ability to listen, and then hear what comes back to us that we didn't realize was our self.

If our children aren't listening to us, then maybe we're not hearing our true self, or them as they truly are. If our children are out of control and destructive, then maybe we're out of control and destructive without knowing it, because we are so focused on the world being something outside of us, that we have forgotten there is so much more going on inside that has influence beyond us. We physically may be spending a lot of time cleaning up our house, dealing with paperwork on our desk, doing laundry, and dishes, but internally, our thoughts and emotions are destructive and out of control. We may be doing the right things, and without this discomfort we would still choose to do them, but it is being driven by discontent, and angst and anger, not peace of mind. And in most people's minds anger is a bad thing, so inside these feelings are being denied, and kept tightly concealed so as to contain them from being what we perceive to be destructive. We have successfully cut ourselves off from our own destructiveness and feelings of being out of control, but look what's being demonstrated all around us! We want it to stop, but we want to stop it outside ourselves, not internally deal with its origin within ourselves.

Maybe, just as our children are trying to get our attention, and not in very positive ways, inside our very self the same thing is going on. Anger is an emotion that every single human being experiences; it is part of our emotional anatomy. If denied and not allowed expression it builds, and gains quite a momentum, until finally it just blows! There is no denying this is destructive. People who have respect and acceptance of these feelings experience anger, but because they are in touch with their emotional anatomy, they recognize anger long before it becomes an outer expression, and *out of control*. Anger recognized as it rises within us, can motivate. It can create a purpose for us, and lead us to discover things that otherwise we wouldn't have had the drive or stamina to pursue. If someone says something to us that angers us, and we recognize our anger, it stimulates thought, and action that can actually fuel growth within us personally. Left denied, and perceived as *wrong* to feel, it harbors, it builds, it gets stashed deeper, and sent to the place we reserve inside ourselves for all the things we believe are wrong to feel, because we believe only *bad people feel these negative emotions.* Then, when we are tired, or feeling the pressure from too many demands being made on us, there's a threshold that gets crossed and before you know it, up flies all this unreasonable RAGE! Unfortunately, I think those kids running around out of control, and acting destructively are often the target for this… and all they are doing is resonating with what has been unknowingly been transmitted on an energetic level all around them. Children act out what they feel. When they're happy they bounce, when they're sad they slump, when they're excited they bop, when they're frustrated they clench up. Watching them shows us what energetic environment is around them, and if we seek answers, we can find those answers in ourselves. To find those answers, we have a few accumulations to deal with as well, and our bodies, energetically and physically aren't quite as clear as children's anymore. Children under the age of seven don't have behavior problems, and those that demonstrate behavior problems are the smartest, clearest, and most confident of us around. They resonate strongly with what they are exposed to, and demonstrate unconsciously what flows through them. Food that is contaminated or full of chemical additives effect them, and people around them who are harboring anger and resentment, or grief without acknowledging it, can see clearly it mirrored in the children's outward expression. What you personally see in a child, be it more one sided to the good, or the bad, is more than likely what you refuse to see in yourself.

Take a few minutes without interruption and spend it with yourself. Imagine you could reach out with your mind into the heavens and ask for God for help in recognizing yourself. Take a leap of faith and imagine that your prayers are answered, but you need to listen, and pay attention to what you hear and feel inside yourself. Chances are the first impression is that of anxiety, as there is fear in most to reach out to the unknown. This is probably where you will first become aware of the ideas you hold about God, and there may be some fear associated with these ideas. This is our unconscious programming, not God. Through hearing and feeling and accepting what you find inside yourself, it may just turn out to be a very beautiful and soft energy that once really felt is quite calming and assuring. The other part may be within you, the part of self that needs to be acknowledged and a little frustrated from trying to get your attention and being repeatedly told to "wait a minute, here, keep yourself occupied with this!" Pay attention to what you hear, and see if there is any coincidence to it being what you often tell your children. It's shocking really how the answers are there all along if we just pay attention to what we're doing, saying and feeling.

It is pretty hard to come up with constructive ways to deal with challenge, if we can't admit or fully embrace what it is we are dealing with. It more than likely will show itself to be something completely different than we have assumed. Where we thought our children need to change, we are reminded that we too require changing how we see and experience them. When we embrace change for ourselves, these perceptions will automatically reflect our own balance in what we experience of them. Our children are not the problem, but they will become one for themselves if they are not honored for their clarity in perceptions.

Our children are the purest, brightest, and most innocent reflection there is- of who we are. Our children have quick and receptive minds, open hearts and exuberant presence. In recognizing their natural qualities, and the things needed to nurture and support healthy development, we are fueled to learn about things beyond what we know has supported our own growth. Nutrition has changed since we were children, education has changed since we were children, children have changed since we were children, and we can no longer assume that everything we want and is available is necessarily safe or good for fostering these things. Sensitivities have increased, not just in the sense of peanut allergies, but to their subtle sensory awareness. Children's ability to feel sensation and subtle impressions has increased significantly with each generation. These qualities if we can recognize them ourselves, enable us to be more conscious in supporting our children to remain healthy in body and mind. By the time many of them have hit school age, we are implementing medications to keep them in check, and on task, in sync with our system of operating, as we insist on holding onto it.

The question I keep coming back to is *whose comfort zone are we keeping intact exactly?* Are we looking to support an environment that our children feel safe to express and nurture their development, or are we looking to justify our current beliefs about what our children need to be successful, in what we believe is *our* external world. It seems to me, that entering our world at this stage of it's development is going to need some very creative and secure input, that incorporates resourcefulness from more than one source of knowledge. *Isolated-self* at the helm is making a mess of things, and the further from our hearts we go, the more we feel depressed, and defeated, and seek to implement tools to deal with damage control. Medications aren't proving to be a very good long term solution. To disregard self is to feed isolation, but to acknowledge self as it exists, serves to move us to embrace more than self currently realizes or wants to acknowledge. There's a whole other dimension of human experience possible, right here, right now, and no medication is going to numb us enough to disconnect completely from it. This new world we keep praying for is ALREADY HERE! We just don't recognize it because like everything else, we're so busy categorizing things, organizing and protecting ourselves from what we perceive as threats to our security, that we don't recognize what is, and has always been inherent right here amidst us, and within us. So much attention is put towards what we don't like, what we don't want to happen, that we completely miss seeing the conscientious and conscious people already present in our communities in plain view.

Children today, in order to anchor their nervous systems and agile minds, need a different type of support to balance our technology advancements if we insist on holding onto them as they are and continue to be developed. We are changing what is organically present to fit our technology, instead of developing technology to support what is organically inherent in our world, children included. Nutrition is a huge part of this, and many are filling their little bodies with sugar, hormones, chemical additives, and genetically engineered food, which is creating havoc inside them. We need to get off our cell phones, and blackberries long enough to receive the transmission of greater dimensions beyond our physical existence, as they may remind us who we are, and what we need to be aware of in order to support life right now. Communicating with one another is part of the solution, but resourcefulness from outside the gene pool of *techno-derived solutions*, may be wise and conscientious to implement at this point. Is it not discomfort, if not outright crisis that drives us to seek God, and realize we have bought into self-importance to guide humanity?

We're trying to reframe things that exist into something more acceptable, more convenient, that fit our technology, instead of adjusting our lifestyles and choices to things that support actual life itself. The *Life* I am talking about is the sacred divinity within us as human beings. The *God*, the ultimate power of *Love,* that is accepting and allowing of experience to know itself. Children carry this knowledge openly, and innocently, so they are a wonderful way to first recognize it. It needs no name for them to know it, but without presence of mind, it finds no acceptable expression or acknowledgment to remain vital.

Holding a newborn baby brings one completely in touch with God, but we don't recognize this as power any more, once it grows enough to become mobile and communicating with its own free will. With our little ones, right from word go, we aim to protect and keep them from experiencing the harshness of this world, we perceive will ruin or hurt them. We have lost faith in our humanity, because we have lost touch with ourselves, and denied our need to experience our own divinity. The *in-love with the baby phase* gets washed over by daily routine pretty quickly when we are materially focused, and *we ourselves* are resisting changing this, because it may ruin us, the way we have become. Crisis is just building, but it will reach undeniable heights before we are willing to reach for different solutions than those that are technology driven. Consciousness delivers the unknown, beyond our current realm of knowledge, so we can better support the development of constructive relationship to all life here on earth.

Chapter 7

Embracing a Humanity
We Don't Know How to Trust

What we have dismissed developing awareness of in our own experience,
is being outwardly demonstrated as vital for us to realize,
in order to nurture the development of our children.

꩜   ꩜   ꩜

We all learn best when we respect the authority that is sharing their knowledge with us, because we believe we are worthy, and a valuable and appreciated part of it. Can we experience in another that which is a void within ourselves? Where we may initially experience our own value in relation to others, once validated, we may move naturally towards extending ourselves to include appreciation for the value of others respectfully. Respect for others comes through experiencing trust and faith in what another honors in us. If the message we receive when we are children only imprints on us with how we don't fit in, or measure up, how are we to gain the confidence and in turn the encouragement to develop the skills to communicate and express ourselves authentically? To become real, is to recognize our humanness and strive to incorporate our divinity into our conscious experience. Our message to many children today is one of not honoring them for their current expression of who they are, or more importantly, what we have unconsciously fostered in them to develop as resources to draw on to go through challenge independently.

If we feed them junk food, and give in to their preferences for entertainment and quick solutions to their boredom, we endorse seeking satisfaction for their desires, but we are also endorsing a limited satisfaction that may just be at the expense of creating a true sense of security within them. Staggering numbers of children are medicated with one thing or another, and those that aren't medicated to be calm, or non-reactive to their environment, are injected full of immunizations to keep them safe. The reactivity of our children, both physically and emotionally to me, is an indicator that there is something fundamentally amiss in our current way of nurturing them. We are not only physically suppressing their immune systems, but we are mentally and emotionally suppressing their ability to recognize challenge and feel strong enough to go through it constructively, rather than destructively, or completely avoid it all together. We handle things for them, and take care of things for them, believing we are protecting them. Possibly what we are protecting is a false sense of self's importance in relation to the *greater resources* available for them to draw on when facing discomfort.

We are approaching a very revealing time right now, as the first seeds of genetically modified food that were planted in the United States in 1996 have been consumed by people for over a decade. The average young woman, who has consumed these foods without knowledge of their hazards or implications for her entire life, is going to be bringing into this world over the next few years, the offspring of this nutritional approach.

There are several things that have been drastically different in our lifestyle choices over the past twenty years. Some of them have been known choices, whereas others have been made for us without our awareness or consent. There are many more children with peanut allergies, autism, developmental delays and attention deficit disorders now than in previous generations and it is difficult to determine the exact factors responsible. More than ever, as adults, we are being given incentive to foster going through challenge constructively, because it is difficult to determine where the truth lies around these issues. Unless we have the ability to feel the resonance of the food we eat, and develop the sensitivity to know when something doesn't support our health, we are reliant upon what we are told is safe. Unless you are a scientist and can test every morsel, you must rely on what you read on the label. If we are too busy doing what *self drives* us to accomplish, we miss the presence of mind to see what our children are demonstrating to us in their behavior and their health, because of what we feed them, both energetically and physically. This alone is enough reason for us to develop our consciousness and sensitivity to life, so we can recognize by the way we feel when something is not right for our wellbeing. Allowing in the *Greater Other Dimensions of who we are,* to direct our attention to what supports not only ourselves but others, gives us a fulfillment that outlasts the momentary high of self's accomplishments.

Children, in my experience, don't connive, manipulate, and act out, unless they are attempting to communicate what is crying out from inside them. Those who whine and cry have learned to illicit a certain response from us this way. Often we respond to this behavior and give in to keep this part of them quiet, rather than recognizing the strength needed on our part to look past their apparent discord to hear the deeper part of them that needs relief. They're seeking our attention, but do we divert them away from their discomfort or do we allow them the time and space, without outer stimulation, to understand where it's coming from, be it something they're doing, something they're eating, or the way they're thinking or feeling about themselves. It's not always because they are from broken homes or physically abusive environments, or lack food, or are deprived of opportunity. Often, unrecognized influences are pushing them to demonstrate their discontent with our *lack of presence* about what is going on with them that they don't know how to relate to constructively. We give in and give them what they want, instead of helping them recognize what they need. Children today have a high level of consciousness, and functioning in our world as it exists is creating uneasiness for them because we aren't hearing what they are communicating through their energy, and we're not always endorsing their tools to help them develop relationship to it for themselves, in awareness and acceptance.

Communication is difficult when it is the *feeling part* of them engaged, and we have culturally dismissed much of the poetry and song of the emotions, in place of fitting in and accomplishing what is valued as acceptable. Their awareness of what is being expressed through them involves our awareness to help them learn to build relationship to a deeper calling within them than self that wants immediate desires obtained. Feminine energy has been thrown into a bag with displayed emotions, and generally most people understand emotions as weakness, but children have fluid emotions, and underlying the outward crying, anger, and grief in them is the ability to work consciously with their *Greater Other Dimensions*! As mental energy is further endorsed as self setting goals, emotional energy is further submerged, because it often first surfaces as the *dark hole* of discontent, rebelliousness, and finally hopelessness and complete absence on our part. In not developing and exercising the skills of our own sensitivity, they become overly sensitive when exposed. It is very threatening to most, because it can pull us in deep, and self feels threatened in that realm, as those *Greater Other Dimensions* enters the picture to help bring our awareness to what we need to change in ourselves.

This emotional energy is necessary in order for us to build consciousness with energy. We need to be able to feel things, and sense their impressions through these feelings if we are to know what is good for us. Sensations are required to take us to this higher consciousness of recognition of true needs, beyond immediate wants and desires. We can't reliably sense if there is a lot of suppressed emotion, for what we feel sensationally *becomes our own resistance*, not what we are introducing to our bodies to access. Now, what I say here may sound absolutely insane to those who aren't aware that body sensation is a frequency of energy within us. If we were to place our intent to be guided by the greatest intelligence that exists, and I mean placing faith in God, however you choose to define your beliefs, would it not be aligned with our vitality and health more surely than any human-made decision? I don't mean that we should just say a prayer. We need to take responsibility for our choices. If we want high quality foods on our grocery store shelves, we have to ask for it and stop making unhealthy choices. As self, we are part of this unfolding process. We are being influenced by a greater intelligence beyond self to take steps that demonstrate what is important to us.

I'm suggesting that we make a clear intent to have our *Greater Other Dimensions* guide us, and actually become conscious enough to feel when things resonate with our own vitality and exercise our ability to choose things accordingly. We can do this for our children and endorse through our actions what is quite natural for them already. We can test these impressions by monitoring their behavior. When something is not aligned with their innate potential, they will tell us with their behavior or by becoming ill. Tell me we don't see the effects of refined sugar on our children just a few minutes after they eat it! In learning to become present, we can observe subtle changes in those around us by the way they act, because we ourselves become clear conduits for feeling these frequencies. You don't have to become psychic overnight, but it may shock you to know that this skill is not very difficult to develop if you begin to observe things outside your own agenda. It is difficult to trust because we are led to believe that there is no such thing as psychic power. By trusting this "energy" we can discern between right and wrong choices at the grocery store. Muscle testing and pendulums have been utilized this way for a long time, as they are tools that outwardly respond to this electromagnetic dynamic in us. Even birds and animals know when something is not safe to eat. Look around and you will see how dysfunctional we all are. If your nervous system is intact then you are capable of sensing in this way, and if it is not, notice what you are feeding your body in thought and nourishment to strengthen your faith in your subtle senses.

We can't solve on the emotional level what is being created on the physical, and most children under the age of seven do not have emotional or mental problems, even though this is where we see them displayed! By the time they reach ten years of age, they have developed emotional imbalances on top of the physical ones and their inability to recognize that they alone hold the power to choose at will what they wish to believe about themselves is bringing them to further imbalances on the mental level. At the age of fourteen, many of our young people have become apathetic and rebellious and we fail to see the true causes of these manifestations of physical dysfunction.

*Possibly this dark hole is just the disguise of an
undeveloped and malnourished creativity,
not wanting to be exposed because of its extreme sensitivity.*

❧   ❧   ❧

With our outwardly abundant lives here in North America, children are enticed into adopting our experience of reality through the gifting of presents. *Isolated-self* is constantly lured in by popular culture. There are endless impulses to feed. As I experienced with my youngest child, Easter and Christmas are all about presents! I was a little shocked to hear this from him, I must admit, until I appreciated what he was sharing with me. I asked my six year old while we were decorating Easter eggs, what Christ had to do with Easter. He looked at me blankly and said, "Nothing, Easter is about having an Easter egg hunt". So, I asked what God had to do with Easter. "What do you mean mom?" was his reply. I was horrified and frantically wondered just where I'd gone wrong with him! Surely we were talking about different things here, or more to the point, I was praying he meant something different than what I was hearing. I wasn't really sure where to go with this, because I wasn't altogether sure I was prepared for what this was showing me about what impression we had given him. So, I continued, "Well, people have special days they celebrate God in different ways". There followed a very long silence in which I was beginning to think he was ignoring me, and not too interested in pursuing this conversation. But I waited, through what felt like eternity, in silence, and finally he very thoughtfully said; " God is everywhere… in *every* day, Mom… so I don't know what Christmas and Easter are for, except that we eat chocolate and get presents… and I like it that way". He was quite sure of this, and not really moved to talk about it anymore. His matter of fact tone stopped me in my tracks, as if I had asked the most obvious question in the world, and it was a complete drain on his patience to explain it to me.

We sat together decorating eggs in silence for some time, comfortable silence for him, uncomfortable for me. While sitting there, stuck in my head with myself, it occurred to me that at six, our full presence is in every moment, and God is actively everywhere beyond any doubt, for life is magical and surprising in all ways, through the unclouded lenses through which we see the world at this age. Things are simple. God just is. As adults, we make things complicated. Our perceptions are clouded by our conditioning. It is rather embarrassing to be caught forgetting such a simple and obviously important thing. His words, delivered with such confidence, made it unnecessary to deliver the lecture of explanation that was forming in my mind. It was as if wisdom of common sense has just landed in our kitchen with a big thud. I often think he isn't listening to me, and really, he's so focused on whatever he's doing that anything that takes him away from that simple state, is irrelevant to him. I hate to admit it, but much of what I am asking him to do is quite irrelevant in the long run, but important to *me* in that moment.

I seem to be constantly juggling the integration of presence in the moment with finding a balance that is in sync with me and the world at large. After all, the school bus comes at eight o'clock in the morning, and its schedule is not going to revolve around my child's personal morning rituals. There has to be some agreed-upon rules of conduct under which we function, otherwise we miss the opportunity of expanding our own awareness through our interaction with others. At six, he is beginning to experience a sense of self, and the openness in which he operates exposes a beautiful naiveté. When he got a watch, he proudly set the time, by his sense of time, not by the standard time. As we drove down the road one day he insisted that his watch was right! It took his Dad fifteen minutes to convince him that other people were not going to set their watches on his time. The rest of us were operating on an agreed time, and that it would be crazy to think we would meet up at the right time, the right place if our watches were all different. My son never did give in to this reasoning, but I see that now he has his watch set correctly. He is still not too concerned about whether he will be at the right place at the right time or not. He doesn't think he'll be missing anything. He has held fast to the idea that everything happens as it should, and his own timing remains important to him. It is interactions like these that one hopes will never be completely lost in the process of entering the world and having respect for its established rules of conduct. I know many adults that, although they have their watches set correctly and understand the concept of time, still operate as if the rest of the world is going to revolve around their agenda and sense of time.

A young child's own rhythm and sense of time is important for us as parents to acknowledge if they are to expand their awareness to include anyone else walking this earth, for if the foundation for understanding others is not established within, it will continue to inadvertently seek acknowledgement throughout their life. The *time* taken at six years of age to establish relationship to this internal rhythm is appropriate, for once confirmed as valid, it naturally evolves into taking other people into consideration. There can be harmony between setting one's own watch and standard time when we personally acknowledge our own needs. For my son at six, his own rhythm, and his sense of timing needed to be acknowledged as it was for him, through his own experience. Having validated his personal sense of time for himself, he expanded his awareness all on his own, to consider how he takes that into the agreed schedule of the larger world. Six and seven-year-olds don't remain self-centered unless they are ignored for having valuable input as they learn these concepts. I believe that for our children it is this *timing* of their internal rhythm which, once acknowledged and honored in them when young, will foster respect and understanding for a timing of a different nature that runs in sync with our concrete world. For when you think about it, how do we know our world, except in relation to ourselves, through our own perceptions and experience? If we fail to learn to value what we are, there is no secure place from which to relate to others. If we start off believing that our *own time* is wrong, then how does that set up our perception of everything outside of us? Acknowledgement and respect for our shared external world is a process of building from our security found within our own internal world.

I constantly have to take a step back, and hear children from where they are at, instead of coming up against their ideas from my own experience and perspective. My son's take on Easter, urged me to think about something that I hadn't considered before. If we celebrated God in every day, in all ways, and reserved a couple of special days to celebrate ourselves, maybe we would maintain a simple and trusting view of the world. Our human nature could be trusted, instead of the insatiable hunger of self seeking acknowledgment, driving us to conquer and have power *over* everything to feel secure and worthy of love. Self on its own is a difficult demon to slay unless we draw our swords and use them to separate illusion from reality, rather than severing ourselves from the greater dimension of our being. We have the choice to draw upon something much, much greater than self that illuminates us so its threat seems preposterous. It becomes our friend rather than our foe. Remembering this greater truth *everyday* may just serve to feed that void inside, in a way than self left to its own devices is not capable of accomplishing on its own.

As children, we believe we know everything, because things seem simple to us, and we aren't attached to self. As we experience life, self accumulates references through experience, and we begin to realize that there is so much more to learn. Challenging others who have more experience is not our intention, but is rather just us stretching our wings so we can claim our innocent self in relation to authority figures and our familiar world. Self's limitations can easily be validated in our culture unless soul's faith can be fostered to lead self to realize where we need to grow when we encounter resistance from others. The boundaries we are taught today aren't necessarily learned in our own backyard while mom bakes brownies and watches us through the kitchen window. Our natural expression of soul, left alone to investigate at our leisure can be frustrated if all of our leisure time is regimented by scheduled activities. Children need unstructured time to be alone with themselves. The cooperative relationship which self can find with soul is replaced by the impressions we take on as limited-self that our personal surroundings provide for us, and we unknowingly accepted as our full reality.

Soul can easily go unrecognized when developing self takes precedence in order to survive in our competitive world. When there is no conscious relationship to soul we develop a void, and unless those nurturing us support developing security of a different nature, we feel lost. Religion has taken advantage of this void in human awareness throughout history by providing a framework for this expression, but our own consciousness has moved past religion's perceptions defining our own. I think we are in our adolescence as a society, caught up in rebellion because we are not recognized for our individuality. This feeling of being lost is being manifested in our collective insistence that we have more and more in order to stand out from the crowd. Of course, there is never enough. We have arrived at a spiritually dark place and we are wandering about in that darkness trying to find our way home. In being left unrecognized in its innocence, and unattended to for what it is, self continues to seek gratification and acknowledgement that is impossible to satisfy. We will continue to seek and fill the void with material "stuff" leaving the emptiness unresolved. When self reaches this threshold of becoming aware of its limitations and we are given diversions and stimulations to keep us occupied and productive, we suffer at a deeper soul level. Any space that once existed in solitude where we might become still enough to center ourselves in faith is avoided out of conditioning. We must be busy and productive! When we do attempt to delve deeper to find meaning and direction, we encounter an accumulation of the layers of self instead of the space where soul resides. Soul can have so many of self's layers covering it that it can be difficult to believe that it is still there under all the senseless debris. There is an inherent drive that keeps us seeking *our innocence* no matter how we try to ignore it.

Today, by the age of three, many of our children have travelled and been exposed to our global community, which is a wonderful thing in itself. The backyard is boring to many, and "down the street" is no longer seen as the huge wilderness to explore that it was when we were children. They have covered that distance in the car on the way to a play group. We experienced childhood differently from our own children because there weren't the same physical threats that we believe exist today. Great care is taken to make sure our children are safe. They are watched like hawks or put in structured environments that ensure they are watched for us. We expose them to every sort of experience through programmed, structured activities. Their exploration is contained to scheduled experiences. Those that haven't physically traveled have been exposed through media to various cultures, environments, and impressions about other places than their home. There are swimming programs, music programs, programs to teach them to read, and programs on computers to stimulate and entertain them. So much seems to be programmed to ensure the maximum amount of information is delivered in the most timely fashion, and it is very easy to overlook the basic honoring of the fundamental needs of growing a healthy child. Hanging out in the back yard with a stick and cardboard box is not enough for most children once they've been exposed to the wonders of modern technology.

Snack time becomes a packaged prepared food in the car on the way to playgroup, not a blanket laid out on the grass with a bowl of cut up apples, a pause for nourishment on different levels. In our haste, their need to develop relationship with their own internal barometer is often overlooked. We continue to be oblivious to this aspect of human development when our children get sick. Current advertising for Children's Tylenol sells us on the fact that despite a fever, their medication will ensure that your child doesn't miss a beat in their regular routine, and neither do you! Maybe our focus on self's efficiency has driven us to do too much, and we are conditioning our children to segregate their own capacity for *being* and *doing* into two separate expressions, not a blended *presence.*

Safety is a concept for most children, not a *feeling* they have learned to trust. The fears they express are based on anticipation or learned criteria, rather than on what they actually experience. A sick body isn't noticed as a signal something needs to change for us, and we don't support taking to bed for the day, or venturing towards understanding our illness. In *our own adolescent awareness*, we have overlooked the origins of these perceptions. We take a pill so we can get on with our day when we should be sitting with our discomfort in order to determine its message, its meaning, and our part in bringing the illness about. We look to *change the content* of the programs that our children are enrolled in, rather than support our children and the people who implement the programs to meet everyone's needs. These programs may be wonderful, but many of our children are not showing up prepared to benefit from them because they are full of pharmaceutical interventions that keep them functional in our idea of an efficient society.

Children today are having a difficult time of it because their nervous systems are on complete overload. Take away the programmed stimulation and they become distracted and agitated. When they are left alone with their imagination, many who have been *plugged in* from day one complain that they are bored. We relieve their boredom by plugging them in. We put them in front of a DVD or video game. There just isn't time in most children's schedules to download or rather *upload* the innate programming of our *Greater Other Dimensions.* We don't trust them to experience this world for themselves, because most of us don't trust this world ourselves anymore, and yet we keep doing what were doing, hoping things will be different for them. On one end of the spectrum, we give our children complete freedom, without boundaries in place for them to discover the effects of their actions, because we solve and take care of most things for them. On the other end of the spectrum, we place extreme physical boundaries that don't allow them to venture out the front door alone, and we endorse mental stimulation that anesthetizes them from having the desire to do so. We think the world is not safe. If every household believes this, then where exactly are all the dangerous people living? We have already decided that anyone outside our circle of comfort is a threat to ourselves, and our children, and we're withholding the nurturance of the tools that will help them learn the art of discernment to determine for themselves what is safe.

Silence to most children is torment and signals to them that something is wrong. I'd like to know how we couldn't recognize this as our responsibility as adults, to help them cultivate a respect for a relationship to silence. How will they know, how will they feel, or sense our world if we sever them from their natural instincts to be with their internal world? Jeopardy to our physical safety is instinctual when we're confronted by a physical threat, and this fear can be recognized more readily from a feeling rather than a thought. Perceived fears are learned, not necessarily naturally derived from experience. Our way of relating to our children is teaching them fear of themselves, as much as of others, instead of respect for careful enquiry. If our thoughts target avoiding what we fear then we miss the experience of dispelling what is real from illusion through feeling it for what it is. It is in learning to acknowledge self in relation to others, and honoring our internal barometer, that helps us continue to stretch our boundaries to go past learned fear as we mature.

At the bottom of it is the most horrible realization of all: We don't know how to trust a world in which we can't trust ourselves, or others, because of what we have all become. Our *conscience* is overshadowed by a plague that believes we are powerful individuals, we are on the top of the food chain, and that *self can control* and *create* our reality. Given the state of our world, self has been very successful. But that success has come at a cost. Reality is already fully created. How we choose to experience reality will determine the richness of our personal and shared experience, and our ability to experience a fuller realization of its potential. If there is no pure water, pure food, nutrient soil, fresh air, or life, we as a physical species will not be experienced. Never mind the individual's survival! Self as small-self, and not connected to any greater intelligence would have us believe that we need to maintain control in order to be safe. Fears are something to be conquered because we must win at the expense of something that scares us because we don't understand it. From what vantage point is this thinking coming from? If it's self-driven, isolated from a faith in something greater, then we are in trouble! If it is soul driven, we will pave our reality with compassion.

We've traded in walking, and feeling, and hearing our own internal rhythm for being more efficient, productive, and safe, in sync with the big wheel of commerce. In not recognizing the need for physical balance, we have literally cut off our connection to the earth and its resourcefulness to support us by ignoring the silent internal rhythm of soul that speaks through our conscience. We all become dangerous people when conscience can't be heard any longer through self's personal agenda.

Chapter 8

The Mother & Father of Entitlement

---

*Entitlement is the illusion we see, when bright, keen, minds arrive
to challenge us to grow with them. What an honor to be trusted
with such a venture. We'll miss the invitation if we don't grow wings
to recognize and harness the potential presented by it for us all!*

᪾   ᪾   ᪾

Many adults in recognized and established positions, be it parents, teachers, or employers, are experiencing this seemingly arrogant attitude being expressed by our youth towards us. We've even labeled it *entitlement*, so that we can all agree to its significance as it opposes us, and keep us from admitting what it reflects about our own adolescent behavior. We need to admit to ourselves that we've gone off track to what our heart knows, and the young ones coming up are challenging us in ways that only an open and receptive heart recognizes. We're being asked to be big now, and step up to the plate from a place of awareness so our young people will experience the best parts of us, and themselves, not a sense of defeat that gets passed down the line. Consciousness is pushing us through a threshold we can no longer ignore as it's walking in our doors presenting itself rather boldly. The very fact that they are walking through our door is an opportunity for us to graciously acknowledge them, and extend our hospitality and capacity to make space to cooperatively work with them, but instead we greet others with our masculine energy and expect them to fit in to what exists for us. We rely on our positions and stature to define us, not who we are on a deeper level that seeks opportunity to grow beyond what exists already for us beyond the currently recognized identity.

Soul is ultimately in the driver's seat whether we acknowledge it or not, and self's survival is reliant on utilizing souls wisdom constructively for the benefit of others, not just self's idea of what should exist. As we learn to build a trusted connection between self and our *Greater Other Dimensions*, we can move beyond the self's current identity to include a graciousness found in the heart, that brings further meaning to our own experience of our shared humanity. What was subtle before has become louder and louder with each generation, and now what appears gutsy and obnoxious is possibly our own rebelliousness to change self's perceptions of what is important. Soul is not going to get buried until old age when we no longer have the energy to exert our physical command in the world, and are forced to take inventory of our internal world, and take responsibility for how our personal choices have affected others.

We are rooted firmly in our own backyards, but not from a place of discovery or expanded awareness, more from a fixed position looking out over what we have accomplished and are able to recognize and be comfortable with, clearly before us. Not unlike our perceived position relative to the youth who come barreling through our doors claiming they have arrived to impart fresh thinking and are able to lead! They can set off a reaction within us if we mistakenly hear what they say as a comparison between their abilities, and what we are currently doing or able to do effectively. Their exuberance is refreshing, and they can be very confident in expressing themselves, but they often have yet to realize how their individual contribution affects others. This is their inexperience presenting itself openly, but we often miss its innocence because of our own insecurity in maintaining control over ourselves with them.

Shifting our perceptions from a position of opposition to one of cooperation is similar to the experience of standing out in the midst of our backyard, and then looking at our self in relation to our backyard from a more objective standpoint. As we stand in our backyard, we believe we have a complete view of everything within our backyard boundaries, and are aware of the things that obstruct our view, so we can change our position relative to these things to see more clearly. We see the whole area, to inspect the grass, our garden, the trees and whatever else exists there as we know them from our awareness in the midst of it. Standing there we feel in control and aware of what surrounds us, because it is visibly there to acknowledge and recognize for us, as we have experience with it. When that youth comes flying in, it's a little disconcerting that they don't realize this, as we believe it is in plain view and obvious to anyone present. We remind our self that it is a nice backyard, and that we have done well for our self, and we are comfortable there, just the way it is.

Now, imagine, we were led into our backyard blindfolded without knowing where we were going, and left to stand alone to gather impressions about our surroundings. In trying to figure out where we were, we would *tune in* to our environment in a different way. We would encounter our fears, our resistance to stand openly to sense the environment, even though part of us knows this place from being there everyday, we may not be aware of that deeper calming influence at our disposal because it is overridden with many conflicting impressions. What confronts us? Is it an adventure in unveiling what we recognize on a deeper level of awareness, to know where we are by the way things sound, and feel to us? Or are we confronted by an internal world that is busy with questions, and insecurity, focused on keeping our self comfortable enough to endure the experience? This exercise reveals to us the gap that exists between what an open heart perceives, and the experience of *isolated-self* defending its position relative to the *unrecognized arrival of growth.* When asked to approach things differently, our fears and doubts create resistance for an authoritative-self.

Now imagine that the blindfold is removed, and we are awakened to what we thought we knew very well before. The backyard has expanded in its experience now for us, and the illusion of security it held for us has been unveiled, even if we don't fully appreciate it yet. We feel a little shell-shocked in that we haven't yet made the connection between our discomfort and the contents of what we know in our backyard. Then we notice there is a ladder leaning against the house, and we decide to climb up the ladder to the roof. The ladder looks very appealing at this point, because standing beside us is this young person telling us everything they know and how they can help us! We decide to get some space and leave them to their own devices for a few moments. Up we go, and when we reach the rooftop, we step off the ladder and stand there looking down at the backyard. Things become apparent that we didn't see standing in its midst. Looking down reveals patterns, relatedness between the elements, and broader awareness of the components of our backyard, beyond what we could appreciate as valid before. When we make an invitation to God to enter our awareness, we are enabling spirit to lift us up and give us this expanded view from the rooftop, beyond what we think we know in its entirety while personally in its midst. Depending on how much trust and faith we place in allowing this broader perspective, the higher the vantage point shown to us, will be. The higher we go, the less significant the threats that confront us appear to be, and it seems almost comical that we could have felt so triggered by that youth entering our space moments earlier.

Looking down from the rooftop, we may begin seeing past our own backyard, to realize the synchronicity and influence your own backyard has in relation to others, and how what personally seems in order in our life, often impacts and influences others negatively beyond our awareness. If we are so utterly convinced that we know everything, and are in control, and when challenged to expand our thinking to include another perspective we become resistant, afraid, or uncomfortable with what we believe it could represent, we miss the gift of the experience to expand our own awareness. We have to be willing to make the choice to climb the ladder when resistance rears its head in our own backyard rather than locking heads by confronting things head on.

That youth standing down there is placed into context from standing here now, and the reflection of entitlement is no longer all you see in them. Although they come in armed with wonderful idea's about changing things, and a whack of information to back their thinking, standing alone, they aren't too aware of what already exists under their feet down there, or acknowledge fully the skills required in implementing and maintaining new idea's. How could they be, as learned knowledge has not yet been given the opportunity to be applied to their experience of their life and its effect on others. As we look down, we see the youth scuffing his foot across a patch of moss we have been gently coaxing along next to our pond, but we continue to observe, and a realization creeps into our mind. We realize this youth has pushed us to retreat to reassess things, and find this new perspective up on the roof, about our self. From the vantage point of the rooftop, there is so much more potential revealed in their sheer enthusiasm, and if nurtured like the moss, we have the ability to bring awareness of this relatedness we now appreciate up here, down with us into the experience of the backyard. Its effects may very well extend out beyond the two of us if there is this newly found compassion implemented.

Entitlement takes on a new meaning when we take our perceptions to a higher vantage point, because we realize that with experience, building relatedness to a shared humanity brings greater meaning and appreciation to us about a new kind of fulfillment beyond our own identity. Having opened our eyes more fully to see what is before us, we climb down the ladder, and introduce our self whole heartedly to the youth. We receive that enthusiasm exuding from them and we ask them to direct it towards a specific task they have ideas about improving. Off they bound to take on the new challenge. The youth returns with an unforeseen problem, and leaves feeling a little overwhelmed with being trusted with taking responsibility for their actions, and given the opportunity to resolve it on their own. Without criticism, or reaction about it, *we decide to be big with them*, so when they return a little disappointed by the outcome of their venture, we share with them our thoughts about a constructive approach that will extend beyond our backyard to benefit others, not just us or them. Faith is a powerful virtue to implement with others. We invite in new dimensions to the situation, beyond both our positions, and suggest they accompany us up the ladder to stand on the roof for a bit. They accept our invitation and we both look at what happened from there, and between the two of us a plan is agreed upon. Their confidence is supported, along with gaining respect for us and their own abilities, when they realize they don't know everything when left to their own devices, and our opinion of them goes well beyond their admission to learning, as we are *both committed to learning together* now.

Some who enter our lives, and we theirs, are not interested in climbing the ladder of greater awareness, and they remain focused on self's agenda, as experience has shown them it is enough to get what they want. When we invite spirit into our life, we also invite compassion for those with different idea's and different priorities than our own. Recognizing those who wish to work co-operatively, and those who wish to impart their ideas without honoring anything beyond self, become apparent much earlier. Whether we are on the youth end of the equation, or the adult end, we can be the ones refusing to climb the ladder of illumination. We will head into another backyard or have the experience of building our own, to realize these boundaries are but an illusion, and that a shared humanity exists whether we acknowledge it or not. Sooner or later we all get pushed to climb the ladder of consciousness, as we just can't resolve things on our own, and run out of backyards to wander into, to have the same experience repeated with the same isolating experience for self.

None of us likes the idea of being led! We are a culture attached to the idea of being leaders, and to *become a follower* is still unconsciously associated with weakness and oppression. When challenge shows up in our backyard, be it in a young person fresh out of school and armed with skills to implement their ideas, our unrecognized emotions greet them, not our enthusiasm for their arrival to share our workspace. When the masculine energy that calls the shots, and chooses direction is greeted with another's approach to infuse fresh thinking to something beyond what we believe currently exists, it must be *allowing* for the feminine in us to receive and nurture it to become manifest. Aligned with a shared, greater consciousness beyond self takes courage, as conditioning of self would tell us otherwise. If our emotional response closes these gates to greater receptivity, and plants us more firmly in our personal position, the feminine cannot receive that seed of an idea and begin gestation through creativity. We miss incredible opportunity to focus our own skills and knowledge towards a new potential born out of cooperation with consciousness beyond our recognized identity.

Unrecognized Self with the masculine engaged, sides with defensiveness and protectiveness over what we mistakenly believe to be our personal property and contribution to the whole. If the masculine is determined to remain in control at the expense of honoring another for their input, then the masculine approaches another from a position of proving its own position, by either humiliating the other, or deciding to personally teach them a lesson. Pride leads, instead of faith in our humanity. This is not a cooperative venture seeking a shared experience of learning or demonstration by self of a compassionate God. Deciding to climb up that ladder is our conscious choice to become *a follower* of a greater guide than the *self* we identify with, or unrecognized self as reflected in another. We want those younger to be followers, and us to be the leaders, and this is not hopefully going to be happening anytime soon, if we are to support a shared and compassionate humanity. We all become resourceful co-creators of our experience, but not because we believe we are leaders, or perceive ourselves or others to be leaders, but because we are *secure enough to follow* our inner conscience, and *allow in* a greater consciousness that supports life itself, in ourselves and others equally.

Patriarchal energy has a history of being a self-serving authority that can't be dismissed for existing, but it does not have to be the model we choose to currently exercise. Through awareness of self, we can choose to get out of our own backyard and get a broader perspective from the rooftop where self is revealed to be isolated, functioning out of fear down there. Once we acknowledge where self believed its position to be, where territory seemed relevant, and others appeared in opposition with it, we are able to let go of the emotional attachment that keeps self's perception real for us. True resolution will come only through transcending the dualism of this masculine versus masculine struggle found there, and it requires allowing the expression of the inherent feminine waiting patiently to birth it. As long as the masculine energies remain engaged when relating to one another, the feminine ability to nurture creativity remains unrealized, and the outdated patriarchal model *remains alive through us*, by how we continue to demonstrate self's authority in the present.

In our own backyard we may feel justified in exercising and demanding respect for our position, so anyone entering has got to abide by our rules, but if the guidelines are developed from a place of compassion, there is no place for opposition to greet us, as it no longer exists as an oppressive expression. As an adult to an adult, to exercise a model of masculine energy that is secure enough in self's own abilities that one is opened to being infused by a higher intelligence that can lead with compassion, where *our self follows* because it agrees to learn from being exposed to new experience. This takes courage of a completely different nature, to admit we don't know everything at this moment as self, and yet the confidence to remain in *control of allowing conception and growth*, not control over others who stand before us who think differently. Through the act of *allowing* we enable a greater dimension of *who we are* to infuse knowledge beyond how self would like to be identified, but we always remain in control to choose how we wish to integrate this with who we currently are capable of being. To allow is not to necessarily agree with another, but rather opening to hear a greater truth that self on its own is unable to do as long it wants to remain right in its current position, and isolated in its own backyard.

Self, not recognized in its shadow within us, seeks validation it never received on the home front, and that patriarchal energy has evolved into an invisible force within us that gets in our way. It appears to be what confronts us in others, but is really our own shadow left unnoticed, looking to be acknowledged for what it is. We will continue to fight it as long as we see it as a threat and don't move beyond that perception to really see what we're looking at. When these young people show up, what we're experiencing of them is what we refuse to accept experiencing in ourselves. We become what we least like in others, to understand what it is, and we rarely recognize it because judgment gets in the way from experiencing anything else but what we choose to believe it represents. The entitlement perceived is our own masculine self's vanity in believing it is right and superior, and more evolved than others because of its experience.

This seemingly *entitled* generation is extremely resilient to overt masculine energy, as if it doesn't even touch them, or alter their course of action, because they don't want it to exist. Who could blame them when what they have experienced of masculine energy has been very opinionated and harsh in its treatment of the creative energy they express. Emotionally, they first appear in control and adaptive because mentally they are very agile, but anxiety can overcome them when challenged, and complete physical exhaustion can overtake them because they become inwardly destructive when emotionally challenged. The outward demonstration *we interpret as entitlement* is really a very clever mask utilized to protect the feminine sensitivity in themselves. They are a very creative and positive generation with high ideals, and capable of profound insight, but it is not integrated with a self that knows how to constructively channel it into the world as it is. They are a more sensitive and more extreme expression of us, their parents, and even better at avoiding discomfort, because many have never experienced any in the material sense. They are unknowingly seeking solutions beyond the materialism that currently exists, but this masculine side being evoked in them, by us, is seeking resolution of a different kind, and finds expression by wanting to prove what it can do and obtain acknowledgement before it can move beyond it. For this reason, they tend to side with technology in expressing themselves because it is impersonal and non-confrontational. This generation is worth growing wings for, for they are very bright lights worth inviting into our life if we're looking to find illumination about self's influence and ability to foster wealth of a different nature for all of us.

I'm doing a lot of listening these days, because our young people speak a truth none of us likes to hear or admit. I'm not sure they actually realize what they are speaking, or if they are speaking it with an understanding of the significance, but non-the-less they are speaking it through their actions, by showing us what we are manifesting. We will miss hearing it, unless we pause for a moment, invite God into our hearts, and give our full attention beyond what we think we know, to invite in these young peoples questions. We are stuck in our positions, in our own backyards without awareness of how we are influencing and receiving others through our limited perceptions. We've known it for some time deep inside ourselves, but we have become our own masters at over-riding any discontent we feel. We think we are removing our blindfolds when we shop, and pack more stuff into our backyards, so we have a sense of experiencing and knowing more, when really we've just jammed more stuff into supporting our own personal comfort zone. We build bigger, and better monuments for our accomplishments, be it our homes, or our businesses, and support self's desire to stay in control, instead soul's hunger for the experience of compassion. No matter what we think standing on the ground, looking around, there are still influences at work beyond what we realize standing here. If we are to evolve more smoothly, with less confrontation, then the masculine and feminine energies need to be acknowledged for their sacred roles. In getting past our idea's of territory, and who's place it is to exercise authority, we may become more allowing of spirit into our hearts where conscience can guide us.

As a mother my heart aches for our children and youth innocently seeking growth when dealing with us. Entering our world at this time, with all of us being so blind to their message because we are so focused on thinking of solutions instead of allowing them to surface from what is inherent already being expressed from them. They don't need to know how to talk, or walk, for their very presence brings this message clearly into our experience. *They are the message*, and if we want them to survive, and thrive, and succeed, we have to clean up our act, and quick, before we sabotage this presence as we have demonstrated doing to ourselves. We too brought the same message, but it is harder to interpret as we have compensated with self's interventions and it is more difficult to unveil with clarity. We're all head, and our hearts can't hear what is right here, with us in this moment, because we are stuck in protecting what we believe is our personal positions relative to them. We *believe* our perceptions are greater than our children's because of our experience, and we believe how we *interpret them* to be correct, when they are often limited to self's vantage point, not aligned with the divine essence in all of us.

Those that are open to taking the blinders off, climbing to the rooftop and taking it all in, are acknowledging the existing truth of our world beyond what they think it represents, by allowing themselves to see and feel what it's currently expressing about its imbalances. We're resisting the temptation to plough over and build again to suit our current way of operating, and instead, we're *inviting in the diversity* that appears to be before us, so we can *hear it for what it is*, not what makes us comfortable acknowledging. As conscious people, we need to implement resources to support what we value in our hearts, not change to fit into what technology would have us believe will make *it* more efficient to take care of us. Would we honestly place greater faith in machines to sustain us, then place trust in life itself to nurture, sustain, and teach us how to care for ourselves and others equally?

Our children are inherent goodness, but do they learn how to hold it, and channel it constructively, when confronted by our insanity? With the realization of our separation from a greater consciousness than self, resilience has taken hold of our young people. It's surfaced as an illusion that gives the impression of *entitlement*, to those adults insistent on staying firmly rooted in their own comfort zones. To stand in judgment of what our young people have adopted from witnessing our example, is to dismiss in ourselves the ability to take responsibility for our own part in experiencing them this way. The receptivity within us needs to claim its power, or it will be overwhelmed by illusion of its inadequacy to withstand transformation, and we will cling to our rooted identities and sheer vanity. We are not celebrating God in everyday, nor are we celebrating our oneness with God, or offering our hands and bodies to act on its behalf, *beyond* where the accomplishments of self are leading us. We have endorsed this behavior in our young people through our example, and now we are upset with them, because they apply these principles to us now in an attempt to communicate with us. It doesn't feel as good to be on the receiving end, because the feminine that receives, nurtures and gives birth to a consciousness beyond duality, is not enabled as long as the masculine is set on defending its current position.

As we grew into adults, we slowly accumulated criteria as to how we celebrate God in our lives. The everyday is focused on the agenda of self asserting its place in the world, separate from God. *Self,* unrecognized, cannot aid in what we as *beings* are being urged to realign with now beyond our current identity. Self remains a threat as long as it is not accepted as who we have become, in relation to who we have the ability to choose to be now.

Where self perceives entitlement,
Soul perceives opportunities to grow
closer to the experience of a compassionate world.

We have modeled how to be direct, set goals, focus on the outcome desired, don't get emotional, don't stop and doubt yourself, just DO IT! We unknowingly keep this cycle alive ourselves, in treating our children as a reflection of who we are as parents out in the world, when we send them out with things beyond their experience or often current ability, to value or care for. We buy them expensive computers, cell phones and games and get upset with them because they lose them, or forget them somewhere, or are careless and break them. We buy them what we believe is the *best for them*, and then get upset because they don't know what is involved in having things belong with them. We don't allow the experience of earning things they choose, or start them with things that enable them to learn these simple lessons without feeling guilty for not realizing the responsibility that goes with caring for them. When they misuse these things because of not realizing what's involved in maintaining them, we talk to them about responsibility, we infuse some guilt into the equation to assure they feel bad for a few moments, and then we buy them new ones. They miss the experience of responsibility not just the first time through in losing or breaking the actual thing, but then we take the experience of figuring out what to do about it, or how they will replace it, from them as well.

How are our actions supporting what we say exactly? What is the influence that takes over us to get us to cave in and solve their discomfort for them? We buy them things *we think* they can use and will appreciate, and we give them to them. From that point on these things belong with them, not us. The decisions about caring for them, lending them, whatever they choose to do with them, is in their hands, and so are the consequences of their choices and actions. We respond emotionally to the situation without realizing it, and we withhold from them the experience of their own discomfort they may go through emotionally in figuring out what to do when they run into problems. They may not care about the cell phone, and replacing it really isn't a priority for them, so they go without. If it's important to them they'll go through the process of figuring it out. We all learn responsibility through *the process of realization*, and as children or adults, it doesn't matter what someone tells us ahead of time, true appreciation for what is involved in taking responsibility for something only happens through our *experience* with it. Through our demonstration of working through a process, they can learn to use these tools to help not only themselves but others, or they can learn to use them destructively because they are unaware of the effects of their actions. Should they be lost, stolen, or broken, they will figure out what to do about it, if we allow them the opportunity without making them feel less for not realizing what's involved in caring for things ahead of time.

It doesn't feel good to fill our own spiritual void with another's gold, and that' pretty much what we're doing when we set them up for failure in our eyes, because we rob them of our faith in their greatness. We pass on our unrecognized *martyr* to be realized through them. Faith in their ability to first of all define what they need to us, help in choosing it because we're helping make it possible, and then to resolve the things that come with having the responsibility of using and caring for these things we give them, because they belong with them now. As parents, we are our children's first experience of feeling accepted, trusted, and valued. If they fail in our eyes, they may just believe they are a failure, and we are unconsciously withholding their own experience of power, because we don't know how to exercise our own true power. By our actions, we give them the impression that without these things they aren't enough on their own, so we arm them unknowingly with things that we believe speak for them materially, to others. We further endorse our concerns over their ability to think and resolve things for themselves by constantly reminding them, and asking where things are, or if they have taken care of their responsibilities. They resist the interference and never have the experience of what happens when they don't remember on their own. Leaving without a lunch for school, or forgetting to complete homework is a small price to pay for bringing them into awareness of what their part in being accountable requires from them.

If we wonder how our actions are unknowingly emotionally driven, then take a look at how we respond to our child when something goes wrong for them. Not what we say, but *what we do*. Do we jump in and fix it, solve it for them, or replace it *without allowing them* the experience of becoming resourceful or accountable by themselves? Does the masculine energy in us take the position of imposing our way on them, rather then encouraging them to discover their way, that leads to a experienced victory? We find our worth, and learn to honor it when we are supported to constructively find solutions because others place faith in us to do so. If we approach our children without becoming students, we miss the lesson in learning about ourselves through observing where they struggle, and being prepared to work through it with them choosing to be a constructive influence. Children unconditionally placed their trust in us to love, protect and guide them to maturity. To reciprocate this trust means openly acknowledging that *they are* gold to us, regardless of circumstance, and they can rely on our faith in their resourcefulness because they are wealthy in our eyes. When consciously giving to our children without strings attached, we are giving them our best, because in our eyes, they have earned and deserve the privilege of our trust to be their best. We have enough faith in them that their mistakes will be allowed by us, as tools to learn about themselves, their choices, and their ability to adapt. Buy them the best if we so desire, but be clear that this is our choice of what is best, not necessarily appreciated by them because they know nothing else to compare it to.

In placing faith in our children, we allow them opportunities to be strong, capable, and brilliant because we aren't threatened by their approach, and we remain open to learn from their expression. Our roles with them stretch beyond the commonly accepted identities that our culture may endorse. The father as provider doesn't hold water in many households anymore, so the mother and father roles are not as easily defined as they used to be for many of us. It's on the spiritual level in which we have to draw from, to broaden our awareness of what position our self is determined to have acknowledged before choosing to move on. The feminine energy of receptivity must re-engage, but not from a place of reliance or surrender, rather from a place of security, not threatened by the expression of the masculine trying to assert itself and hold its position at the expense of another. The feminine in us is unable to birth creative solutions beyond our own position, if we hold onto the idea that we are not being honored or recognized by another. This thinking is from believing that another has the right to determine who we are, and our worth. If we wait for another to do this, we will all be stuck in opposition with others for a long, long time, when the true opposition lies within us. The masculine energy within us is what we resist recognizing, and seeks permission to align with, without becoming the patriarchal expression our self. If we can all accept, and mature in the expression of our own masculine energy it is much easier to let the feminine expand to receive higher guidance beyond duality, because it is backed with strength and conviction about what true presence is, in support of growing into a compassionate self.

Great solutions exist beyond the duality of the masculine and feminine. Just like a baby; the feminine receives and nurtures the conception until it is delivered, and then it is born and exists as an individual expression, beyond the separate component of the male and female union that allowed the manifestation to take place. The *it* is an energy beyond duality, as it is divine. We all carry this energy, and in unveiling its potential we are challenged, to recognize how the masculine and feminine play sacred roles in allowing its expression. If we look at the signs present in our world, we see conflict, and even those not living in awareness cannot deny this. If we are to acknowledge our relationship to the *Greater Other Dimensions* of our being, and seek guidance beyond the experience of self, we may transcend what small people we have all become. What our young people appear to be from a place of recognizing a *common passion*, is very different than putting a label of *entitlement* to what is ultimately a misguided understanding of *privilege* on our own part, and in many cases, theirs.

Entitlement is possibly a mask we all adopt,
to hide an unexpressed emotional-self
in the face of authority we don't respect or trust anymore.

≈   ≈   ≈

We are reaching out with one hand to develop greater consciousness for our planet so our frequency will be elevated. No sooner have we placed our focus on this goal, then seemingly overnight we wake to find our other hand full of accumulated garbage that resonates with a lower frequency that we don't recognize as belonging within us. As adults, we don't want to assume the responsibility for the clean up required by us in response to accepting this higher state of awareness. The emotional energy that has been suppressed and overridden by our intellect can send us into overdrive when we haven't developed the tools to recognize its influence, and work with it constructively to understand the value of acknowledging it. When youth decide to walk through the gates of our backyards, we get overwhelmed by their enthusiasm and their *dive right in to take action* approach, before properly observing or acknowledging what already exists. We get upset at them for not honoring our current positions, when really they need direction, and compassion, for they are merely doing what we've shown them creates successful people. We, not them, want to blame our parents, our grandparents, and our ancestors for their collective impressions that have molded us. Well that's well and good, but all that does is prolong getting down to *entering the process* of growing from our current situation, and taking the responsibility to own what resides with us now, and choosing to expand where self believes it knows everything, into a shared appreciation of everyone's ability to grow together, without feeling personally compromised.

It doesn't really matter where the mess we find ourselves in came from at this point, it's here, and once accepted it may be expressed and demonstrated differently because we consciously choose to heal our perceptions of it. Hindsight is a wonderful thing, especially when we realize we know something now we didn't know then, and it becomes a blessing to have gone through the experience, because of what it challenged us to develop as a result of it. We're being asked to emotionally mature, so we recognize the incredible role we're being asked to assume in relation to the young people in our lives.

We alone, as individuals make choices for ourselves. No one else has the ability to ultimately decide what you choose to make of things, and how you choose to see yourself in any circumstance. The more we act from self's agenda without awareness, the more shocking it is when misfortune arrives at our doorstep, because we don't realize the path we paved that led us there. It will remain cruel and unforgiving in our eyes, as long as we fail to assume responsibility for having been unknowingly part of its creation. For a society that thinks that emotions are the muck and nonsense of life, we are without acknowledging it, being overly influenced by them. If it weren't for these unrecognized, or suppressed emotions being present, then changing our minds would not be perceived by us as a weakness, but rather a demonstration of our security in being open to adapt our positions to include greater possibilities that go beyond our personal experience, or awareness. Let's not forget that today's youth, the ones we see as adopting an attitude of entitlement, have parents, and we are among them!

It has nothing to do with putting children in daycare, private school, public school, staying home with them, placing them in many extra curricular activities, or exposing them to none. It has everything to do with allowing them the experience to know how their choices affect themselves and others within a safe environment. What we do allow to happen is for our children to emotionally blackmail us. They play us without knowing they are responding to the one place we feel vulnerable and unable to operate with clarity, our emotions. We appease their discontent with things we know are not good for them, so they *like us*, and feel appreciated and acknowledged by us satisfying their desires. We give them candy, in full knowledge that it is not a good substitute for healthy food, but it is easier for us in the moment to agree with them, them face the resistance in being guardians of them.

There is no *emotional conflict for us*, or opposition in the moment of appeasing them, but deep down, do they learn to respect us, or feel safer because of how we respect them? Parents are guardians, not always friends to young children. Being guardian is not popular always, but when the chips are down, our children trust us to observe their best interests, even when they don't appreciate it at the time. We demonstrate our respect for higher ideals, and don't cave in when it's inconvenient or time consuming to implement them. Learning to go through challenge constructively starts in the home, and as long as we attempt to keep everyone happy, we're missing the gift of experience to show them and us a path that leads to a sense of wellbeing, not momentary satisfaction. Children who feel secure naturally take responsibility for their own wellbeing because we have demonstrated discipline in following what is right in our hearts, not what the immediate mirrors to us about satisfying self's desires. We hear their hearts, not react to their emotions when we acknowledge we seek what is best for them, not just what supports our own comfort zone.

In teaching them through our example, to close their circle, based on what they internally know to be right, not what others necessarily acknowledge or validate as worthy in the moment, gives them security in trusting themselves. We often give them freedom of expression without imparting simple boundaries that enable them to experience the effects of their choices beyond themselves, and then we wonder why they seem so inconsiderate of others. We tell them to honor others, but we deprive them of the experience of taking on small responsibilities that can *show them* how to honor themselves, and give them the experience of seeing the effects of their choices. Getting them to think beyond *what's in it for me* and to consider the effect their choices have on others requires them sometimes standing in the receiving position, and experiencing it from there, not because we do it to them, but rather allow their own choices to demonstrate this back to them. It's not pleasant to feel left out, or ignored, but we shield them from these experiences before they go to school, believing it is harmful, when it is constructive to recognize the origins of such experiences, and become aware of not creating the experience for them. Children can learn from being allowed to have their own experiences, and in turn choose wisely their friends, and people that operate with a conscience, because they realize there is more than *being liked* in the moment.

That candy, we gave in to feeding them, comes back to bite *us* where *we recognize it hurts; watching our children choose situations, people and experiences that hurt them, because self seeks momentary validation from them.* Where we fail to recognize their true needs, we unknowingly satisfy our own emotional needs in the moment. Giving the candy satisfied our emotional need to keep them comfortable, when physically we bailed on doing what was best for them. When we keep our children from accepting discomfort as an invitation to invite growth early on, it is devastating for us to witness when they arrive home from school feeling rejected by friends, believing something is wrong with them. It makes one wonder the tentacles we create when we act from a place of protecting self, rather than reaching through our initial discomfort to follow our heart and do what is right *beyond our own experience* in the moment.

There is incredible stimulation of the nervous system that our technology and our external and our internal environments are creating that is not conducive to our wellbeing. Few in relation to our global population are committed to investing in solutions that support the development of our inner resources. These examples exist, but we have to take the time to work with our children to develop these qualities constructively. Music and dance, painting and drawing all work to integrate the brain and body through creative expression, and taking three year olds to dance class once a week, at the expense of having a nutritious dinner with family, does not necessarily nurture a child's ability to recognize their own needs, or to value life. To have our children entertained and in structured programs every evening of the week does not compensate for missing a shared experience of dancing in the kitchen *with us* while the rice is cooking, or reading together before bed. Expressing oneself comes naturally when the physical foundation is secure, and the pathways to feeling the flow of life within us are open. As long as we allow video games and computers to be competition for learning to care for their more fundamental needs, their desire to be with their imagination, or experiencing nurturing relationships within family, or eating wholesome food, will continue to evoke large-scale reactions. We can't just keep putting chemicals, genetically engineered food, and toxic material into our bodies without it affecting our ability to function mentally, emotionally and physically. Consciousness is rising, but do we have in place a foundation physically and energetically that can support and nurture it to be a constructive expression of who we are *with others?*

As air breathing organisms we can't manage without having the support of a healthy earth, and an awareness of ourselves that keeps our ability to regulate and adapt in order. It's what most can't see or acknowledge as valid to health that these young people are sensitive to, because they have entered our world with higher consciousness. Higher consciousness means greater sensitivity, and without the wisdom passed down from others it is difficult to know how to grow in our understanding of how to care for these *sensitive* needs for ourselves. Maybe as adults, with our own experiences in hand, and volumes of history books to remind us what has happened in previous civilizations, we could choose differently now, and adjust our seats to get a better view of what we are *doing to ourselves* and in turn conditioning in our children.

Are we compromising our own higher ideals because of our need to feel love and be popular with our own children? If we can be still enough, to become witness to see what our actions are telling us about our own duality, maybe we will transcend our need to *do* for ourselves, and learn how to *be* for all of us. With the soul's wisdom comes the ability to recognize true gold, in its many alloyed forms, and not have to control it all, to feel valued or honored for who we are relative to it. Emotional blackmail only works when not recognized, so in becoming aware of our own emotional discomfort, and learning not to be threatened by it, but moved to transform it with understanding, we are better able to stand authentically present for those we have the ability to influence constructively.

Chapter 9

*Opening our Heart
to Realize Greater Truths*

---

*The masculine energy in us must decide to evolve in its current expression
before the feminine is allowed to birth new expression and knowledge
of who we are: Self integrated with Greater Other Dimensions.*

ﬞﾑ   ﾑ   ﾑ

We've greatly underestimated our potential as human beings because our
hearts can't *hear innocence* clearly anymore. We're all little islands bobbing
about, clinging to our posts and positions because we don't trust anything we
can't see. Feeling life is difficult when we are afraid of our own darkness inside.
Our hearts have closed in hopes of keeping us functioning effectively. When
we bog ourselves down with so many negative thoughts and unrecognized
emotions- that light gets very dim inside us. We buy into believing it is our
inadequacy that confronts us, but perhaps it is our vanity instead. The all-
important, set-in-its-ways self, holds us hostage, because we have forgotten
our innocent nature as human's learning to *be* who we really are beyond self.
If we were to feel past this illusion, we would realize that what appears to be
opposition is really just our own inability to listen and continue being students
of life. In our accumulation of material wealth, we've become spiritually
inept. Emotional energy is what makes us human, and integrating with our
Greater Other Dimensions requires the movement of these feelings to bring
us into spiritual awareness. What we can't initially see comes through us
as feeling, and as we embrace this movement, we become aware of greater
depths in ourselves and in others.

Learning to read through word recognition was popular in schools ten
years ago. Rather than learning to sound out words, children were taught
to read by recognizing a word to which they had already been introduced.
A teacher would tell a student what the word was and then the student was

expected to remember the word when he saw it again. There was nothing in place to help them go beyond what they already knew. When I was in school we learned to sound out words phonetically. Reading a word in print for the first time was often a humbling experience. They were words that I wasn't exposed to, other than in print, so even though I didn't learn them through what was spoken about around me, I gained knowledge of them. In abandoning approaches of previous generations, rather than building on them, I'm not sure we're helping build skills to take on unknown situations.

Surely learning how nature exists and learning the foundations of basic skills can only help build confidence in approaching new challenges. It is interesting to think that we are going to go through life applying what we know to everything we encounter and not seek to know or experience anything beyond it. It seems rather ridiculous to think that if someone hasn't already identified something or told us about it, it doesn't exist. If we are encouraged to accept that there is more beyond what we currently recognize, then these basic skills are going to give us the confidence and experience to begin building conscious relationship to the unknown. Whether we sound things out, or feel our way through them, or develop a new viewpoint by allowing in another perspective, all of these approaches will reveal new possibilities that we didn't know existed before we explored them.

Now the school curriculum integrates the two approaches towards reading and the children's reading abilities are benefiting. Moreover, the combination of the two approaches to reading builds confidence to take on new tasks and investigate new approaches independently when faced with the unknown. When children use a word that they've read it is very humorous sometimes, but it shows initiative and courage to implement new things for others to experience from them, albeit in an unusual context sometimes. It seems to me that evolution depends upon people believing there is more beyond what we already know, and faith that with perseverance we will unveil it, even though it initially may appear out of context, knowing that *with practice* it becomes part of everyday experience.

Children ask so many questions when they are in the car. They want to know what the road signs say and when we will "get there". We tell them what the signs say and get them to count street lights as we answer the same questions over and over again. Then they begin to recognize and read the signs on their own. When they encounter the copy on computer game screens, directions for building Lego or recipe instructions, they build upon their "street sign" skills to decode the new text. It is only a matter of time before we start sharing how we figure out what words say, by sounding them out with them. They are motivated because they want to build or create something. They will walk through fire intellectually to learn these skills because they are focused on the successful outcome of their learning. Before we know it, they are independently reading books they choose themselves and beginning to write down some of their own ideas. It's very exciting to watch how adaptive and creative they become in leaps and bounds when skills are developed that bring meaning to their relationship with their outer world.

As adults, are we so different in choosing what skills to develop in ourselves? Once self realizes it can never be truly satisfied, we seek greater means to find fulfillment in our relationship to life. We begin to ask questions again. What surfaces through the awareness of our discomfort is an awareness of our own spiritual dimensions because we seek answers to further our understanding. We also become aware of the inherent spiritual dimensions in our partners, friends, co-workers, and children who have always been there and require fostering in new ways, beyond just reading the signposts that people currently acknowledge exist.

Compassion opens doors
and tests the boundaries of who we think we are,
bringing us to new levels of awareness.

⁃⁃⁃

Maybe it's time we gave up our idea of power as a conquering and owning phenomenon and embraced a power that liberates the love of humanity towards itself as a whole. There are many active bodies who are aligned with this thinking now, but without owning our passion as an unfolding process are we missing the experience of actualizing greater potentials for ourselves and others. I am often disheartened to realize that many are completely oblivious not only to our global community, but also to what they are oblivious to as they step out their own front door. The ability to take concepts and make connections with something that exists within their personal experience is avoided because it requires putting the heart and mind together. It's like leaving the public washroom with toilet paper trailing from your shoe, realizing it is there and then scraping your shoe along the sidewalk to get rid of it, hoping no one has witnessed your embarrassing experience. These are the people who can't be bothered to stoop down, pick it up and take care of it because in their eyes it's someone else's problem and they don't want to be associated with it. These things seem to happen at the most inappropriate times. Not unlike having toilet paper stuck to our shoe, the call to become responsible to spiritual ideals is never going to arrive at appropriate times, in appropriate places, and be witnessed by people we choose. It's easy to do what is right, but oh so difficult to do it if it requires stooping down to take care of things when we are concerned about how we may appear to others in that moment.

I see a parallel between the dynamics of our outer and inner worlds today. Within us, the duality, the shadow, the deep cavern of unknown territory that beckons us in, is the same as our perceptions about the devastating state of some of our global communities. We don't have to cross the ocean to see poverty. Poverty is on our doorstep. We do what we can, providing food and shelter and clothing as a band-aid but do little beyond this to make a significant difference. How are we supporting the less fortunate among us to build a foundation that supports their needs relative to ours? Are we basing our assumptions about their needs on our shared existing resources? Many of these people do not want to accept our food and shelter. There's a trust issue here, and possibly it is as simple as shedding our vanity about what we think exists among us. We believe we know better, and more, and we hand over what we think others need, and with every handful we give, we often take a piece of their dignity in return.

If we stop for a moment and listen to the internal dialogue and drop our assumptions about what our thoughts represent, is it possible that we will recognize the shadow side of our inner-dragon seeking our attention? If alienation, rejection, defeat, and hopelessness are what we insist on clinging to in our inner-world, are we missing the expression of our innocent passion that is needed in our outer-world? Emotional influences will have us become our greatest fear in order that we may transform it into harnessed fire! The fire of passion is transforming when it burns through the illusion of inadequacy and hopelessness and gives us knowledge of our wings that will take us to greater heights of consciousness. Giving others what we think they need is different from hearing with our hearts what they're telling us is needed by us all to cultivate differently. With an open heart we feel another as our soul. With this acceptance we are able to respond with compassion which brings integrity back to the fabric of our society. The dragon has wings which enable its power, and often in focusing on our position relative to the existing kingdom, we miss the true nature of the dragon to show us new potentials only we can invite in.

The Power of God is in us all, but we have to know it,
as surely as we know it took an actual father and a mother to conceive us.

❧   ❧   ❧

In a young child's wisdom when he was sick with a bad cold, crying and upset, he said to me, " My feet are too heavy to carry me through this world". I thought to myself, "I'm right there with you child!" But the following is where his sentiments about *the feeling so heavy* intuitively took me in resonating with his words:

When Jesus walked the earth, I imagine that he felt privileged. Not because he felt superior to every other man, but because he was humbled to know and accept that he was the Son of God. He knew that God was in him in the same way that we know our birth mother and father are in us. He knew he *was privileged* to live in full knowledge of this Truth. He lived in awareness that there were *Greater Other Dimensions* working through him. When he observed his fellow man, he recognized God in them too, but he was so humbled to walk in full knowledge that the grace of God had trusted him to live the reality of this truth. He did not see himself as a leader, but rather a *true follower* of this greater truth for others to come to know and experience in them. The message he lived, was for others to experience the grace of God through his presence on earth, until they recognized these *Greater Other Dimensions* in themselves.

Within Jesus himself, there must have been times, when all the odds were against him personally, that it felt like this truth was an incredible burden to carry. To keep his faith in tact when everyone around him was clinging to another way of being must have been overwhelming at times. He was an outcast. His knowing was in complete contradiction to the way in which the world was operating at that time, and yet he kept moving forward and openly sharing his love as he was guided by God to do. Amidst adversity, he continued to be faithful to what he knew in his heart to be the greater truth of humanity.

This child's grief and heaviness is from living in a world that has forgotten the true meaning of privilege. He did not know how to reconcile what he felt in his being with what was being demonstrated all around him. Privilege is traditionally associated with the idea of recognized stature based on material wealth and personal power. To reconcile the idea of privilege as our culture currently demonstrates it with the experience of *sacred privilege* is difficult if we have no recognizable or honored model to follow. Whether our children know how to express it verbally or not, they naturally act from it. It often appears as inappropriate behavior to us, but then, our behavior is often inappropriate to the expression of a free innocent being. Limited-self when it takes hold of us, pulls us into a personal experience, rather than integrating self with the innate knowledge of our transcended truth as beings. We can help our children to integrate what they already embody of their magnificence with a positive experience of self, by honoring the *privilege* of life itself. *By one's small self we can do nothing.* In accepting the grace of God, our self hands over the use of its eyes, ears, hands, voice and whole bodies, including its feet, to stand firmly on this earth, and *Be* the likeness of the GOD presence here, to the best of our ability. These *Greater Other Dimensions* are part of us, as people, as all the parts of self, learning about our *being* in manifest form. In surrendering our false ideas about privilege we are open to receive the truth about walking humbly with honor and integrity regardless of material security.

Without the integration between self and God, the meaning of privilege remains one dimensional and as long as we insist on clinging to one side of its expression, we miss the opportunity to embrace greater understanding when younger, less affected minds ask us to re-evaluate what we're doing. Do we walk with open arms for others to see what we carry in innocence, or do we clench our fists tightly to conceal what we believe others want to steal from us in our vanity? We may think that the clench-fisted is the privileged one with much to protect and miss the spiritual presence of the one with open arms. After all, we are conditioned to recognize when someone is protecting something of value. The one with open arms embodies privilege beyond what we can see as outward displays of wealth or prestige. It has everything to do with what we carry in our hearts and our knowledge and experience of life, as rich or poor, we become privileged in embodying this magnificent grace of God. In identifying solely with self, we may feel inadequate, and become resentful of those who appear to have more than we do. We abandon our own right to true privilege when we adopt limited-self's misguided idea of wealth. With our *Greater Other Dimensions* embraced, we may hold gold one day, and rice the next, for it is only in our hands for the time it serves its purpose to help us realize the potential of these *Greater Other Dimensions* in us. There is a greater purpose in serving humanity, not just our limited-self's identity with it.

There is great privilege and responsibility, in being a vessel for God's Grace in the many forms it takes. Self is no longer isolated or separate from anyone else when we hold the truth of this gold in our hearts openly. So, walking through life with our arms open wide in innocence, many things pass through them, each and every one of them carrying this grace in the experience of the everyday. The gold of consciousness cannot multiply if it is held tightly in our fists, concealed from others we fear might steal it from us. You can live in abundance and enjoy the experience of wealth without the fear of losing it. The very gold that is offered unconditionally paves the road for us all to knowingly take each step guided by God's grace.

Opening our minds through prayer or meditation, or simple intent, brings us back into awareness of *self in relation to God.* The illusion of self in relation to a fuller reality can only be seen when we are not entrenched in it. We need to see from a vantage point that goes beyond our own experience. With open arms we remember how to listen with our hearts and minds to greater existing dimensions because we begin to feel the presence of magnificence being liberated from within us and visible in others. When we embody spirit, self evolves, and carries the truth of this grace into the world. The only box that has the ability to contain us is our own fears of being revealed in our humanness, which is a self-imposed limitation.

I had a discussion with a woman in my office recently who was a healer. In spite of her healing abilities, she was suffering from serious heart problems. She told me about her work with people, her great faith in God, and how she opened herself and could see and feel energy to help alleviate the pain in others. We talked about how she cared for herself and I asked her if she ate organic food. She hesitantly confessed that no, she didn't, because she thought it was over-rated and she thought that the organic movement was one catering to the privileged, as it cost more and only people who were well off could afford it. This really interested me, and obviously surprised me, as I had never thought of it that way. I asked her how she came to this conclusion. She told me of a spiritual group of women she had joined which she felt acted as if they were somehow better than she as they had successful husbands and spent a great deal of time at home caring for their families. They had the time to shop in specialty stores and prepare more labor-intensive meals. The women in the group didn't have to *work*, as she put it, so she felt they couldn't relate to her or her situation. She had taken time off from her job, a job she hated, because of her health, but had yearned to be able to make a living doing her healing work. I asked her if, hypothetically, organic food cost the same as other food, what one would be supporting if one chose to buy organic. She admitted that she would prefer to eat organic as she was already taking a few prescription medications and the pesticides and preservatives from regular food was adding to the chemicals that the pharmaceuticals were putting in her body, but that it was a lot of work to cook and prepare food from scratch. Her exposure to organic food had been at the supermarket, and the women in this group talking about where they shopped. She perceived organic food as a fad and the fact that the women in her group were buying it allowed her to criticize them. She felt superior and inferior to them all at the same time.

I shared with her my experience in our community. There are an increasing number of independent farms that are committed to growing and selling organic food. When I've talked to these farmers at our local market and listened to their stories, I've learned how much patience and hard work these people have put into creating what they believe to be a worthy contribution for us all. They have forfeited the luxury of producing on a large scale to large distributors in lieu of *investing* in being steward's our earth, growing healthy and nutritious vegetables and raising healthy livestock. What was one farm at our local market has grown into five or six small farms producing organic food, and they are selling out Saturday mornings at our market. When I see what they are doing, and the passion and commitment they have to see it through despite what the bank may advise, I am further moved to support their efforts. Our community is but one example that this is becoming more visible.

I shared with her that many of the farmers are young University Graduates. Today, unlike ten years ago, it hasn't cost me a significant amount more to buy their produce, and what difference there is in price I know I am investing in the health of my family and even the health of the planet. When I buy their organic produce, I am investing in the healers of society. If it's a numbers equation, then it is bound to become profitable for them as more consumer dollars go to purchasing their goods. When we invest in a healthy lifestyle, we are less likely to have to spend later on illness. It seems like common sense to me that our economy will shift to produce what people want, so if it is trend that shifts people into doing more sustainable practices like buying organic produce, then the momentum shifts us a little faster. I don't think there are any supermarkets that don't carry some organic food now, but this was not the case five years ago. Organic food in our supermarkets is only marginally more expensive than other produce at this point in time here in Canada, and often there is no difference in cost when sold at the Farmer's Market on our main street each Saturday. From a spiritual standpoint, how we feel about the people who are supporting these efforts towards *healing* our planet and society is not the point. Doesn't everyone benefit from supporting our ecology and physical health?

Entering this dialogue with her illuminated how her own emotional response to the women in that group had colored her perceptions towards them as something separate she fought from becoming herself. She perceived their choices to be at home rearing children and managing their households as a privilege that she too deserved but wasn't afforded in following her own dreams. In not supporting the healers of our planet, be it those women, the farmers, or in her case hands-on healers, how was that reflecting her choice to support and nurture in herself what she told me was important for her? She saw these women as dependent on their husbands for their experience of independence, and this is her own unrecognized shadow being projected onto them. In not admitting to her own perceptions about being dependent on *another's approval* to follow her dreams she saw these women's circumstance as *wrong* and compromising to them. In projecting her own shadow onto others, she was further separated from experiencing her abilities as a healer beyond the hands-on healing that she currently identified with. If we become our dragon without realizing it, and mistake our shadow as our dragon to slay, we miss the potential left unrealized in owning and acting on our fire constructively because it is in our hands alone to do so. This fire is our passion for what we believe in. This fire we experience as anger is not against what we believe threatens us in others. This anger is a signal we have denied our self the experience of holding and learning to harness our unique expression of our souls passion for life.

We've all found ourselves here at one time or another, probably more than we care to admit. We stay committed to a truth about ourselves and others without realizing that our actions are in complete contradiction to what we claim we place faith in. We often miss the message of our discomfort because we have judged the messenger, rather than aligning with our magnificence to openly express our perceptions. We can't hear the message because we don't like the messenger. When we consciously choose to experience something in one way, we miss investing in making it our reality by acting in complete contradiction. We spend our time consumed in thought with what we don't like about our life, and continue to take actions that further invest in keeping it that way. When we are baffled by others who suggest that we create our experience of reality this is more than likely what we are unconsciously playing out. Our passion can become something positive for us to experience when we admit it is our self who is holding our dragon hostage in the dungeon, or banished from the kingdom to live in isolation. Humility is a powerful virtue to have the courage to implement. We yearn to experience a different reality for ourselves, be it our job or health, and yet we spend our energy trying to survive our current situation, instead of investing what we do have in the reality we choose to experience.

Privilege and abundance in spiritual terms
is opening one's heart to loving where we are.

⚬ ⚬ ⚬

I meet many people who are involved in spiritual pursuits. They often tell me how they wish they could quit their jobs and do something more spiritual in nature, like healing, or counseling, or mentoring, but can't financially afford to make the change. They claim there just aren't the jobs that pay what they are currently earning, to allow them to do what they want to do. My answer to this is to simply continue doing what you do, but begin doing it spiritually! When we awaken to our dragon and begin to experience our passion to change the way things are for others, we perceive ourselves as the only dragon in existence. We see our outer-world as one that we must enter independently, and we miss the infrastructure of interdependence that exists at this level of consciousness. Our inner and outer worlds are still perceived separately, and it is in this perception that we look for entry, rather than realizing we are already there on a level yet to be realized. Whatever job you currently have, be yourself and show up as who you are to be an inspiration for others to show up in the same way.

We all have a dragon, just as we all have a hero, a martyr, a victim and a queen and king, and many, many more identities. Everyone's instincts are to wait until things are set up and running smoothly, with proven viability before we are willing to choose the role we want to be relative to what exists. Investing in a new reality takes a lot of courage because our old expressions no longer define us or guarantee our security. Money, just like energy, comes and goes and flows with as much ease as the person working with it. Spirituality and materialism do not need to be on opposite ends of the pole. What you personally place value on becomes what you become aware of, so if your desire is to be more spiritually involved in life, then stop waiting for a place that already exists that you somehow will magically be given entry into and honored for your place. Start where you are, and begin *being* the spiritual person you choose to be in your fullest capacity. Accept that you already have been blessed with the innocence to live spiritually, and open the door right in front of you no matter what you believe exists on the other side.

The most fulfilling and unexpected spiritual experiences are on the other side of the doors that few recognize as spiritual in nature. So begin with energy, and if your pockets are empty, then give who you are with integrity to whatever you do. Buy what you need, not want, and support the needs of those producing commodities with spiritual consciousness and a conscience. Put consciousness into whatever your current *job* is, and bring your *conscience* to work with you. The possibilities emerge for it to become what you would like it to be when you bring your conscience and faith with you, because you change, and the very businesses that require consumer dollars to sustain them, will change too if they are to survive. How we do our work is a reflection of who we are, and there is great fulfillment in approaching life this way. The idea of the job disappears, and our participation in making it what we would like opens us to our creative energy. If we learn to realize the happiness in what already exists in our life, then it will soon reflect back to us all the inherent spiritual possibilities. Acceptance, growth, and change all naturally happen with ease, because we're living what is important to us and gives meaning to our lives.

We have conditioned ourselves to believe that hard work is what pays off, and we're really not up for the challenge of it. The concepts of *hard work* and *immediate gratification* have overshadowed our faith in *being and doing our best with what we have*. If what we have shows us no potential, then maybe our victim needs to hand over the *clump of clay* that we believe we hold, over to our magician who can mold it and help us explore its potential through us. If we don't practice making the most of what we have, how are we to handle our magnificence, or even recognize it when it first appears separate from us? Now that we have all become experts at being victims, even the bible's, "do unto others as you would have others do unto you", has us remembering all the times we have been done wrong, and giving ourselves an excuse as to why we shouldn't get involved or extend ourselves unconditionally to help another. Without consciousness, we let other's opinions of us determine are worth. Only you can determine if you have really put your true self into something, and somehow another's opinion isn't as important as the feeling you have inside that you've done what you know to be the right thing in your heart, even though it felt hard to push past your fears and self-doubts. As adults, we may become true advocates for our children's innocence, when we realize we have the ability to hold and own our own again. You more than likely will surprise yourself with how much you got out of allowing yourself the process of growing, when your expectations were not focused on the acknowledgement it would bring you. You might just begin to realize the beginnings of your true magnificence taking form. Without innocence, we want everything to arrive neatly packaged and identified before we are willing to hold it or entertain the idea of making something with it.

When we always hold back that little bit rather than take that extra time to really do what we feel is our best, we hear the voice inside that urges us with, " Ah, that's good enough!" or "It won't make any difference so I'm not wasting anymore time on this". We can all do with less stuff, and more of that feeling that fills us in a way that no other can do for you. Monetary or otherwise, abundance as energy carries a generosity that helps fuel giving more, and focusing less on the engrained *what's in it for me* mentality. In aligning with abundance, our personal reserves step out of the way and we channel in the boundless reserves of the universe. If we can bring integrity back to our internal relationship with heart energy, then outward relationships will support a shared abundance, not compromises made that serve only to safeguard our interests. There will still be those who exhibit the material signs of privilege and those who are slave to it, but by walking in step with our soulful dreams and ideals, we become examples for others to follow. They follow *not us*, but rather the hope and faith we demonstrate in human nature. Materialistically we can be identified as privileged and abundant, but if spiritually we are impoverished, then there is great loneliness and paranoia that keeps us imprisoned in our perceived reality. What good is experience without a community of others to share with us an abundance that enriches our faith in trust and love?

With Liberation, the outer world no longer defines us,
instead our inner world opens us to accept who we are
beyond the current identity of self.

To break free of our conditioned ideas we must lose our emotional attachments to them. Even more importantly, we must nurture our physical capacity to allow in abundant energy to transform us. Free flowing emotions are the very nature of spiritual energy, and our physical bodies need to be functioning efficiently if we are to support this process. Where our focus was once on keeping pace with the frenetic world around us, we become attuned to a deeper sense of rhythm that brings life through us. Just like bringing awareness to our breath, we develop our ability to feel life as a presence we allow into ourselves. Have you ever noticed after a good cry, you see things more clearly and your part in them. The weight of the heavy heart bearing down on us in times of distress, once released, gives your heart space to receive clarity for your own part in choosing to be separate from a greater experience.

Facing spiritual or material bankruptcy brings us ultimately to face the biggest void of all, the lack of development and faith in our internal resources. We forget to breathe deeply; we forget to feel ourselves open to hear inner guidance, which will gently lift the veil of the illusion that tells us we are alone. In placing our focus on everything outside ourselves that is validating us, we miss what has been calling from within us to develop in awareness of ourselves. As the backlog of unheard, unrecognized self within us reaches that critical threshold where the polarities of who we have become, and what we have chosen to be, come crashing together, we find ourselves caught in the undertow of our own wave. Part of us, rooted deeply in our subconscious, can go no further without inflicting extreme discomfort in its fight to survive in its current state. It is yearning to be integrated with our current conscious choices, but because of the confrontation within, our masculine energy is engaged and we won't give in and listed to the feminine within that can birth freedom. It's akin to the experience of drowning. In our unrecognized fear, gasping for air, we struggle and miss utilizing *our ability* to be supported by the breath within us. We become so attached to the belief that we will be swallowed up by the sea of life's circumstances that we continue to fight and struggle. We thrash about in hopes of being recognized by the ripples we send out to all those around us, forgetting that *we have the ability to float.* We remain oblivious to our ability to float and stay committed to sinking to the depths of life's sea where we remain attached to the reality of our suffering.

Instead of embracing the power of *Greater Other Dimensions* to support us, we see it as an act of weakness and in contradiction to claiming our personal power. Others see that we are gasping for air in panic, but they don't know how to affect a rescue without being pulled under with us. Few are able to summon the strength or courage to see past the illusion while caught in the throws of such waves. There is such strength and conviction on our part in this place, but it is complete contradiction to the trusting nature of our true being. We have to know the strength of our own being, and self's innocence, through developing faith in it, before we can support someone without jumping into their illusion, as they delve deeply within themselves to resurrect their own innate power. It takes placing faith in something greater than our small-self alone, to trust and know how to be, when confronted with the fear of the unknown in ourselves and others.

We naturally float, but we have to allow trust to enter the picture so we will not disappear into the depths of despair when we find ourselves there. We willingly have to enter the unknown, because we consciously decide not to fight what we believe to be the truth of our position anymore. God enters in that moment of surrender, and we become a listener to a new voice that can lead us, as self chooses to hear a greater guidance that we're being asked to follow. To be swallowed up, never to be heard, is the illusion of the feminine energy within us when it does not recognize its inherent strength to embody truth in all its power. The masculine within us, that wants to be honored in its ability to assert its position and be right, must not be threatened if the feminine is to emerge and blossom. Our perception that self is drowning makes us struggle to stay afloat and separate from our ability to surrender to our true innocent and trusting nature.

We must go through the struggle to get to the other side where the true self waits. The "dark night of the soul" is the prerequisite for the birth of a radiant light within us. Not knowing what is beyond the darkness, we resist its pull. We avoid accepting this perceived gloom by occupying ourselves with endless *business* in an effort to avoid disappearing into the depths of our own dreaded despair. We set goals for ourselves in our attempts to realign with our chosen roles. But the goals are based on what we believe we need to accomplish, not necessarily on an acceptance of who we are, or what already exists that reflects our true light all around us. To trade what we believe to be power based on our position relative to others, for a power relative to something self won't acknowledge, creates incredible conflict within us. We are completely blind and deaf to anything beyond our identity with the shadow-dragon in this place of despair.

Accomplishments bring acknowledgement, praise, respect, and admiration from others. This is the masculine energy validating itself. *Being* who we are brings fulfillment we recognize within ourselves, and with it comes an appreciation for others, because we don't see our separateness anymore. This is the power of the feminine integrated with the masculine.

If we stop for one moment and listen to this inner dialogue of self-loathing, we realize that it's not who we choose to be anymore. It's like walking into a crowded room where many people are talking and we can't relate to anything they are saying. We are sure we have missed something. Worse than that, in that moment of isolation is the paralyzing fear of being exposed in our confusion and hopelessness. Everyone else seems to know what they're doing. In this place of alienation, our greatest fear is in stepping towards a new beginning for ourselves and leaving our old identity with self behind. Our fear of being abandoned is what keeps us from discovering the truth that lies in the depths of that dark hole. This is the void within us that yearns to be recognized as belonging in the light. As the sun rises higher in the sky, our shadow diminishes. We seldom stop to think about the signposts that nature shows us daily as road maps to recognizing and knowing the process of realizing self.

No matter what continent we stand on, the sun rises and sets, and our shadow rises and diminishes in a continuous cycle. Have you ever noticed that no matter where you stand on one side of a body of water, ocean, lake, or pond, or a puddle for that matter, there is a straight line of reflection coming from the sun and moon directly to your feet? The person standing beside you sees the same thing, although they occupy a different place with a unique perspective. A person facing you sees their shadow at that same time of day. Your shadow may be behind you, unrecognized or overlooked for the most part, but that path of light is directly in front in plain view at that moment. It is always in a direct line to our feet no matter where we stand in relation to it. If we switch places with the person facing us, we turn our back to the sun or light source, and we will recognize our own shadow in that moment as we face them in their position of light. They both always exist; for our shadow is merely the parts in ourselves we have yet to realize. As students, we can appreciate the learning this offers us, but as teachers, it can be a menace to deal with if it challenges us to change our chosen position relative to another so our light is what we share with them.

In our life, when we get turned around unexpectedly, we are stripped of the identity of who we believe we are, and there is a sense of loss of what we mistakenly adopted as our identity. We naturally have an emotional response to being disoriented, and it is usually grief, or anger or just general confusion. In accepting our feelings as valid for us to feel, they are acknowledged and then they disperse because they have served their purpose. As soon as the emotions clear, the illusion of what we believed was underlying them is exposed. We begin to realize that we have ventured outside of the accepted mode of operating, and expanded our awareness of self. It is completely sobering to open our eyes to see past the illusion of what we believed to be real in our life. But having arrived here, and having accepted it, there is light brought into it by those who face us. Once we adjust, we will slowly be able to see what really exists beyond our fear of it. Without accepting self, it is very difficult to get beyond its limits to embrace a greater part of ourselves, where we accept the love of God's reflection in another to illuminate our own humanness.

As a global community, we are in the throes of a struggle that is not unlike "the dark night of the soul" on an individual level. We are in between what currently exists and what could be. Misunderstanding and conflict exist on so many levels and in so many arenas. There are political liberals and political conservatives, religious zealots and religious conservatives, Western Medicine and Eastern Medicine, Capitalists and Socialists, and the list goes on. We will destroy ourselves or we will accept who we have become in order to move beyond the status quo into a broader view of who we have the choice to be. The struggles exist because neither side will move toward the other. Just like our experience on an individual level, there is a strong resistance to change. Underlying the resistance, of course, is fear. The level of tension between these opposing forces is high and ready to snap, it seems. Until we begin to accept, not agree, but accept one another for what we are, there will be no resolution.

Initially, what appears to be in opposition to our own perceptions turns out to be another expression of the same underlying values we hold in our own hearts. We can't move beyond this duality unless we accept that there is more than our personal perception of things. In our anger we see nothing but what we have to protect and we cling to being right even though it doesn't make sense anymore. We see only what we have to lose and we cling to the familiarity of our lives even though it is painful. We would rather suffer than admit that changing our minds might be good for us.

When we can look at our children, our spouses, our homes, our occupations, and contributions, and see ourselves in relation to them, we are moving towards acceptance of what we currently are. There may be great love and gratitude within each of these relationships, but do we feel separate from really enjoying the experience they offer us, and the potential of what we can authentically bring of ourselves to the relationship? Do we actually embrace what they are here to teach us about ourselves? We may be very busy, and have many responsibilities and duties to fulfill each day, but is there a loneliness that creeps in when we are alone? Have these relationships become our reference to measure our worth, or the significance of our contribution? When we rest our heads on our pillows each night, is there peace, or is there white noise in our minds that reminds us of a dinner party where everyone is talking but we can't understand what's being said?

Accepting what is, is not the same as becoming complacent with it. Accepting what is requires *learning* to hear again, and reassessing whether we take a step towards further understanding or head in another direction with our thinking. There is always one student during my workshops who corrects me when I say that we are learning. They are quite correct when they remind me that we don't learn anything but rather *remember*, as creation already exists, and at some level of consciousness there is knowledge of it. I can relate to what they say with my intellect, but in all honesty, only about the things I have already realized because once becoming aware of them I see how they have been there all along without my acknowledging them. The more I realize the more I also realize I have *not* realized. Curiosity keeps me open to actualize more, and this feels like learning to me. In every moment there is always something that I feel, but can't yet identify or see in its entirety, and it is with the *perception of learning* that I am taken to a greater depth of perception, not remembering. It seems the further I go with my awareness, the more I realize I don't know, as the depths of our reality seem infinite. Possibly, as a soul, it is all remembering as time does not exist at that dimension of our reality. But for me, operating in this realm as self, learning about myself, it is hard to take ownership beyond being anything but a student relative to something that vast.

When we are engaged in the tension between the polarities, it is difficult to be a listener and an admitted learner, because we are moved to want to express the validity of our position. Becoming a listener who is open to learning takes the threat out of what we don't want to hear because we are not defending our current knowledge. We can inadvertently put all our energy into keeping the discomfort of something we believe to be in opposition to us at bay, when in becoming curious about what it is, beyond our assumptions, we open the doors to see more clearly what is being shown to us, and move beyond our own limitations. As the diversity in cultures and beliefs approaches a middle ground between the polarities, there is more friction, more resistance, and more defensiveness. The two opposite sides begin to broach the critical line of dissolution. The desire to hold on to what we do know keeps the tension alive with others, but more importantly, inside us.

This apparent outward expression of others' resistance is merely reflecting back to us our own unrecognized internal struggle. As awareness increases, and our ability to be conscious of what we are experiencing internally, the duality within us reaches a critical point. Like a pressure boiler, its expression can no longer be contained. The outward expressions we recognize as *conflict* are merely a reflection of the fight that is ultimately within. In our resistance, we believe that we are not understood, accepted, appreciated, or valued for our individual contributions. It feels like a personal slight when we meet opposition, and these unrecognized perceptions unknowingly fuel great resentment from us. Before we know it, we are unintentionally expressing our discontent towards everything and everyone outside of ourselves. We become the relentless complainers and grumblers in society. To look within is the last place we expect to find the source of our discontent, let alone the solution.

Throughout history, the artist has demonstrated this struggle through great works of art by embracing the creative energy of liberation. Before its emergence though, there is great grief. There is deep, dark loathing for one's current existence. We become very attached to our suffering, not because we desire pain, but because we unknowingly create it in our resistance to be liberated to greater awareness. Change and internal exposure is a threatening venture, and rarely do we associate it with the act of liberation. Yet, it is in these very depths of realization, that we open ourselves to stepping beyond what most are currently able to perceive. That deep dark hole is an incredible portal to dimensions of our being that we have yet to realize. It is symbolic of how we are birthed into this physical dimension as infants, but because it exists on the spiritual level, it reaches far beyond the physical, and envelops consciously entering into the realm of imagination. Liberation of self takes great courage, because it turns our insides outward for the world to see, and possibly pass judgment upon. There is great sense of responsibility that comes with liberation, not to mention the fear of what emerges from within us that appears to be in opposition to what is acknowledged, endorsed, and accepted, as a valid or worthy expression by society. With the truth of liberation, no longer are we at the mercy of everything that exists outside of our control, and things outside of us being able to define who we are, for we have found the core within that assures us of our faith and trust in a grace beyond self.

There is a power with liberation,
that emerges as a presence greater than self.
This shift in our perceptions opens us to reassess
with clarity just who we are.

≈ ≈ ≈

The self-important bubble bursts, and we are left with the initial reality that we are nothing. This experience is sobering, and within us there is complete quiet. The noise of the crowd that has been consuming our minds is silent. There's no applause, no emotion. All that remains is complete stillness. It is as if we have entered a new world in which there is no point of reference that can tell us who we are that seems rational. We don't actually know anything here but there is a distinct absence of fear in the nothingness. Then we realize we are still breathing, we are indeed feeling, but in a sensorial, surreal way, and at complete peace with our surroundings. The seemingly complete isolation that we were resisting, once accepted, leads us directly to its polarity, complete peace and connectedness with everything. Our own walls have vanished and we instantly cross the threshold that keeps these polarities separate and in place for us. This transition, referred to "as a door into another reality" by others throughout history, can also be experienced as a rebirth. It's as if we are given a clean slate, but with a repertoire of memories that give us substance, and backing to venture forward trusting we are able to experience, forgive, and grow even more, because we are returned to our innocence. This symbolic journey through the threshold of our minds allows us to realize that any obstacles we once perceived were merely within us. This new territory we find ourselves experiencing is beyond separate self in the realm of the *Greater Other Dimensions* of our being, where we are one with all.

Right now, as consciousness is reaching this threshold in large numbers, our own intellect is desperately trying to hold on. We will be carried across this threshold kicking and screaming, terrified of losing what has kept our personal world together for us thus far. We fear that all our hard work, our accomplishments and creature comforts are inextricably linked to who we are. The illusion, of course, that we all resist dispelling is that these very markers of identity may dismantle completely if we let go of what we currently are, and what we believe to be our shared reality. Crossing the threshold would not feel as liberating as it does, if it weren't for the accompanying destruction of this illusion. These things with which we identify ourselves are not what bind us. Rather it is our perception of their value that imprisons us. It is these perceptions that we resist letting go of, as the fear of the unknown seems far more threatening than anything we believe to be the truth.

Most of us have more than what we need for our physical survival. But emotionally and spiritually we are sorely lacking. We are tormented by the intellectual framework through which we identify, judge, and experience ourselves. Once we pass over this threshold, self dissolves from its current state to re-emerge as a broader, more expansive expression of who we are. We are not really leaving self behind, but rather embracing a fuller experience of an existing reality that self needs to accept. Self doesn't disappear, or get squashed, or beaten into submission… it evolves into a fuller expression of who we ALREADY are as a soul! This unraveling of our identity is what makes us grow as conscious human beings. Self has to go through that symbolic door of transformation in order to free itself from its current belief in its power over us. But evolution as a theory is much more palatable than trying to go through it as a mental exercise of relinquishing our current position to expand where self is not in complete control anymore. The process of unraveling is disorienting, and fuels our desire to find a new way to fit into our life, as it exists for us. Self, as it is now, wants to remain in control, and it is painful and demoralizing to hand over our perceived personal authority for the idea of GOD, or *Greater Other Dimensions* of our being taking the helm.

We need to stop for a moment, and become listeners again, to just hear the part of self driving us from within. If we keep bulldozing our way forward, attempting to forge new territory for ourselves, we miss the opportunity to truly expand and deepen our personal experience in our existing homeland. It takes faith and courage to move past the discomfort of who we believe we are, to awaken to our truth. After all, the existing authority of self, does not like the threat of challenge, being unraveled or being dismissed!

Chapter 10

Finding Grace in Growing Wings

Self, facing a world of uncertainty and discord,
follows its own lead,
and becomes further isolated from its true purpose to
show us who we are as a shared humanity.

Our actions can reflect our inability to do what is best for everyone, in an attempt to stay on track with what we feel we are justified in receiving for ourselves. We often aren't even aware that achieving our personal goals is at the expense of another's wellbeing until we reach our goal and find ourselves rejoicing alone. Who's kidding who? As adults we know at some level when we're doing this, but we often don't consider the consequences of our actions except in relation to ourselves. We see this same behavior in children. As adults, our role if we choose to accept it, is to help our children make connections beyond self's perspective to include the needs of others as well. This is a difficult task if a child's interests are perceived as being in competition with our own. From the time they begin school, we juggle to fit them into our routines. Years later, when they become adults, one wonders how daily life for many still focuses on *what's in it for me?* We'd like to think we have moved beyond this, but apparently we are very influenced by this one-dimensional thinking. Advertising and marketing counts on this ingrained vanity. Our competitive natures are encouraged when our livelihood is influenced by the bigger wheels of commerce and by what are led to believe is important to us. The need for external authority thrives on the fact that individual's are unable to exercise a deeper acknowledgment of an authority that is beyond the personal agenda of self. We continue to speed along in our cars unaware of the effect our actions are having on others because we are so focused on where we are going. Out of unrecognized arrogance we ignore the speed limit.

We have inadvertently turned off our *conscience* because it slows us down in obtaining our goals. Our vanity is not an outward strutting of our power as much as a completely unrecognized ability to take into account anything aside from our own personal agenda. Those of us who see our children off in the morning and wave goodbye as they ride away in the school bus, hope others on the road will take care so our children will be safe. As parents, we count on others having a conscience when driving. But when we are behind schedule, the same concerns about who else shares the road don't occur to us.

We live in a goal-oriented society. How our actions affect others moment to moment is of little consequence to most, as it is through the achievement of self alone, that we seek security, recognition, and acknowledgement. We become careless, through being unconscious of anything beyond our own immediate focus. Until we realize something important to us is involved, we probably won't stop to become conscious of the actual journey we're on. Moving from careless to careful requires acknowledging our relatedness to life beyond just the perspective of self. We all have moments where we don't realize others are affected by what we think and do. Unfortunately, it isn't until tragedy hits us personally, or something of value to us is affected, that we come to appreciate the value of awareness. As a child, when a toy gets broken, or we fall and hurt ourselves, we develop awareness of our actions because emotionally and physically we feel the pain of the experience. If our feelings are frozen from being experienced as adults, our conscience seems to get frozen right along with them. Self chooses to remain in control as it is, and prove itself to be beyond the authority of anything outside itself. We feel quite justified and will do what we need to do to maintain the illusion that we are the ultimate authority- until someone who is innocent is hurt and we cannot deceive ourselves any longer. When we are forced to slow down to hear what's actually driving us, we are shocked that we were so blind and ignorant that we failed to have taken into account those who are innocent and trusting and rely on us to be conscientious *with them.*

It is in our most humble moments when we
realize we actually know nothing.
We are forced to admit that we need help.
This is how grace finds its way into our heart.
In this new state of mind, we experience revelations.

My own limits are constantly being pushed to expand as our children expand into their own sense of self, developing their own likes and dislikes and challenging what previously existed as the known and accepted for them. Without realizing it, I often place boundaries that keep my world intact, rather than from a place of nurturing our children's development. I find it difficult to remain flexible when their individual needs are so different from one another because their stages of development range from age seven to eighteen. I've been plunked into the many expressions that the role of authority and role of mother have exposed in so many different ways, in my own world. There are many times that we aren't functioning as one family unit. Instead, we are in what appears to be complete opposition. There might as well be a railroad track running through our kitchen at times, judging by the sound we all make getting our point of view across to each other. On one particular evening I reached my limit. On one side was me, preparing dinner after getting home from work. On the other side, was the authority supreme, outwardly demanding what and how he wished me to serve him dinner. There he sat on his throne, informing me that I don't know anything and that he, knows everything. There was nothing subtle in his proclamation of my ignorance. In fact, he suggested that I read more non-fiction books so that I too may know the things he does. He wasn't telling me this in anger. His delivery was eloquent and matter-of-fact. He was the observer, perched at the counter, overseeing my frantic attempt to fix an evening meal.

This voice of authority belonged to my six-year-old son! My eldest was seventeen at the time, and I don't remember her pushing my buttons about what I knew, or my position of authority as her mother. She was my first-born and I was figuring things out as I went. I didn't actually know very much about being a mom, and in hindsight, at thirty, I was definitely more flexible and receptive to what she was showing me. Everyone seemed to be an authority to me during this time, and it was getting the best of me by the end of the day, arriving home to a different pace and the varying needs of our kids greeting me at the door each day. At six, my son was operating secure in his magnificence. As his mother, I am grateful that this image of himself had not been dampened, but as a child who knows no limits to his magnificence there is much he had yet to experience that would help him see that he too is a student of life, and not an authority. I can appreciate his exuberance when dealing with a household of siblings and parents who are busy and sometimes don't have the patience to listen to his jokes and urgent questions about everything that's going on for him. I did recognize that this perception of his believing he was the authority over me, belonged to me alone, but it got me thinking. Through my eyes, while making dinner, I was mulling over the idea of authority as a difficult concept for young people to grasp.

Maybe I should mention that authority has been a recurring theme throughout my entire life, and it is through my personal relationships that it has been loudest. It just seems to keep coming around in different disguises and just when I think I am beginning to understand, it rears its head in another more subtle form. The well runs deep with this authority theme in me, and it seems to permeate the places I least expect to find it. My youngest son is just the latest expression to reveal itself to me, so I am more than willing to admit it is my thing, not his. When I step out of my shoes as mother, I face the fact that I am the one who has a problem relinquishing my position of authority. It stings a little to face the realization that these perceptions are self-inflicted. Integrating the higher truths of what we are in our magnificence, with the potential that as humans we have weaknesses that leave room for growth is not really an easy bridge to cross no matter how old we are.

The rearing up of the part of self that believes it to be the authority is often not recognized by us because we often fail to really hear where it is coming from. When we hear the judgment arise from within us in opposition to another's position in relation to us, we aren't listening to ourselves or them anymore. We're listening to the *judgment* and not really hearing what they're really responding to *in us*. We miss the higher more evolved authority within us that could take us past these parts of self to where we can hear objectively another's truth. Instead, we hear how another is not honoring our position as one of knowledge and experience relative to them. My son is magnificent always, but he too is learning the art of negotiating with a world which sometimes opposes his idea of self.

That sense of magnificence in young people is not going to be easily relinquished, nor should it be, in order for the world to evolve and become aligned with this higher truth of our being. The sense of authority we adopt with experience is not going to be easily relinquished either, but maybe it should become more flexible in order for our world to evolve and become aligned with the magnificence at the core of us all. Self grows from experience, and our inner magnificence, the God within, often gets forgotten when we buy into our experienced inadequacies as we learn. Those hard knocks in life color our perceptions, and maybe it is these buried wounds that we secretly seek to have another honor so we can justify holding onto them. The pain of who we have become that we can't reconcile, gets put onto someone else in hopes of justifying our own burden, or possibly it is just to ease our feeling of isolation with it.

Our children, in their naiveté, are our teachers if we allow them to be. The railroad tracks that run through our relationships, separating the positions of self, are but an illusion we make real for them by continuing to demonstrate it with them. Children openly express their resistance to adopting a limited sense of self, that we are unknowingly impressing on them through our reaction to their innocent observations. They aren't always kindly expressed as innocent observations. Instead they are delivered as outright demands to get our attention. Children have not yet accumulated the baggage that, as adults, we believe define us and give us the right to keep our current position. At six, they are still actively engaged with the sensorial experience of this world. The music, the poetry, the beauty of the light and color of life and patterns of synchronicity that life is continuously expressing in its ability to adapt, flow, and keep balance, remains amazing always to the child in us all, through imagination. On the other end of the spectrum, the grief, the anger, the resentment, and the frustration within us, is also what the child picks up on and responds to. These wonderful sensory perceptions are not limited to the experience of our children, but most adults have forgotten how to engage with life in this way. Life is absolutely captivating and magical if we see it for what it is, beyond our conditioned perceptions. The boundlessness of children's perceptions is multi-dimensional, so when we restrict their behavior, they see us as limited in our appreciation of their carefree expressions. In the experience of division, we may not only learn about our own shadow from our children, but exercise honor and appreciation for a greater authority that is liberating for both beyond the boundaries of our roles with them.

Self, with age, I have come to realize, gets set in its ways. Self gets defensive and grumpy and doesn't like to be challenged to expand, especially when time becomes such a critical factor. Self unrecognized really doesn't like to be questioned, because it is standing on very unstable ground. In the face of my *mother-self* being challenged over making dinner, I offered to give up my position in the kitchen and hand over my personal authority, as self perceived it, to a greater authority within me. It wasn't easy coming to this decision, because in my own head I had the voice of the mother trying to get dinner ready on time after a day at the office! This voice could belong to every mother, after arriving home from work to face the diverse needs, or more to the point, outward demands of her family, without cooperation or help being offered. Once I accepted that I had to change my perception from one of opposition to one of hearing, I found a solution to the standoff. I must admit, it was preceded by an initial reaction inside me of wanting to throw in the towel, and walk away while proclaiming, " If you know so much, do it yourself!" Fortunately, I didn't really want to become that destructive force that I would regret later. So I bit my tongue, and sighed, then listened and accepted this first reaction that reared up from within me, and soon recognized, hey, hold on just a minute, *I'm not the child here!* As a mother, it wouldn't be safe to hand over the responsibility of cooking to a six year old who has no fears and no experience with a gas stove. My initial reaction quickly dissolved into an, "O.k. How about getting off that chair and come help me put something together that you might like as well?" *Time* isn't part of a six year olds equation, but he certainly had ideas! I had to let go of my *idea of time*, and open myself to receive his ideas.

I really needed to embrace that there was another way to see my position in relation to him in that moment. The mother, as authority, needed to step aside. I listened to his ideas and then we looked in the fridge to see how the food we had could be used to create them. I decided to cooperate and allow him the experience of putting together dinner for the family and what transpired became a family event. My ability as Mother to educate, along with my ability to provide a safe environment, could make plenty of room for him to experience the role of cooking for himself. He was quite capable of learning for himself what he needed to know through the experience, and an introduction from me, to the tools we had to work with. He climbed off his throne of authority. I shed my position of assumed authority, and between the two of us we actually attracted the others to join in and put together a good dinner that we all liked and enjoyed preparing together. Dinner was late of course, very late actually, but it was timely in that everyone was part of it in his or her own unique way. The idea of raw food has become increasingly more appealing to the whole family as a result. That extra time invested in relinquishing authority shifted us all out of our roles and into a shared experience that the magnificence within us all found constructive expression. The initial effort which, at the time, felt like the last thing I wanted to take on that evening, has proven to be a great time saver in the long run.

Dinner isn't a source of opposition very often anymore, and when the potential arises that it could be, I'm not the only one able to problem solve without creating discord. How I see this, and the others involved, is through what I know, through my own life experiences. Our children see the part they are ready to take on, and we often miss, the positive impressions we can make on each other when we fail to look at the larger picture of what's being demonstrated. Time and space can create great conflict when we allow them to define who we are in any moment. My youngest son, learning about himself and his abilities, is at an important stage right now. For me, on a different level, recognizing when a part of self is engaged, and learning to get out of the way of my own prejudices, so I can expand my own capabilities, is an important stage right now. I've earned his respect from being open to hear what he is saying, not how an unrecognized part of me is hearing him.

Manners are entering the picture now because he is learning better to express what he means from a place of appreciation. When he says *thank you*, he sincerely means it. It is not a learned and automatic response that is expected of him in order to be in my good graces. The throne he once occupied in my eyes, has transformed into an ordinary bar chair at the end of the kitchen island again, and the voice emanating from it loud and clear, I love and appreciate more each day, as truly magnificent.

Opposition brings resistance.
Acceptance opens the door to rapport.
With rapport comes cooperation.
We discover things we didn't know existed before
through openly shared experiences.

꜁ꜚ   ꜁ꜚ   ꜁ꜚ

We often have the most enlightening experiences from the people and places we least expect. In setting our focus on obtaining clarity, we also filter out all the things that are showing us what we seek because we have ideas about where we will find it. In consciously placing intent to seek resolution about a current dilemma, or struggle we're experiencing, we miss all the ways clarity is being offered to us. By remaining set on how we are prepared to receive what we've asked for, we miss its existence being already within our grasp. It can be delivered in many forms, not just the one we had our mind set on. Seeing ourselves, and where we have unconsciously placed these limitations, it becomes apparent in the resistance we experience with the people closest to us in our life. We are around them most, and don't realize that we have set responses, and unrecognized assumptions worked out with them unconsciously.

Moving beyond our experience of resistance with others requires us to really listen to them and to hear within ourselves what part of us is responding to them. This unconscious self filters how and what we hear from them as long as it is engaged and we aren't aware of it. The experience of cooperation helps mold our own relationship to knowledge because we accept we are going to learn something *with* them. It brings acknowledgement of our own authority into perspective when we integrate what another has to show us about our resistance with expanding our self to include a broader perspective. Whether we choose to cooperate with others in relationship to us, or develop cooperation with the parts of self that are engaged in us doesn't matter as they both serve to move us past our resistance towards a common understanding we hold in our hearts about how we choose to experience a common passion. Not everyone in relationship with us is always willing to enter such a process, so sometimes we have to bring awareness to it all on our own. But help is never far away as long as we ask for it. Others benefit also when we take these leaps of faith to ask for help; be it a prayer, a friend, or our invitation to be illuminated from the unseen dimensions of life.

When someone confident, creative and irresistible appears,
We are tempted to find and expose a flaw in an attempt
to hide our own feelings of intimidation.
If only we realized that we are being prompted to
step up to the plate to be who we are,
big right along with them in our ability to shine
brightly in our own unique way.

❧ ❧ ❧

Self integrates with who we really are when it is given room to stretch and expand itself beyond our adopted positions of authority. Of course, there is always the option to unknowingly engage our will power to hold a chosen position in relation to everyone and everything around us so we remain in control and off the hook for taking any responsibility for how they experience us. The voice of "How dare you challenge my authority!" can easily take over within us without our realizing it. Often, as parents, this voice does not belong to the adult in us, but rather our own unrecognized child that never got expression in the face of absolute authority growing up. In that moment, the polarities are strengthened in us, and we look for alliances! These alliances take the form of yet other parts of self that have a vested interest in keeping things just as they are. The *victim-self* would have loved for me to throw in the towel when challenged with making dinner because it would have summoned up memories of all the times in my life when I was not appreciated, respected or valued for my contributions. Don't we all have a list of those hanging in the back of our minds, just waiting to leap out for some exercise? What we don't have in our own experience, we have many examples that others have experienced and imprinted on us throughout history, and we wear them like our own. It becomes a lonely place when we engage the voice of despair. It's got a charge that draws others into our illusion of hopelessness, but the experience of it is like sinking in mud, soggy and draining of any will to get unstuck. We completely justify holding our position, through the reassurance we attract in others that draws them into recognizing our isolation. We feel further isolated from our magnificence, rather than encouraged to seek it, by what we engage in others in response to us. It is a roadmap full of dead ends. We want a route that offers the experience of hope and passion for life; and we know this at some level, but just can't bring ourselves to listen inwardly. If you have a strong will like I do, then chances are you plummet, until you are exhausted, or have exhausted all available avenues that justify your position. The long way or the short way leads us to face the same experience, loneliness, and defeat. With our will power exhausted in keeping this illusion alive within us, we're just too tired to defend it any longer. That deep, dark hole pulls us in…because we feel powerless to stop it.

I can't tell you how often that's where I've gone, and even though I know where it leads, I fight it to the end, every time. As with any perceived ending, there is its polarity, ready and waiting to be embraced, a new beginning, *if we allow it.* With acceptance, thought dissolves, and in its place we engage our sensory perception. That same nothingness becomes everything. That pause before the dawn of *everything* appears, feels like eternity though, because we are suspended outside how we have defined ourselves in relation to time and space. In that moment of true surrender we are opened to a greater other dimension in which we become one with all, the GOD of our being. We have to accept existing self as it is, as much as we are upset with ourselves, in order to enter this other dimension that exists within us that knows a greater truth about us. It's always there, but reaching it requires relinquishing how we are set on seeing ourselves, and we won't recognize it, if we won't stop to hear it out inside ourselves, before reclaiming who we really are relative to it.

This inner dialogue usually revolves around believing we are right, or misunderstood, because we are hurting. Most of us experience great physical pain, emotional, or mental anguish before we are willing to explore the seemingly impossible to overcome self. Our resistance, relinquishing our will to be in control of our destiny, our right to choose our experiences, and mostly our instincts to be right, all must be given acceptance before they soften their hold on us, enough to reveal the threshold we must pass through. We don't recognize our shadow self, or know how to relate to it, because we have somewhere along the line developed disdain for this expression of self, as we have experienced it in another that had great influence on us. We resist, and resent it, without really knowing it for what it is in its entirety. If we are able to just stop and listen to what we don't want to hear in ourselves, its power is placed in the context of who we really are. Just as a six-year-old can appear demanding and righteous about what they know one minute, and through hearing them, beyond our own limited child-self, they become the most innocent and open children in our eyes the next minute. By opening ourselves to get past their being a threat to our position, we too have the ability to relinquish our assumed authority to embrace our own innate magnificence in relating to them. It was a full year later when I heard where my son got the idea about reading more nonfiction books. One of the teachers mentioned to me about how they have increased boys' reading abilities by encouraging them to read more non-fiction books to capture their interest. The connection between nonfiction books and his trying to capture my interest in his preferences for dinner had completely baffled me before I heard this.

Self is part of us, but difficult to embrace and accept as it is, in its limited state. We share collectively many aspects of self, and we can become infused with many others experiences without recognizing we are resonating with an idea about ourselves, not the whole truth. The process of self-loathing is also, unfortunately, a shared experience, that we are all susceptible to adopting when we fail to listen to all that is unpleasant that emerges from within. We tune in to the experience of loathing, and pull up all the mental images of ourselves that resonate with it, and others that resonate with it, are also unfortunately drawn to us. When we are so weary of ourselves, and exhausted from the struggle of saving ourselves from being totally consumed and tormented, we can choose to relinquish our position and decide to accept our current experience for what it is. In accepting to hear it out, *we aren't committing to agreeing,* just listening fully before deciding whether to make an alliance with it. It is here that we become sober to what we have been avoiding. In that moment of dissolve, out of that dark hole within us, we begin to see our shadow emerge in form, and we actually clearly hear what has been yammering away inside, trying to get our attention. That shadow within comes into our conscious awareness. It is not any great voice of God that greets us. It's a dialogue we know very well and have spent a great effort to ignore. But now, we actually begin to hear it as a voice within that needs our attention.

To attentively listen with every part of our being, the dialogue begins to fall silent, as the light of consciousness penetrates its essence. Our frozen emotions thaw, and movement begins towards sensations that wash into our awareness. Those sensations are not unpleasant and they beckon us to just go with them. It's like finding ourselves on a voyage that seems to last for hours because of the amount of detail and knowledge that instantly enters our awareness. We pass through the waves of our personal experience to the bliss of the open ocean where everything makes sense in a way that would be hard to explain to anybody else. There is a sense of aliveness here that goes beyond our physical reality, but it is in complete synchronicity and acceptance of all parts of self, as they exist in their limited context. Our own limited-self emerges, out of the shadows where is has been hiding unrecognized, into the light of our conscious awareness. We realize in that moment what we had unknowingly become, because we see it for what it is. We had become set in our ways, and become what, as a child, we couldn't understand was being demonstrated in the adults and world around us: *Absolute Authority*. It's our own inner child that has become the absolute authority that we seek to have acknowledged inside, not our conscious adult who knows better beyond the emotion of our personally perceived injustice. In this realization, the voice of judgment about others no longer has a hold on us, because we see clearly what they were mirroring to us about our self. Ironically, in disowning the voice of authority within us we unknowingly fail to model a constructive model of a matured adult authority for our own children. When we implement boundaries, *we perceive how we felt as children*, not what strength and courage our own children require from us as adults to implement in relation to them in this moment, as their guardian.

So begins our conscious journey that opens us to the depths of our minds where we may begin accepting our reality knowingly, rather than passively, or manifesting symptoms to get our attention. Inner sensory awareness opens us to the unlimited experience of our true being. Self may be observed and merge with the realization that we are so much more beyond our assumptions, from the vantage point of light. It can be as simple as proclaiming who we are in our own innocence when facing adversity. The harsh projections coming from another can be dissolved with a simple, "I am a good listener", or "I am thoughtful and considerate", when another tells us what we are NOT in response to them. Our children carry the gift of bringing us back to the experience of our own naiveté, if we allow them. As adults, in accepting their innocent gift of liberation, we engage our true nature of inquiry, and playfulness to get past what we have inadvertently relinquished over the years to gain acceptance by others… and awaken to experience our own innocence. By revealing ourselves in awareness, we give back to them the gift of growing into accepting and developing their own selves, beyond our personal experience and assumptions about what is possible for them. We become guardians of all that is in harmony with their own soul's magnificence, and unveil more of ours in the process.

As a conscious adult there are times that the word NO is the most compassionate response we can have to our children's requests. In spreading our wings for them, they learn to expand their own in response to constructive challenges backed by our emotional security.

❧   ❧   ❧

We may not have control over our children, our lives, our partners, but we do have control over ourselves and how we choose to be relative to others. We alone *choose* how we wish to express ourselves and experience ourselves in relation to others. Implementing consistent boundaries that support security and growth in our children becomes possible when we are clear about what we choose to express and how we choose to express it with them. If there was one word in my opinion that can be exercised constructively for the sake of creating consistency and security for our children, it is the word *NO*. There are times this word when used with discernment, is the only one that is needed. If children were to be left in charge of deciding what is best for them, and were allowed to dictate how things work in the family home, we would be bowing to their limited experience of self, and handing the role of guardian over to them. Some children don't know enough to honor the word *yes* when respect is attached to it from us. The word *no* is needed to be brought forward sometimes, and when exercised with compassion it gives stability to children. It gives respect not only for adults, but respect for them and their ability to harness the expression of self constructively in relation to others. As a developing child's internal world is shifting to and fro, as they become aware of themselves, how they feel, what they think, and as they learn about their unique relatedness to life, their outer world remains consistent through secure adults who are clear about boundaries and how they are exercised and implemented. There is a much better chance of their finding their conscience and inner core that guides them when they wander too far in one direction when they meet consistent boundaries that redirect misguided focus into constructive outlets.

Masculine energy often expresses boundaries with a clear "*no*", period. A concrete wall is erected and nothing can cross the boundary under any circumstance. Feminine energy often expresses *no*, and then offers a reason or explanation for the decision, often delivered like an apology for having to implement restriction. The feminine energy expressed this way is possibly seeking to be alleviated of guilt over not wanting to go along, breaking the illusion of peace, or appeasing resistance experienced by another in a confrontational situation. 'No", expressed purely from the masculine, is a statement. 'No", expressed purely form the feminine communicates disagreement and unwillingness to go along. Yes, expressed purely from the masculine is approval, whereas from the feminine expresses support. In avoiding confrontation, rather then transcending it, both the masculine and feminine exercised this way is not being utilized to their potential to birth greater awareness for the child or ourselves. When we deny the use of constructive masculine expression, we implement the feminine in areas that open us to debate or negotiation that can foster doubt in our children to trust us to act in their best interests, until they demonstrate to us they are able to do so for themselves. If the *masculine within us is allowing*, then the feminine is not expressed in an appeasing manner, and a greater compassionate expression is born, beyond the dogmatic masculine authority that most of us cringe at thinking about exercising ourselves. We may implement boundaries by *being the conscious adult*, demonstrating the art of discernment for them, whether our children agree or not, and we remain strong for them knowing we hold greater knowledge about what is necessary for health, for learning, for remaining physically safe for them beyond their ability to recognize in the current situation. Through the approach of *relating through a common passion* with them, we blend the strengths of the masculine and the feminine and implement boundaries that may be honored because the child is respected for being an important consideration. We may then stand securely in the role of being guardian of greater potential beyond the immediate goal or desire the child is demonstrating by extending our own awareness in relating to them. Often when a child understands something they are willing participants in helping to make it happen, whether it's cleaning up their toys or helping to set the table for dinner. Rather than feeling confined by restrictions they are encouraged to be a meaningful part of family life.

As parents, and as adults in a child's life, recognizing our own inner child helps eliminate imprinting our own injustices and unresolved issues through our relationship with them. Emotion is not self, but it certainly fuels staying in the experience of limited-self, if we choose to resent it and deny it as a component of human experience. Without being trapped by emotion, self is put into context, and fails to get the better of us or find inappropriate expression with our children and partners. There's a righteousness that holds the hand of self in its hurt, and as long as we allow emotion to dictate who we are, not how we express ourselves, we continue to see a distorted and personal world that is against us and doesn't honor us. When emotion takes over, and we are completely captivated by the energy of its expression, we forget the compassionate person we really are underneath it and the word "no" springs to our lips to shut down all that threatens our own sense of order. Our emotions can act as a beacon, to find the part of self that is trying to get our attention, if we allow ourselves to internally accept them, so we can move past them to reveal the perception that little piece of us is holding onto. Emotions have been underestimated for their many roles in furthering us as individuals and as humanity.

If we fail to recognize our own inner child emotionally responding to our children's natural expressions of growth, and get past the idea that they are personally taking us on, we may model an adult authority that is liberating for them rather than demoralizing. Growing wings and children in today's world requires reassessing our roles and how we serve others constructively beyond what we may currently see demonstrated around us. If we learn to be constructive adults in our actions and eternally youthful in our eagerness to remain receptive to new ideas, then we may become secure enough to enter the realm of greater dimensions that embody a compassionate authority that inspires not only self, but a shared humanity. "Yes" and "no" are powerful words, and represent very distinct polarities of choice if one seeks to be validated by another. Each one, implemented in awareness keeps the other open to be expressed and experienced without conflict. A "no", wisely spoken, allows a *yes* to be experienced. A "yes" voiced, invites a "no" to be transcended into mutually respected boundaries.

So often, we fail to say no when we *feel* no in our hearts because there is emotional attachment to being accepted and pleasing those we care about. Yet for all the unspoken no's we fail to express, where we feel compromised as a result, we then compensate with voicing a dogmatic *NO* in situations that deserve our discernment. We miss the opportunity a *yes* could provide in opening us to new and richer experiences with others by assuming ahead of time their response to us. What if we stopped doing the dance to maintain an appearance of harmony because *no* can unleash emotional responses in those close to us, and instead, decided to engage our own emotional security and stand by our heart in daring to respond with a compassionate *no*, because we honor our ability to make choice for ourselves in the situation. In consciously becoming aware of our ability to make choice for ourselves, we transcend guarding our position with a *no*, and engage movement of those seemingly immoveable brick walls we encounter with others, that opens us to experience the *yes's* of possibility in life, shared in appreciation of others ability to honor us, and us them for their chosen path.

The other day, I had the all too familiar experience of being on the receiving end of a verbal tirade from someone headed in the opposite direction than I was at the time. They were long gone, without missing a beat or giving me a second thought. I was left alone to clean up the mess they had unknowingly made of me. I sat for a few moments to get my bearings, dumbfounded and wondering what just happened, and thinking about how things could be different the next time it happens. I wrote this silly story to work it out for myself. The whole incident became rather ridiculous to me as this unfolded, and honestly I'm came to the conclusion that I too can be the "No" in the story, although I was sure initially that I am always the "Yes". The word "no" is a very good word to include in our vocabulary if we are to honor who we are beyond self in the moment, when others' actions demonstrate that they are oblivious to the idea of a shared humanity.

YES AND NO BECOMING A TWO WAY STREET

One day, NO was walking down the street and bumped into YES. YES, got back on its feet, smiled sweetly, and without a word continued on its way with a skip in its step.

NO stood there watching YES skip away wondering what happened.

The next day, NO was running down the same street, not looking where it was going, and ran right into YES coming from the opposite direction.

They both fell to the ground.

When YES and NO got to their feet, YES wasn't as polite as the day before, and No was angry because it felt that YES had gotten in its way.

YES looked at NO and said "Don't do that again!" and continued on its way.

NO was confused and stood there for a moment wondering just where YES thought it was going.

The very next day YES and NO found themselves in each other's way on that same street.

This time, they stopped before knocking each other down and thought it might be a good idea to *cooperate* with one another before someone got hurt.

After *sharing* their ideas about where they were coming from,

and where they were going, and how they were going to get there,

they decided that putting some *rules of conduct* into place would serve them both.

They decided that they could be on opposite sides of the same street, but there could be respect for the other's right to be there, without creating conflict.

They named the street "Conscious Street" and it was agreed that they would each stay on the right side of the street, no matter what direction they were travelling in.

This would keep the whole street useable by both, and others, and they could choose which direction and how they wished to travel suited to their own preferences, but everyone could freely move about without running into one another.

NO liked this idea a lot because it was getting confused the other way.

And YES liked this idea as well because it was getting tired of being run into every day. They both decided to head in the same direction after meeting that day, skipping along side by side in agreement about traveling on Conscious Street their own way, together but independently. We've all heard the saying, "Let's agree to disagree", and now we can add without the feeling of defeat from not being appreciated for our individuality, "And travel together cooperatively so we can cover the same ground differently, in a shared experience together".

There are times when "no" must be expressed and honored, and times when "yes" must be heard and acknowledged *before* "no" is expressed. Respect is a shared pathway with honored rules of conduct that include the advantages of "yes" and "no" and the ability to change one's mind about how one wishes to make the journey. Whether we walk, skip or run is not the point. But acknowledging that for one to reach their destination there is no need to bulldoze over anybody because each has an honored right of passage. Depending on the direction in which you choose to travel, right can be either side of the same street, and has the ability to serve everyone on their journey. Respected rules of conduct can support the yes's and no's in life because they both belong on the same shared path of consciousness.

Rules of conduct keep *boundaries* respectful rather than building brick walls that separate us from appreciation of another's chosen way.

The yes's and no's of our world exist, and although equal, they are different. They approach things differently. They see things from different perspectives, and often miss the necessity of their counterpart to maintain balance. It is so much nicer to face another that we honor and respect for their unique approach because we honor who we have chosen to be on a shared path.

Most of us are uncomfortable with emotions, and it's not because they are outrageous, it's because they are honest, intimate, and personally revealing about how we experience ourselves.

❧ ❧ ❧

As a little girl I was terribly emotional, and it got me into trouble on several fronts. I remember being sent to the Principal's office in grade one because a boy in my class had put a frog down the back of my blouse and I was completely beside myself. Coming in from recess, I felt something slimy go down the back of my blouse. As it jumped around wildly to free itself, I completely lost control. In front of everyone in the middle of a crowded hall there must have been a lot of jumping around, crying, and screaming coming from me. I don't really remember that part, but I do remember my imagination getting the best of me about what horrible thing was going to hurt me. By the time I got my blouse un-tucked and the frog fell to the floor, it was too late for me to find any composure. I was already being marched down to the principal's office, and I was angry.

The principal had very specific advice for me. He was very stern in explaining how important it is to be in control of myself. I knew he was right, but this seemed terribly unfair to me under the circumstances. His advice was to push out your bottom jaw and clench you teeth to keep from crying. Well, that attitude just made me even more angry. If I had just one moment *after* that frog was released I could have slugged that kid, because fear left as soon as I saw the frog! Maybe I would have felt better about myself getting into trouble sitting across the desk from the Principal, but hindsight always has me feeling more courageous than I actually was at the time. I don't know which was scarier, not knowing what the slimy thing was, or sitting there feeling so small, on the opposite side of the principal's desk, wondering what he was going to do with me. He was immovable. I wondered why I was the one who was in trouble.

I learned to keep my mouth shut and not question authority or express discontent with the way people handled things, even when it negatively affected me. In that moment I internalized a new definition of self control. I learned that getting emotional got you into trouble. It seems I've spent a good part of my life fighting my emotions as if they were the enemy. The tears would well up and before I knew it, I was hysterical and out of control. Hysteria does nothing for your credibility. It wasn't until I consciously decided to accept them as part of who I am that I came to love and appreciate them. Having acknowledged they are important to me, and they exist whether I acknowledge them or not, I don't think I will ever understand them, and I certainly don't expect anyone else to understand them either.

Had I stood my ground and punched the kid who put the frog down my blouse, I might have developed confidence in my own abilities to handle things. We accept fights between boys where they learn to know their strength and the negative effect it has on another. But for little girls, fighting was never allowed, nor was emotional outbreaks, or arguing, or expressing any grievance of any kind. There were times in my twenties when I fantasized about slugging some jerk for his derogatory remarks or arrogant behavior should I ever experience it. I finally got it out of my system when I realized, that if the need arose, I could and would physically protect myself, or someone else in the face of physical threat. I never actually had a guy treat me that way, so the need to defend myself never came up. The idea that the boy with the frog might have had a crush on me had never occurred to me and the principal hadn't informed me of that possibility.

Giving myself permission to protect myself if need be was liberating. I haven't actually felt like physically tackling anyone or anything on since. In fact, no similar situation has presented itself since then. I was somehow relieved of the need to defend, once knowing I had my own permission to do it, if needed, and realized there is a much greater power than brute force. We all have it, and it rests with the feminine energy of diffusion. For that kind of energy to emerge, our masculine energy must be secure enough to stand in support and allow it, knowing it can step in at anytime and take control because the opposition is no threat. The *need* to prove a point, or win against another, or save face, must not exist for the feminine to birth a presence that has the effect of dampening the opponents need to fight. Until we honor our ability to decide for ourselves what *we choose to think about ourselves* that need to defend is going to rise up from within us when others don't agree with us. There is something to be said about mastering our confidence in dealing with external power at a young age, when a punch educates us to its consequences without really hurting anyone. It is better to learn this lesson when we are young than later in life when we are bigger and stronger and have a backlog of emotion to express. We might develop confidence in the power of the feminine energy, beyond tears and anger, to cushion and extinguish the fire of the directed masculine energy sooner rather than later.

The real threat is within us because we are afraid of what we don't know of ourselves in our true power. In our true power, self is honored as existing, and we are able to extend out beyond self to know more without letting self's assumptions dictate our experience. No wonder many of us have felt intimidated by physical and energetic aggression. Where emotional wisdom can be brought into play we are frozen, unsure of our ability to stand our ground confidently. As females, in not having constructive outlets to know our actual physical strength and ability to defend ourselves, the confidence to know we are capable of standing in stillness feeling safe is difficult to develop. Today's young women learn self-defense at school and in martial arts, which is a much more constructive approach than learning to grit one's teeth and bear it. An adopted posture of being in control when emotionally we are stuck carries a stoic energy with it that tends to evoke distance with others.

This outward appearance, and controlled quiet, is a very different thing than actually being at peace with what stands before us because we perceive more than what is evident. As women we might not have specific memories of being coached to maintain our composure, but we are experts at responding rationally. When asked if anything is wrong, we know just how to say, "Nothing." I'm fine". Everyone understands that this marks the end of the conversation and the beginning of the game of trying to find out what will please us, because until that is figured out there will be no communication. For me, as it happened, I was destined to be pushed to explore my internal world because the, "I'm fine", response only works if someone asks if things are all right with us. My own feminine energy developed silently, as it does for many females, and the masculine energy got its workout when I went out into the world and learned to stand up as myself.

Today, I would have something to say to that principal. It took many years to have the courage to proclaim my faith in this: Those same emotions, once accepted as personally valid, become fluid, and open us to the *Greater Other Dimensions* of our being. Hysteria expressed by a child, once experienced and transcended, can lead to emotional stability and confidence in handling fear and aggression positively. I'm not suggesting we should allow females to become hysterical every time they felt an emotion, but surely if emotions were not thought to be the enemy, a calm response, not complete dismissal of them, could take the drama out of being caught up in them. It only takes a couple of episodes for a child to get it and move on, without becoming stuck in the fear and self-doubt that takes over the mind in the form of emotions. I don't think clenching one's teeth through life promotes developing a compassionate expression of the masculine energy within us. If anything, it severs us completely from acknowledging it exists in us in a constructive state, and we avoid igniting the masculine energy in others so we can maintain the illusion of being peacekeepers.

If we are cut off from acknowledging our emotions within ourselves, then we are also completely void of what sensation, subtle energy, and the very life force within us has the ability to communicate to us, through our intuition and compassion for our humanness. Emotion is personal, but in its freeform state, links us firmly to the experience of the universal. I walked out of that principal's office completely dismissing him as an adult that I respected or wanted anything to do with again because I didn't trust him, or accept his ability to help me learn to resolve the situation. In that few minutes looking at my lap as he told me what to do, without listening to what happened from me, set in stone my idea of what authority was all about.

When others authentically express their emotions, it touches us deeply. In ourselves, emotion honors our perceptions as our own, and disintegrates the masks we hide behind. Of course, emotions can be a vehicle of destruction, as much as healing. They become destructive when they build up into an unknown, untouchable force that even we become afraid of within ourselves. Fluid emotions that reflect our ability to love are universal, and empowering. The fluid emotions I'm talking about are the tears of joy, the flush of gratitude, the joy of inhibition, and laughter of appreciation, not the hysteria of frogs down our blouses. An open heart *feels life* like waves rolling in on the shores of the ocean. They wash in and they wash out constantly, and in tune with this rhythm, we move as souls to merge with the masculine and feminine energies of the heavens and earth. Emotions are what carry us through this process of integration of the two qualities within us, for we feel alive and empowered by grace. Our faith in humanity finds assurance in this place of awareness. Most people are uncomfortable with emotions, and it's not because they are outrageous, it's because they are honest, intimate, and personally revealing. Illusions are hard to keep in place when the hard truth, delivered straight from the heart, hits you square in the face as another looks you straight in the eye and allows you to look back into them.

If you have faith backing emotional energy, you have passion, and you have authentic expression that incorporates the humanness of experience, beyond the factual delivery of a message. Poetry is emotional. Music is emotional. Creativity unleashed is free flowing emotional energy, fueled by the focus of the masculine energy, supported by the faith of the feminine energy to birth it. There is both movement and grace in its expression. We don't need to slug anyone to prove a point, because the field of energy created around us replaces words, and stabilizes both polarities to a common passion, for clear expression. Aggression is stopped in its tracks because in that moment, there is no longer anything to attack, or fuel its expression. The engagement of feminine energy has been greatly under-rated when we face the aggression of the masculine. It's not because the feminine has greater ability to solve it, but because without its presence honored, a *greater presence* cannot be known. The key to it is that we need both the masculine and the feminine engaged and present cohesively to implement such omnipresent energy. It's beyond confidence, it's beyond faith, it's an unquestioned *known*, gained only through trust. Those *Greater Other Dimensions* must be present in harmony with self, to act through us with love that expresses such compassion that transcends the dualism of oppression and aggression.

CPSIA information can be obtained at www.ICGtesting.com
Printed in the USA
BVOW03s0647200415

396697BV00001B/1/P